Fresh Raspberry-
Spinach Salad,
page 295

Southern Living

ULTIMATE
QUICK & EASY
COOKBOOK

Compiled and Edited by
Jane E. Gentry

OXMOOR
HOUSE®

© 2004 by Oxmoor House, Inc.
Book Division of Southern Progress Corporation
P. O. Box 2262, Birmingham, Alabama 35201-2262

Southern Living® is a federally registered trademark belonging to
Southern Living, Inc.

ISBN: 0-8487-2825-4
Library of Congress Control Number: 2004091416
Printed in the United States of America
Fifth Printing 2005

Editor-in-Chief: Nancy Fitzpatrick Wyatt
Executive Editor: Susan Carlisle Payne
Art Director: Cynthia Rose Cooper
Copy Chief: Allison Long Lowery

Southern Living®
Ultimate Quick & Easy Cookbook

Editor: Jane E. Gentry
Nutrition Editor: Holley Contri Johnson, M.S., R.D.
Editorial Assistant: Shannon Friedmann
Proofreader: Diane Rose
Senior Designer: Emily Albright Parrish
Senior Photographer: Jim Bathie
Photographer: Brit Huckabay
Senior Photo Stylist: Kay E. Clarke
Photo Stylist: Ashley J. Wyatt
Director, Test Kitchens: Elizabeth Tyler Luckett
Assistant Director, Test Kitchens: Julie Christopher
Recipe Editor: Gayle Hays Sadler
Test Kitchens Staff: Kristi Carter, Jennifer A. Cofield, Nicole Lee Faber,
Kathleen Royal Phillips, Jan A. Smith, Elise Weis, Kelley Wilton
Publishing Systems Administrator: Rick Tucker
Director of Production: Phillip Lee
Associate Production Manager: Leslie Wells Johnson
Production Assistant: Faye Porter Bonner

Contributors:
Copy Editor: Carmine Loper
Recipe Consultant: Leah Marlett
Indexer: Mary Ann Laurens
Photo Stylist: Missie Crawford
Interns: Amber Ballew, Leigh Ann Laney, Julie Perno

Cover: Molten Chocolate Cakes, page 362
Back Cover: Blue Cheese-Stuffed Chops, page 53; Fresh Raspberry-Spinach
Salad, page 295; Chicken Parmesan, page 220; Caramel Pie, page 137

To order additional publications, call 1-800-765-6400.

For more books to enrich your life, visit **oxmoorhouse.com**

contents

Southern Salutations

Imagine finding all of your childhood favorites in one source revised into simpler, more streamlined recipes. With *Southern Living® Ultimate Quick & Easy Cookbook*, you've discovered just such a collection of our best recipes with fewer steps and quicker times without sacrificing flavor. With this edition, you can put dinner on the table in no time, and have your family and friends believing you've spent all day in the kitchen.

Revisit your childhood memories in Southern style using these recipes that will leave you with more time to spend with family and friends.

- **Chicken-Fried Steak 'n' Country Gravy** (page 10) is on the table in 30 minutes flat.
- **Caramel-Nut Pull-Apart Bread** (page 199) is a treat for the whole family—and easy on the cook with just 4 ingredients.
- Pop some fries in the oven when you start preparing **Fried Catfish Sandwiches** (page 284), and you'll have dinner finished in 25 minutes.
- **Spiced Pecans** (page 150) are sure to disappear quickly at your next party...good thing it only takes 15 minutes to whip up a second batch.
- **Pan-Seared Steaks with Roasted Red Pepper Sauce** (page 204) offer unbelievable flavor with only 5 ingredients and 10 minutes start to finish!

Reflections of family, traditions, and favorite foods flood our memories when we think back on meals from our childhood. Whether it's the home cooking or the cozy feelings we relish, it's great to have these simple versions of the foods we grew up with. They bring us back together again—quicker than ever.

The Editors

Beef Fillets with
Orange Cream,
page 204

Basil Okra 'n'
Tomatoes, page 33

chapter one

Streamlined Southern

From okra and tomatoes to fried chicken to peach cobbler, memories abound of the Southern foods we've grown up with. Find these comfort-food favorites in this chapter, and prepare a classic Southern meal for your family tonight.

Chicken-Fried Steak 'n' Country Gravy

Prep: 14 minutes • **Cook:** 16 minutes

This all-time classic is quicker than you might think!

Menu Makings
Be sure to serve this Southern steak with mashed potatoes for soaking up the gravy. Cook potatoes in the microwave for mashing, or stir up frozen mashed potatoes, if you'd rather.

2¼ teaspoons salt, divided
1¾ teaspoons ground black pepper, divided
4 (4-ounce) cubed steaks
1 sleeve saltine crackers (about 38 crackers), crushed

1¼ cups all-purpose flour, divided
½ teaspoon ground red pepper
½ teaspoon baking powder
4¾ cups milk, divided
2 large eggs
1 cup peanut oil

• Sprinkle ¼ teaspoon salt and ¼ teaspoon black pepper evenly over steaks. Set aside.
• Combine cracker crumbs, 1 cup flour, 1 teaspoon salt, ½ teaspoon black pepper, red pepper, and baking powder.
• Whisk together ¾ cup milk and eggs. Dredge steaks in cracker mixture; dip in milk mixture, and dredge again in cracker mixture.
• Pour oil into a 12-inch skillet; heat to 360°. (Do not use a nonstick skillet.) Fry steaks 2 to 3 minutes. Turn and fry 2 to 3 minutes or until golden. Remove steaks onto a wire rack in a jellyroll pan. Keep steaks warm in a 225° oven. Carefully drain hot oil, reserving cooked bits and 1 tablespoon drippings in skillet.
• Whisk together remaining ¼ cup flour, 1 teaspoon salt, 1 teaspoon black pepper, and 4 cups milk. Add to reserved drippings in skillet; cook, whisking constantly, over medium-high heat 10 minutes or until gravy is thickened. Serve over warm steaks. Yield: 4 servings.

Smoked Sausage with Warm Potato Salad

Prep: 20 minutes • **Cook:** 20 minutes

*Because it's so meaty, this potato salad can be served
as a main dish or as a hearty side.*

3 pounds small red potatoes,
   quartered
2 pounds smoked sausage, cut into
   1-inch-thick slices
¾ cup dry white wine, divided
2 (8-ounce) packages sliced fresh
   mushrooms

¾ cup olive oil, divided
1 tablespoon pepper sauce, divided
1 bunch green onions, chopped
⅓ cup chicken broth
2 tablespoons Dijon mustard
½ teaspoon salt
⅓ teaspoon pepper

Secret Ingredient Savvy

No need to peel the potatoes. That'll save time and lend a great rustic look to this chunky salad.

• Cook potato in boiling water to cover in a large Dutch oven over medium-high heat 15 to 20 minutes or until tender; drain and cool slightly. Cut into ¼-inch-thick slices, and place in a large bowl.

• Meanwhile, brown sausage in Dutch oven over medium-high heat, stirring occasionally, 5 minutes. Add ½ cup wine, and cook 5 minutes. Drain sausage, and add to potato slices.

• Sauté mushrooms in 2 tablespoons hot oil in Dutch oven 5 minutes or until liquid evaporates. Sprinkle with 1½ teaspoons pepper sauce, tossing gently. Add mushroom mixture and green onions to potato mixture.

• Process remaining ¼ cup wine, 1½ teaspoons pepper sauce, chicken broth, and next 3 ingredients in a blender or food processor until blended. Turn blender on high; add remaining oil in a slow, steady stream. Pour over potato mixture, tossing gently to coat. Serve warm. Yield: 8 servings.

King Ranch Chicken Casserole

Prep: 13 minutes • **Cook:** 32 minutes

Rediscovering the "King Ranch Casserole"
brings back fond childhood memories.

Make Ahead
Freeze It

Fix It Faster
We've published several versions of this family favorite, and this one's the quickest yet. No sautéing is needed; just stir the ingredients together and pop them in the oven.

1 (10-ounce) package frozen seasoning blend – *onion & peppers*
2 cups chopped cooked chicken
1 (10¾-ounce) can cream of chicken soup, undiluted
1 (10¾-ounce) can cream of mushroom soup, undiluted

1 (10-ounce) can diced tomatoes and green chiles
1 teaspoon chili powder
½ teaspoon garlic salt
12 (6-inch) corn tortillas
2 cups (8 ounces) shredded Cheddar cheese, divided

• Stir together first 7 ingredients.
• Tear tortillas into 1-inch pieces; layer one-third of tortilla pieces in bottom of a lightly greased 13- x 9-inch baking dish. Top with one-third of chicken mixture and ⅔ cup of cheese. Repeat layers twice.
• Bake at 350° for 32 minutes or until casserole is thoroughly heated and bubbly. Yield: 6 servings.

Note: Freeze casserole up to 1 month, if desired. Thaw in refrigerator overnight, and bake as directed.

30 Minutes or less Chicken and Dumplings

Prep: 9 minutes • **Cook:** 19 minutes

*The best chicken and dumplings yet! Your family will think
you worked all day in the kitchen to prepare this favorite of the South.*

3 celery ribs, sliced (about 1 cup)
2 carrots, sliced (about 1 cup)
3 (14-ounce) cans chicken broth
½ teaspoon poultry seasoning
½ teaspoon pepper
1⅔ cups all-purpose baking mix
½ cup milk
3 cups chopped cooked chicken

• Combine first 5 ingredients in a large Dutch oven. Bring to a boil; cover, reduce heat, and simmer 6 minutes or until vegetables are tender.
• Meanwhile, stir together baking mix and milk. Turn dough out onto a lightly floured surface; roll dough to ⅛-inch thickness. Cut into 3- x 2-inch strips.
• When vegetables are tender, stir in chicken. Bring to a boil; reduce heat to medium-low. Drop dough strips, 1 at a time, into simmering broth. Cover and simmer 8 minutes, spooning broth over dumplings occasionally. Serve immediately. Yield: 4 servings.

Editor's Favorite

Kid Friendly

Secret Ingredient Savvy
Use chopped cooked chicken from the freezer section, or pull the meat from a deli-roasted bird. One roasted chicken yields about 3 cups chicken.

Crispy Fried Catfish

Prep: 10 minutes • **Cook:** 3 minutes per batch

*Frying fillet strips instead of whole catfish greatly speeds up the process.
Three minutes, and these golden nuggets are ready to eat.*

1 cup all-purpose flour
1 tablespoon salt
2 teaspoons ground black pepper
2 teaspoons ground red pepper
2½ cups cornmeal mix
1 tablespoon garlic powder
2 tablespoons dried thyme
10 (6- to 8-ounce) farm-raised
   catfish fillets, cut into strips
1 cup buttermilk
Peanut oil

• Combine first 4 ingredients in a shallow dish.
• Combine cornmeal mix, garlic powder, and thyme in a zip-top freezer bag.
• Dredge catfish fillets in flour mixture, and dip in buttermilk, allowing excess to drip off. Place catfish fillets in cornmeal mixture; seal bag, and shake gently to coat.
• Pour oil to a depth of 1½ inches into a large cast-iron or other heavy skillet; heat to 360°. Fry catfish fillets, in batches, 3 minutes or until golden. Drain on paper towels, and serve immediately. Yield: 10 servings.

Frying Success
1. Select an oil with a high smoke point, such as peanut oil.
2. Use a deep-fat thermometer to maintain an accurate temperature. When the oil is hot enough, the cooking process seals the outside of the fish to lock in flavor and moisture.
3. Fry in batches to prevent the oil temperature from dropping too low.

Layered Cornbread-and-Turkey Salad

Prep: 25 minutes • **Other:** 2 hours

No-Cook
Creation

Make Ahead

**Secret
Ingredient
Savvy**
Use premade cornbread from your grocer's bakery. You only need two cups, crumbled, for this recipe, so serve the rest with Easy Texas Chili (page 24) later in the week.

Some brands of precooked bacon are crispier than others. For extra crunch, sizzle the bacon in the microwave at HIGH for 1 to 2 minutes.

1 (15-ounce) bottle roasted-garlic dressing (we used T. Marzetti's)
½ cup buttermilk
1 head romaine lettuce, shredded
1½ cups chopped smoked turkey (about ½ pound)

8 ounces crumbled feta cheese
1 (12-ounce) jar roasted red bell peppers, drained and chopped
2 cups crumbled cornbread
8 fully cooked bacon slices, crumbled
5 green onions, chopped

• Stir together dressing and buttermilk, blending well.
• Layer a 3-quart glass bowl with half each of lettuce and next 6 ingredients; top with half of dressing. Repeat layers with remaining ingredients and dressing. Cover and chill 2 hours. Yield: 6 to 8 servings.

Blackened Tomato Salad

Prep: 20 minutes • **Cook:** 8 minutes • **Other:** 1 hour

Make Ahead

The juice from the tomatoes creates the fantastic marinade for this salad.

4 large tomatoes
1 tablespoon olive oil
3 tablespoons sliced fresh basil
¼ cup olive oil

1½ tablespoons red wine vinegar
½ teaspoon salt
¼ teaspoon freshly ground pepper
Garnish: fresh basil leaves

• Cut tomatoes into quarters; remove and discard seeds. Pat dry, and brush sides evenly with 1 tablespoon olive oil.
• Cook tomato quarters in a hot cast-iron skillet over high heat 1½ to 2 minutes on each side or until blackened. Remove from skillet, and cool, reserving juice from skillet.
• Toss tomato with reserved juice, basil, and next 4 ingredients in a large bowl. Cover and let mixture stand, stirring occasionally, 1 hour. Garnish, if desired. Yield: 4 servings.

Blackened Tomato
Salad

Dilled Potato Salad

Prep: 15 minutes • **Cook:** 20 minutes • **Other:** 2 hours

Make Ahead ▶

Secret Ingredient Savvy

There's no need to cook the peas for this salad. Just thaw them, and stir them in.

2 pounds new potatoes, cut into wedges
1 (10-ounce) package frozen petite sweet green peas, thawed and drained
½ cup mayonnaise

½ cup plain yogurt
1 tablespoon Dijon mustard
1 teaspoon garlic salt
¼ teaspoon pepper
1 small sweet onion, chopped
3 tablespoons minced fresh dill

• Combine potato and water to cover in a saucepan; cook 20 minutes or until tender. Drain and add peas.
• Meanwhile, stir together mayonnaise and next 6 ingredients in a large bowl. Add potato mixture; toss gently to coat. Cover and chill at least 2 hours. Yield: 8 servings.

Dilled Potato Salad

Creole Potato Salad

Prep: 20 minutes • **Cook:** 12 minutes

Leaving the peel on the potatoes adds nutrients and color—and speeds up the prep time.

Make Ahead

3 pounds red potatoes, cubed	1 teaspoon prepared horseradish
½ cup mayonnaise	½ teaspoon dried thyme
½ cup Creole mustard	¼ teaspoon ground red pepper
1 tablespoon red wine vinegar	6 hard-cooked eggs, chopped
1¼ teaspoons garlic salt	1 medium-size sweet onion, diced

• Combine potato and water to cover in a saucepan; cook 12 minutes or until tender. Drain and cool slightly.

• Stir together mayonnaise and next 6 ingredients in a large bowl; add potato, egg, and onion, tossing gently. Serve at room temperature or chilled. Yield: 8 servings.

Colorful Coleslaw

Prep: 10 minutes

No-Cook Creation

Super Fast and Fresh

1 (10-ounce) package finely shredded cabbage	1 medium tomato, seeded and chopped
4 green onions, chopped	3 tablespoons mayonnaise
1 medium-size green bell pepper, chopped	½ teaspoon salt

• Stir together all ingredients. Cover and chill, if desired. Yield: 6 servings.

Menu Makings
Serve this cool side with Crispy Fried Catfish (page 17).

Jalapeño Coleslaw

Prep: 5 minutes

No-Cook Creation

Make Ahead

Gadget Magic
You can quickly snip the jalapeño peppers in a cup using kitchen shears.

⅓ cup sour cream
⅓ cup mayonnaise
¼ cup chopped pickled jalapeño peppers
2 tablespoons red wine vinegar
2 tablespoons vegetable oil

1 garlic clove, minced
¼ teaspoon salt
⅛ teaspoon black pepper
1 (16-ounce) package shredded coleslaw mix

• Stir together first 8 ingredients in a large bowl; add coleslaw mix, tossing to coat. Cover and chill, if desired. Yield: 4 to 6 servings.

"Fried" Green Tomato BLTs

Prep: 10 minutes • **Cook:** 6 minutes

Oven-frying speeds up the cooking process and minimizes the cleanup compared to the traditional frying procedure.

Ideas for Two

Super Fast and Fresh

Menu Makings
Serve these sandwiches with sliced fresh fruit.

1 medium-size green tomato, cut into ¼-inch-thick slices
⅛ teaspoon hot sauce (optional)
1 egg white, lightly beaten
1½ tablespoons self-rising cornmeal

2 Green Leaf lettuce leaves
2 (1-ounce) slices mozzarella cheese
4 bacon slices, cooked and halved
4 (1-ounce) slices white sandwich bread, toasted

• Sprinkle tomato slices with hot sauce, if desired; dip in egg white, and dredge in cornmeal.
• Place slices in a single layer on a large baking sheet coated with cooking spray. Lightly coat slices with cooking spray. Broil 3 inches from heat 3 minutes on each side or until tender and golden.
• Layer lettuce, cheese, bacon, and tomato slices on 2 slices of toast. Top with remaining 2 slices of toast. Serve immediately. Yield: 2 servings.

Spicy Tortilla Soup

Prep: 5 minutes • **Cook:** 23 minutes

Stovetop
Solution

½ cup chopped onion
1 garlic clove, minced
1 tablespoon vegetable oil
3 medium zucchini, sliced
4 cups chicken broth
1 (16-ounce) can stewed tomatoes, undrained
1 (15-ounce) can tomato sauce

1 (11-ounce) can sweet whole kernel corn, undrained
1 teaspoon ground cumin
½ teaspoon pepper
Tortilla chips
½ cup (2 ounces) shredded Monterey Jack or Cheddar cheese

• Sauté onion and garlic in hot oil in a Dutch oven over medium heat until onion is tender. Add zucchini and next 6 ingredients; bring to a boil. Cover, reduce heat, and simmer 15 minutes.
• Spoon soup into individual bowls. Top with tortilla chips and shredded cheese. Yield: 2¼ quarts.

White Bean Soup

Prep: 5 minutes • **Cook:** 15 minutes

Stovetop
Solution

Ham gives this soup a punch of flavor.
Using the canned kind keeps things simple.

1 (16-ounce) can navy beans, undrained
1 (15.8-ounce) can great Northern beans, undrained
1 cup water

¼ cup chopped onion
½ cup preshredded carrot
¼ cup butter or margarine, melted
1 (5-ounce) can chunk ham, drained and flaked

• Combine beans in a large saucepan; mash slightly with a potato masher. Stir in 1 cup water, and cook over low heat until thoroughly heated.
• Meanwhile, sauté onion and carrot in butter over medium-high heat until onion is tender. Add sautéed vegetables and ham to bean mixture. Cook over low heat 10 minutes, stirring occasionally. Yield: 1 quart.

Secret Ingredient Savvy
Preshredded carrot, found in the produce section, speeds up this simple soup and is handy to keep around for sprinkling into green salads.

Chunky Beef Chili

Prep: 7 minutes • **Cook:** 37 minutes

This chili is handy to keep on hand in the freezer for when you're late getting home. Just defrost it in the microwave while you set the table.

Freeze It
Ideas for Two
Big Batch

Menu Makings
Serve this hearty chili with Old-Fashioned Skillet Cornbread (page 26). Prepare the cornbread while the chili simmers.

2   pounds ground round
2   large onions, chopped
1   small green bell pepper, chopped
3   garlic cloves, minced
1   (16-ounce) can pinto beans
½   cup ketchup
1   (14½-ounce) can diced tomatoes
2   (8-ounce) cans tomato sauce
2½ tablespoons chili powder
1   teaspoon black pepper

• Cook beef and next 3 ingredients in a Dutch oven over medium heat, stirring until meat crumbles and is no longer pink. Drain; pat dry with paper towels. Wipe drippings from Dutch oven. Return meat mixture to Dutch oven. Add beans, ketchup, and remaining ingredients. Bring to a boil, reduce heat, and simmer, uncovered, 25 minutes. Yield: 10 cups.

To Freeze: Place 3⅓ cups chili in each of 3 labeled airtight containers. Freeze up to 3 months.

To Serve Two: Thaw 1 (3⅓-cup) container in refrigerator or microwave oven. Cook chili in a medium saucepan over medium heat until thoroughly heated.

Easy Texas Chili

Prep: 3 minutes • **Cook:** 25 minutes

If your beef is lean enough, there's no need to drain it after browning.

Make Ahead
Stovetop Solution
Freeze It

1   pound lean ground beef
1   small onion, chopped
1   (16-ounce) can pinto beans, drained
1   (6-ounce) can tomato paste
1½ cups water
1½ teaspoons chili powder
½   teaspoon garlic salt

• Cook beef and onion in a Dutch oven over medium heat, stirring until meat crumbles and is no longer pink. Add pinto beans and remaining ingredients; cover, reduce heat, and simmer 15 minutes, stirring occasionally. Yield: about 5 cups.

Chunky Beef Chili and
Old-Fashioned Skillet
Cornbread (page 26)

30 Minutes or less

Old-Fashioned Skillet Cornbread

(pictured on page 25)
Prep: 15 minutes • **Cook:** 15 minutes

Editor's Favorite

Bacon drippings add extra flavor to this crispy, down-home cornbread.

3 bacon slices
2 cups buttermilk
1 large egg
1¾ cups white cornmeal

1 teaspoon baking powder
1 teaspoon baking soda
1 teaspoon salt

• Cook bacon in a 10-inch cast-iron skillet until crisp; remove bacon, and drain on paper towels, reserving drippings in skillet. Crumble bacon, and set aside.
• Heat skillet in a 450° oven 3 minutes or until very hot.
• Whisk together buttermilk and egg. Add cornmeal, stirring well.
• Stir in bacon, baking powder, baking soda, and salt. Pour batter into hot skillet.
• Bake at 450° for 15 minutes. Yield: 8 servings.

Jalapeño Hush Puppies

Prep: 15 minutes • **Cook:** 7 minutes per batch

Big Batch

Freezer Fresh
If you have any of these leftover, pop the puppies in a zip-top freezer bag, and freeze for up to a month. Crisp them in a 400° oven until hot.

If you like more spice in your hush puppies, simply mince the jalapeño pepper without seeding it—it'll save a little time too.

1 cup self-rising flour
1 cup self-rising white cornmeal
½ teaspoon sugar
¼ teaspoon salt
1 small onion, grated

1 small jalapeño pepper, seeded and minced
1 cup buttermilk
1 large egg
Peanut oil

• Combine first 4 ingredients; stir in onion and jalapeño.
• Whisk together buttermilk and egg; add to flour mixture.
• Pour oil to a depth of 3 inches into a Dutch oven; heat to 375°. Drop batter by tablespoonfuls into oil; fry, in batches, 5 to 7 minutes or until golden. Drain on paper towels. Yield: about 2½ dozen.

Broccoli Cornbread Mini-Muffins

Prep: 10 minutes • **Cook:** 20 minutes

Mini-muffin pans speed up the cook time for these cheesy cornbread bites.

1 (8½-ounce) package corn muffin mix
1 (10-ounce) package frozen chopped broccoli, thawed
1 cup (4 ounces) shredded Cheddar cheese
1 small onion, chopped
2 large eggs
½ cup butter or margarine, melted

• Combine first 4 ingredients in a large bowl; make a well in center of mixture.
• Stir together eggs and butter, blending well; add to broccoli mixture, stirring just until dry ingredients are moistened. Spoon into lightly greased mini-muffin pans, filling three-fourths full.
• Bake at 325° for 15 to 20 minutes or until golden. Let stand 2 minutes before removing from pans. Yield: 2 dozen.

Creamy Grits

Prep: 10 minutes • **Cook:** 10 minutes

Cream cheese and half-and-half put the "cream" in this Southern favorite.

2 cups half-and-half or whipping cream
¼ teaspoon salt
⅛ teaspoon garlic powder
⅛ teaspoon pepper
½ cup uncooked quick-cooking grits
2 ounces cream cheese, cubed
¾ cup (3 ounces) shredded sharp Cheddar cheese
¼ teaspoon hot sauce

• Bring first 4 ingredients to a boil in a Dutch oven; gradually stir in grits. Return to a boil; cover, reduce heat, and simmer, stirring occasionally, 5 to 7 minutes or until thickened. Add cheeses and hot sauce, stirring until cheeses melt. Serve immediately. Yield: 4 servings.

Stovetop Solution

Secret Ingredient Savvy
Quick-cooking grits have the germ removed, which gives them a longer shelf life than regular. They're a great pantry staple.

Hot Tomato
Grits

Hot Tomato Grits

Prep: 10 minutes • **Cook:** 25 minutes

Stovetop Solution

Everything cooks in the same saucepan, so there's minimal cleanup with this cheesy main dish or side dish.

2 bacon slices, chopped
2 (14-ounce) cans chicken broth
½ teaspoon salt
1 cup uncooked quick-cooking grits
2 large tomatoes, peeled and chopped
2 tablespoons canned chopped green chiles

1 cup (4 ounces) shredded Cheddar cheese
Garnishes: chopped tomato, cooked and crumbled bacon, shredded Cheddar cheese

• Cook bacon in a heavy saucepan until crisp, reserving bacon and drippings in pan. Gradually add broth and salt; bring to a boil.
• Stir in grits, tomato, and chiles; return to a boil, stirring often. Reduce heat, and simmer, stirring often, 15 minutes.
• Stir in cheese. Garnish, if desired. Yield: 6 servings.

Quick Double-Cheese Grits

Prep: 10 minutes • **Cook:** 5 minutes

Stovetop Solution

Make Ahead

Quick-cooking grits make this cheesy dish a 15-minute marvel.

6 cups water
½ teaspoon salt
1½ cups uncooked quick-cooking grits
1 cup (4 ounces) shredded extra-sharp Cheddar cheese

1 cup (4 ounces) shredded Monterey Jack cheese
2 tablespoons butter or margarine
½ teaspoon pepper

• Bring 6 cups water and salt to a boil in a large saucepan. Gradually stir in grits. Cook 4 to 5 minutes, stirring often, until thickened. Remove from heat. Add shredded cheeses, butter, and pepper, stirring until blended. Serve immediately. Yield: 8 servings.

Two Meals in One
Grits can be chilled and reheated. When reheating, whisk a tablespoon or two of warm water into grits over medium heat, adding more water as necessary.

Bacon 'n' Herb Butterbeans

Stovetop Solution

Prep: 8 minutes • **Cook:** 34 minutes

Fry the bacon, and stir up the other seasonings while the butterbeans simmer; you'll be able to toss everything together in a jiffy.

1 (16-ounce) package frozen butterbeans	1 large garlic clove, minced
4 bacon slices	½ cup chopped fresh parsley
4 green onions, sliced	¾ teaspoon seasoned salt

• Cook butterbeans according to package directions; set aside.
• Cook bacon in a large skillet until crisp; remove bacon, and drain on paper towels, reserving drippings in skillet. Crumble bacon, and set aside.
• Sauté green onions and garlic in hot drippings 2 minutes or until tender. Stir in butterbeans, parsley, and seasoned salt; cook 1 minute or until thoroughly heated. Sprinkle with bacon. Yield: 4 servings.

Black-Eyed Pea Cakes

No Fuss Entertaining

Big Batch

Prep: 20 minutes • **Cook:** 3 minutes per batch • **Other:** 1 hour

Secret Ingredient Savvy
Canned black-eyed peas and packaged hush puppy mix make this recipe a snap to prepare.

1 small onion, chopped	½ teaspoon salt
1 tablespoon olive oil	1 teaspoon hot sauce
2 (15.5-ounce) cans black-eyed peas, rinsed, drained, and divided	1 (8-ounce) package hush puppy mix with onion
1 (8-ounce) container chive-and-onion cream cheese, softened	Olive oil
1 large egg	Toppings: sour cream and green tomato relish

• Sauté onion in 1 tablespoon hot oil in a large skillet over medium-high heat until tender.
• Process onion, 1 can of peas, and next 4 ingredients in a blender or food processor until mixture is smooth, stopping to scrape down sides. Stir in hush puppy mix, and gently fold in remaining can of peas.
• Shape mixture by 2 tablespoonfuls into 3-inch patties, and place on a wax paper-lined baking sheet. Cover and chill 1 hour.
• Cook patties, in batches, in 3 tablespoons hot oil (adding oil as needed) in a skillet over medium heat 1½ minutes on each side or until patties are golden. Drain on paper towels, and keep warm. Serve with desired toppings. Yield: 30 appetizer servings.

Bacon 'n' Herb
Butterbeans

Saucy Green Beans

Prep: 10 minutes • **Cook:** 15 minutes

Secret
Ingredient
Savvy
Purchase one of
the flavored
tomato sauces for
a change of pace.

1 pound fresh green beans, trimmed*
1 small sweet onion, chopped
1 large garlic clove, minced
2 tablespoons olive oil
1 (8-ounce) can tomato sauce

1 tablespoon sugar
½ to ¾ teaspoon salt
½ teaspoon freshly ground pepper
1 tablespoon red wine vinegar

• Cook green beans in boiling water to cover 5 to 10 minutes or to desired degree of doneness; drain and set aside.
• Meanwhile, sauté onion and garlic in hot oil in a large skillet over medium-high heat 5 minutes or until onion is tender.
• Add tomato sauce and sugar; cook, stirring often, 5 minutes. Add green beans, salt, pepper, and vinegar; cook 5 minutes. Yield: 4 servings.

* Substitute 1 pound frozen whole green beans for fresh green beans, if desired. Cook according to package directions; drain well.

Corn Pudding

Prep: 10 minutes • **Cook:** 20 minutes

2 cups milk
½ cup yellow cornmeal
1 (16-ounce) package frozen whole
    kernel corn, thawed

½ teaspoon salt
2 tablespoons whipping cream

• Bring milk to a boil in a heavy saucepan; gradually add cornmeal, stirring until blended after each addition. Cook, stirring constantly, just until mixture begins to boil. Reduce heat, and cook, stirring constantly, until thickened.
• Add corn, stirring until mixture is consistency of whipped potatoes. Stir in salt and whipping cream. Yield: 6 servings.

Basil Okra 'n' Tomatoes

30 Minutes or less

Basil Okra 'n' Tomatoes

Prep: 5 minutes • **Cook:** 20 minutes

Basil adds an aromatic twist to this traditional side dish.

4 bacon slices
1 (16-ounce) package frozen sliced okra, thawed
2 tablespoons all-purpose flour
1 large onion, chopped

2 tomatoes, chopped
2 tablespoons minced fresh basil
½ teaspoon salt
½ teaspoon pepper

• Cook bacon in a large skillet over medium heat until crisp; remove bacon, and drain on paper towels, reserving 2 tablespoons drippings in skillet. Crumble bacon, and set aside.
• Dredge okra in flour.
• Sauté onion in reserved drippings until tender. Add okra; cook, stirring occasionally, 5 minutes or until lightly browned. Stir in tomato and basil; cook over low heat, stirring occasionally, 6 to 8 minutes. Stir in salt and pepper. Sprinkle with bacon. Yield: 4 servings.

20 Minutes *or less*

Crunchy Fried Okra

Prep: 6 minutes • **Cook:** 3 minutes per batch

*Pick small, tender okra pods, and skip the traditional
slicing step to speed up this time-honored favorite.*

1½ cups buttermilk
 1 large egg
1½ sleeves saltine crackers, finely
      crushed

1½ cups all-purpose flour
 1 teaspoon salt
 1 pound small fresh okra
Peanut oil

• Stir together buttermilk and egg. Combine cracker crumbs, flour, and salt.
Dip okra pieces in buttermilk mixture; dredge in cracker crumb mixture.
• Pour oil to a depth of 2 inches into a Dutch oven; heat to 375°. Fry okra, in
batches, 3 minutes or until golden, turning once. Drain on paper towels. Yield:
4 to 6 servings.

Crunchy
Fried Okra

Okra Creole

Prep: 15 minutes • **Cook:** 25 minutes

This spicy okra concoction will have you coming back for more.

3 bacon slices
1 (16-ounce) package frozen sliced
   okra
1 (14.5-ounce) can diced tomatoes
1 cup frozen onion seasoning blend

1 cup frozen whole kernel corn
½ cup water
1 teaspoon Creole seasoning
¼ teaspoon pepper
Hot cooked rice (optional)

• Cook bacon in a Dutch oven until crisp; remove bacon, and drain on paper towels, reserving drippings in Dutch oven. Crumble bacon.
• Cook okra and next 6 ingredients in hot drippings in Dutch oven over medium-high heat, stirring occasionally, 5 minutes. Reduce heat to low, cover, and simmer 15 minutes or until vegetables are tender. Top with crumbled bacon. Serve over rice, if desired. Yield: 4 servings.

 # Savory Stuffed Tomatoes

Prep: 6 minutes • **Cook:** 4 minutes

Super Fast
and Fresh

How-To Hints
If your tomatoes
are too rounded
to stay still on the
jellyroll pan, place
them in a muffin
tin instead—the
cups will cradle
the tomatoes.

Use a small spoon to scoop the pulp out of these tomatoes.

1 (1.5-ounce) slice whole grain bread
4 medium tomatoes
¼ teaspoon salt
¼ teaspoon freshly ground black
   pepper

2 tablespoons chopped fresh basil
2 tablespoons chopped pitted
   kalamata olives
1 garlic clove, minced
2 teaspoons olive oil

• Place bread in a food processor; pulse 10 times or until coarse crumbs measure ½ cup, and set aside.
• Cut top off each tomato. Scoop out pulp, leaving shells intact. Discard tops and pulp.
• Place tomatoes on a jellyroll pan lined with foil. Sprinkle tomatoes with salt and pepper.
• Combine breadcrumbs, basil, olives, and garlic. Spoon crumb mixture evenly into tomato shells. Drizzle each with ½ teaspoon oil.
• Broil 3 to 4 minutes or until thoroughly heated. Yield: 4 servings.

Soufflé Potatoes

Prep: 5 minutes • **Cook:** 5 minutes

The instant potato flakes in this recipe make for a super-quick soufflé.

2⅔ cups instant potato flakes
1 egg, beaten
1 (2.8-ounce) can French fried onion rings

¼ teaspoon salt
½ cup (2 ounces) shredded Cheddar cheese

• Prepare potato flakes according to package directions. Add egg, onion rings, and salt, stirring until blended. Spoon mixture into a lightly greased 2-quart baking dish; sprinkle with cheese. Bake, uncovered, at 350° for 5 minutes or until cheese melts. Yield: 8 servings.

Microwave Directions: Prepare potato flakes in microwave according to package directions. Add egg, onion rings, and salt, stirring until blended. Spoon mixture into a lightly greased 2-quart baking dish. Microwave at HIGH 4 to 5 minutes. Sprinkle with cheese; cover and let stand 2 minutes or until cheese melts.

Bourbon Yams

Prep: 10 minutes • **Cook:** 25 minutes

One-half teaspoon allspice will make a flavorful substitution for the three spices in these yams.

1 (29-ounce) can cut sweet potatoes, drained and cut into ½-inch-thick slices
3 tablespoons butter or margarine, melted
3 tablespoons brown sugar

3 tablespoons orange juice
3 tablespoons bourbon
¼ teaspoon ground cinnamon
⅛ teaspoon ground cloves
⅛ teaspoon ground nutmeg
¼ cup chopped pecans, toasted

• Place sliced potato in a lightly greased 8-inch square baking dish. Combine butter and next 6 ingredients; pour over potato. Sprinkle with pecans. Bake at 350° for 25 minutes or until thoroughly heated. Yield: 4 servings.

Note: If you're partial to fresh sweet potatoes, substitute 3 medium-size fresh (about 1½ pounds) for canned sweet potatoes. Cook in boiling water to cover 30 to 45 minutes or until tender. Let potatoes cool to touch; peel and slice.

Easy Oven Rice

Prep: 10 minutes • **Cook:** 35 minutes

*Sometimes it's nice to get rice off the cooktop and into
the oven to bake alongside an entrée. No tending needed.*

1 cup sliced celery	1 teaspoon poultry seasoning
¾ cup sliced green onions	½ teaspoon salt
¾ cup chopped green bell pepper	⅛ teaspoon black pepper
2 tablespoons olive oil	1½ cups uncooked long-grain rice
2¾ cups chicken broth	¼ cup chopped pecans, toasted

• Sauté celery, green onions, and bell pepper in hot oil in a large nonstick skillet over medium-high heat until vegetables are crisp-tender. Stir in broth and next 3 ingredients; bring to a boil.
• Spoon rice into a shallow 2-quart baking dish; add hot broth mixture. Cover and bake at 350° for 30 minutes or until rice is tender and liquid is absorbed. Sprinkle with pecans. Yield: 6 to 8 servings.

Cream Gravy

Prep: 5 minutes • **Cook:** 5 minutes

1 cup milk	2 tablespoons all-purpose flour
1 (¼-inch-thick) onion slice	⅛ teaspoon salt
1 fresh parsley sprig	⅛ teaspoon ground white pepper
2 tablespoons butter or margarine	Dash of nutmeg

• Bring first 3 ingredients to a boil in a small saucepan; remove from heat. Pour milk mixture through a wire-mesh strainer into a small bowl, reserving the hot milk and discarding solids.
• Melt butter in a large skillet over low heat; whisk in flour until smooth. Cook, whisking constantly, 1 minute. Gradually whisk in reserved hot milk, and cook, whisking constantly, over medium heat until thickened and bubbly. Whisk in salt, pepper, and nutmeg. Yield: ¾ cup.

Menu Makings
Serve with vegetables, pasta, or chicken. If you have drippings from fried chicken or steak, you can substitute those for the butter.

Meat Gravy

Menu Makings
This gravy is as rich as one that begins with a roast. Serve over rice or potatoes.

1 medium onion, halved and sliced
2 celery ribs, sliced
2 tablespoons vegetable oil
1 (10½-ounce) can beef consommé, undiluted
1¼ cups water, divided

1 beef bouillon cube
2 tablespoons cornstarch
¼ teaspoon browning-and-seasoning sauce (we used Kitchen Bouquet)

• Sauté onion and celery in hot oil in a medium saucepan over medium-high heat 10 minutes; stir in consommé, 1 cup water, and bouillon cube. Bring to a boil; cover, reduce heat, and simmer 25 minutes or until onion is tender.
• Stir together cornstarch, remaining ¼ cup water, and seasoning sauce until smooth. Stir into gravy mixture. Bring to a boil over medium heat, stirring constantly; boil, stirring constantly, 1 minute. Yield: 2 cups.

Sausage Gravy

5 Ingredients or Less

Menu Makings
Serve thick sausage gravy over buttermilk biscuits or grits.

8 ounces ground pork sausage
¼ cup all-purpose flour
2⅓ cups milk

½ teaspoon salt
½ teaspoon pepper

• Cook sausage in a large skillet over medium heat, stirring until it crumbles and is no longer pink. Remove sausage, and drain on paper towels, reserving 1 tablespoon drippings in skillet.
• Whisk flour into hot drippings until smooth; cook, whisking constantly, 1 minute. Gradually whisk in milk, and cook, whisking constantly, 5 to 7 minutes or until thickened. Stir in sausage, salt, and pepper. Yield: 2 cups.

Come Back Sauce

Prep: 8 minutes • **Other:** 1 hour

Pair this sauce with your favorite fried chicken strips for a meal that's quick and easy. You'll want to "come back" for more!

1 cup mayonnaise	2 teaspoons coarsely ground pepper
½ cup olive oil	¼ teaspoon hot sauce
⅔ cup chili sauce	1 medium onion, minced
1 tablespoon Worcestershire sauce	2 garlic cloves, minced
1 tablespoon prepared mustard	

• Stir together all ingredients. Cover and chill 1 hour or up to 2 days. Yield: 3 cups.

Make Ahead

No-Cook Creation

Big Batch

Quick Corn Relish

Prep: 2 minutes • **Cook:** 12 minutes • **Other:** 4 to 8 hours

The microwave can cut the time for this 12-minute recipe nearly in half.

1 (11-ounce) can yellow corn with red and green bell peppers	⅓ cup sweet pickle relish
⅓ cup sugar	2 tablespoons instant minced onion
⅓ cup cider vinegar	½ teaspoon celery seeds

• Combine all ingredients in a small saucepan; bring to a boil over medium heat. Reduce heat; cover and simmer 10 minutes.
• Remove to a serving bowl; cover and refrigerate relish 4 to 8 hours, if desired. Yield: 2 cups.

Microwave Directions: Combine all ingredients in a 1-quart casserole. Cover and microwave at MEDIUM HIGH (70% power) 5 to 7 minutes. Cover and refrigerate 4 to 8 hours, if desired.

Make Ahead

Microwave Miracle

Menu Makings
Serve this zesty relish with beef, pork, or poultry.

Shortcut Pralines

Prep: 5 minutes • **Cook:** 12 minutes

*The microwave is magic when it comes to pralines.
It cuts your cook time in half. If your oven is 1000 watts
or more, use the lower time option.*

Make Ahead
Microwave
Miracle

Gadget Magic
Scoop the mixture
into a spoon for
portioning, and
use another
spoon to quickly
push it off onto
the surface.

1½ cups granulated sugar
½ cup firmly packed brown sugar
2 cups pecans, chopped
1 (5-ounce) can evaporated milk

¼ cup butter or margarine
1 tablespoon vanilla extract
⅛ teaspoon salt

• Stir together all ingredients in a 4-quart microwave-safe bowl. Microwave at HIGH 5 to 6 minutes; stir well. Microwave 5 to 6 more minutes. Stir for 2 minutes or just until candy begins to become opaque.
• Working rapidly, drop by tablespoonfuls onto greased wax paper; let stand until firm. Yield: 2 dozen.

Raisin-Oatmeal Cookies

Prep: 10 minutes • **Cook:** 12 minutes per batch • **Other:** 8 hours

*Convenience is key for cookie bakers. Mix and chill this dough ahead,
and then you can bake however many cookies you want at a time.
You can even freeze the dough up to 3 months. No need to thaw,
but the cookies might take a minute or two longer to bake.*

Freeze It
Make Ahead
Kid Friendly

1 cup butter or margarine, softened
1 cup granulated sugar
1 cup firmly packed brown sugar
2 large eggs
2 cups self-rising flour

2 teaspoons ground cinnamon
3 cups uncooked regular oats
1 cup raisins
1 cup chopped pecans

• Beat first 3 ingredients at medium speed with an electric mixer until fluffy. Add eggs, beating until blended. Gradually add flour and cinnamon, beating at low speed until blended. Stir in oats, raisins, and pecans. Cover and chill dough 8 hours.
• Divide dough into 2 equal portions. Roll each portion into a 12-inch log. Cut each log into 1-inch–thick slices. Place slices on ungreased baking sheets.
• Bake at 400° for 12 minutes or until golden brown; remove to wire racks to cool. Yield: 2 dozen.

Pecan Squares

Prep: 10 minutes • **Cook:** 25 minutes

2 cups all-purpose flour
½ cup powdered sugar
1 cup butter or margarine, cut up
1 (14-ounce) can sweetened
    condensed milk
1 large egg

1 teaspoon vanilla extract
1 (10-ounce) package almond toffee
    bits (we used Heath Bits 'O
    Brickle)
1 cup chopped pecans

• Combine flour and powdered sugar in a medium bowl. Cut in butter with a pastry blender until crumbly. Press mixture evenly into a lightly greased 13- x 9-inch baking pan.
• Bake at 375° for 10 minutes. Combine sweetened condensed milk and remaining ingredients; pour over prepared crust.
• Bake at 375° for 15 minutes or until golden. Cool and cut into squares. Yield: 3 dozen.

Editor's Favorite

Secret Ingredient Savvy
Find Bits 'O Brickle in the baking section of your supermarket.

Honey-Pecan Pie Fingers

Prep: 10 minutes • **Cook:** 35 minutes

1¼ cups all-purpose flour
1 cup sugar, divided
½ cup butter, softened
½ cup honey
3 tablespoons all-purpose flour

¼ teaspoon salt
2 eggs, lightly beaten
2 tablespoons butter, melted
1½ teaspoons vanilla extract
1 cup chopped pecans

• Combine 1¼ cups flour and ⅓ cup sugar in a medium bowl; cut ½ cup softened butter into flour mixture with a pastry blender until mixture is crumbly. Press flour mixture firmly and evenly into an ungreased 9-inch square baking pan. Bake at 375° for 10 minutes or until edges of crust are lightly browned.
• Combine remaining ⅔ cup sugar and remaining ingredients in a medium bowl; stir well. Pour evenly over prepared crust. Bake at 375° for 20 to 25 minutes, shielding with aluminum foil the last 5 minutes, if necessary. Cool on a wire rack. Cut into 1½- x 1-inch bars. Yield: 4½ dozen.

Big Batch
Kid Friendly

Gadget Magic
If you don't have a pastry blender, use two knives to cut through the butter and flour mixture until crumbly.

Blueberry-Pecan Cobbler

Prep: 10 minutes • **Cook:** 33 minutes

Gadget Magic
Use a fluted pastry wheel to quickly cut the pastry into strips.

The pecans in this cobbler provide a surprise middle layer.

3 pints fresh or frozen blueberries
1 cup sugar
⅓ cup all-purpose flour
¼ cup water
1½ tablespoons lemon juice

1 teaspoon vanilla extract
1 (15-ounce) package refrigerated piecrusts
½ cup chopped pecans, toasted
Vanilla ice cream

• Bring first 6 ingredients to a boil in a saucepan over medium heat, stirring until sugar melts. Reduce heat to low; cook, stirring occasionally, 10 minutes.
• Spoon half of blueberry mixture into a lightly greased 11- x 7-inch baking dish. Roll 1 piecrust to ⅛-inch thickness on a lightly floured surface; cut dough into an 11- x 7-inch rectangle. Place dough over blueberry mixture; sprinkle with pecans.
• Bake at 475° for 10 minutes. Spoon remaining blueberry mixture over baked crust. Roll remaining piecrust to ⅛-inch thickness; cut into 1-inch strips. Arrange in lattice design over blueberry mixture.
• Bake at 475° for 10 minutes or until golden. Serve with vanilla ice cream. Yield: 4 servings.

Blueberry-
Pecan Cobbler

Quick Peach Cobbler

Prep: 10 minutes • **Cook:** 25 minutes

Ideas for Two

Kid Friendly

Try substituting apricots, cherries, or apples for the peaches.

1½ teaspoons cornstarch
1 tablespoon cold water
1 (8.5-ounce) can sliced peaches, undrained
½ cup buttermilk baking mix (we used Pioneer)

2 teaspoons sugar
2 tablespoons milk
1 tablespoon vegetable oil
Vanilla ice cream

• Dissolve cornstarch in 1 tablespoon cold water in a medium saucepan; add peaches, and cook over medium heat about 5 minutes or until mixture is thickened and bubbly. Pour into a 1-quart baking dish.
• Combine baking mix and sugar; add milk and vegetable oil, stirring to form a soft dough. Drop dough by spoonfuls on top of peach mixture. Bake at 400° for 20 minutes or until golden brown. Serve hot with ice cream. Yield: 2 servings.

Texas Star Pecan Pie

Prep: 10 minutes • **Cook:** 27 minutes

Menu Makings
Serve this
decadent pie
with vanilla ice
cream and
caramel sauce
on top.

This pie is sure to be a star on your favorite recipes list.

4 egg whites
⅛ teaspoon salt
½ teaspoon vanilla extract
½ cup granulated sugar

¼ cup firmly packed brown sugar
1 cup chopped pecans
1 (9-ounce) ready-made graham cracker crust

• Beat egg whites in a small bowl at high speed with an electric mixer until foamy; add salt and vanilla, beating until soft peaks form. Gradually add granulated sugar and brown sugar, 1 tablespoon at a time, beating until stiff peaks form. Stir in chopped pecans.
• Spoon mixture into crust. Bake at 350° for 25 to 27 minutes or until pie is done. Cool on a wire rack. Yield: 1 (9-inch) pie.

Coconut Cream Pie

Prep: 12 minutes • **Cook:** 6 minutes • **Other:** 1 hour

**No Fuss
Entertaining**

*Use a refrigerated or frozen piecrust to keep
this recipe quick. It'll be ready in less than 20 minutes
other than the stand and chill time.*

¾ cup sugar, divided
¼ cup cornstarch
2 cups half-and-half
4 egg yolks
3 tablespoons butter
1 cup sweetened flaked coconut

2 teaspoons vanilla extract,
   divided
1 baked 9-inch pastry shell
1 cup whipping cream
Garnish: toasted coconut chips

• Combine ½ cup sugar and cornstarch in a heavy saucepan; gradually whisk
in half-and-half and egg yolks. Bring to a boil over medium heat, whisking
constantly; boil 1 minute. Remove from heat. Stir in butter, coconut, and 1
teaspoon vanilla.

• Place plastic wrap directly over custard mixture, and cool to room temperature.
Spoon custard mixture into pastry shell, and chill 30 minutes or until set.

• Beat whipping cream at high speed with an electric mixer until foamy; gradually
add remaining ¼ cup sugar and remaining 1 teaspoon vanilla, beating until soft
peaks form. Spread or pipe whipped cream over pie. Garnish, if desired. Yield:
1 (9-inch) pie.

Grilled Gorgonzola Rib-Eye Steaks

Prep: 5 minutes • **Cook:** 19 minutes

*Coarsely grained kosher salt adds nice texture
to the seasoning blend slathered on these steaks.*

30 Minutes or less

No Fuss Entertaining

Secret Ingredient Savvy
You can prepare this recipe without kosher salt by substituting 1 teaspoon regular salt in place of 1½ teaspoons kosher salt.

1 tablespoon minced garlic	4 (8-ounce) rib-eye steaks
1 tablespoon minced shallot	4 ounces Gorgonzola cheese
2 tablespoons olive oil	¼ cup fine, dry breadcrumbs
1½ teaspoons kosher salt	(commercial)
½ teaspoon ground white pepper	8 large green onions

• Combine first 5 ingredients; stir well. Brush about two-thirds of mixture evenly over both sides of steaks. Grill, covered with grill lid, over medium-high heat (350° to 400°) 6 to 8 minutes on each side or to desired degree of doneness.
• Remove steaks from grill, and place on a rack in a broiler pan. Crumble cheese evenly over steaks; sprinkle breadcrumbs evenly over cheese. Place green onions around steaks on rack. Brush remaining garlic mixture over green onions. Broil 5½ inches from heat 3 minutes or until cheese is lightly browned. Yield: 4 servings.

Asian Grilled Flank Steak

Prep: 10 minutes • **Cook:** 20 minutes • **Other:** 8 to 24 hours

Make Ahead

How-To Hints
Score steak diagonally across the grain at ³/₄-inch intervals to encourage the marinade to seep in.

1½ pounds flank steak	2 tablespoons honey
¼ cup soy sauce	½ teaspoon ground ginger
¼ cup vegetable oil	¼ teaspoon garlic powder
2 tablespoons cider vinegar	

• Score steak diagonally across grain at ¾-inch intervals. Place steak in a large zip-top freezer bag or shallow dish. Combine soy sauce and remaining 5 ingredients. Pour ½ cup marinade over steak; seal or cover, and marinate in refrigerator 8 to 24 hours, turning occasionally. Cover and chill remaining marinade.
• Remove steak from marinade, discarding marinade in bag or dish. Grill steak, without grill lid, over medium-high heat (350° to 400°) 8 to 10 minutes on each side or to desired degree of doneness, basting with reserved marinade during last 5 minutes. To serve, slice diagonally across grain. Yield: 4 servings.

Peppered Flank Steaks

Prep: 13 minutes • **Cook:** 16 minutes • **Other:** 8 to 24 hours

¾ cup olive oil
⅓ cup red wine vinegar
¼ cup Dijon mustard
2 green onions, chopped
4 garlic cloves, minced

1½ tablespoons coarsely ground pepper
1 tablespoon minced fresh thyme
1 teaspoon salt
2 (1½-pound) flank steaks

• Combine first 8 ingredients in a large zip-top freezer bag. Add steaks; seal bag securely.
• Marinate in refrigerator 8 to 24 hours, turning occasionally.
• Remove steaks from marinade, discarding marinade. Grill, covered with grill lid, over medium-high heat (350° to 400°) 8 minutes on each side or to desired degree of doneness.
• Slice steaks diagonally across the grain into thin slices. Yield: 8 to 10 servings.

Molasses-Grilled Pork Tenderloin

Prep: 5 minutes • **Cook:** 20 minutes • **Other:** 8 to 24 hours

¼ cup molasses
2 tablespoons coarse-grained Dijon mustard

1 tablespoon cider vinegar
4 (¾-pound) pork tenderloins, trimmed

• Combine first 3 ingredients, and brush evenly over tenderloins. Cover and chill 8 to 24 hours.
• Grill, covered with grill lid, over medium-high heat (350° to 400°) about 20 minutes or until a meat thermometer inserted into thickest portion registers 160°, turning once. Yield: 8 to 10 servings.

◁ **Make Ahead**

No Fuss Entertaining

Secret Ingredient Savvy
No fresh thyme? No problem. Almost any herb works well with this tangy pepper-based seasoning.

◁ **Make Ahead**

5 Ingredients or Less

Gadget Magic
Resolve the "doneness" dilemma— purchase one-time use, disposable thermometers from your local grocery store.

Blue Cheese-
Stuffed Chops

Blue Cheese-Stuffed Chops

Prep: 13 minutes • **Cook:** 19 minutes

Ask your butcher to cut pockets in the loin chops
for you—it will save time and keep the recipe easy.

½ cup crumbled blue cheese
2 green onions, thinly sliced
4 (1-inch-thick) bone-in pork loin
    chops, trimmed and cut with
    pockets
1 tablespoon all-purpose flour
¼ cup sour cream

½ teaspoon chicken bouillon
    granules
⅛ teaspoon pepper
¾ cup milk
Crumbled blue cheese (optional)
Cracked pepper (optional)

• Toss together ½ cup crumbled blue cheese and green onions in a small bowl. Stuff mixture into pockets of chops; secure openings with wooden picks. Grill, covered with grill lid, over medium-high heat (350° to 400°) 8 minutes on each side or until done. Remove wooden picks. Set aside, and keep warm.
• Combine flour and next 3 ingredients in a small saucepan, whisking until smooth. Gradually whisk in milk. Bring to a boil over medium heat, stirring constantly; reduce heat, and simmer 3 minutes, whisking constantly, until mixture is thickened and bubbly. Serve chops with sauce; top with crumbled blue cheese and cracked pepper, if desired. Yield: 4 servings.

No Fuss Entertaining

Menu Makings
Serve these cheesy chops with a crisp green salad topped with grilled red peppers for a splash of color. Simply cut bell peppers in half, remove seeds, and flatten peppers with the palm of your hand. Grill 8 minutes on each side along with the chops, and they will all be ready at the same time.

20 Minutes or less

Ham 'n' Cheese Kabobs

Prep: 16 minutes • **Cook:** 4 minutes

Leftover ham becomes a feast threaded onto skewers alongside chunks of pineapple and Swiss cheese. A simple orange marmalade sauce lends a tangy touch.

1 (20-ounce) can pineapple chunks
  in juice, undrained
½ cup orange marmalade
1 tablespoon prepared mustard
¼ teaspoon ground cloves

1 pound cooked ham, cut into
  1-inch cubes
8 ounces Swiss cheese, cut into
  1-inch cubes

• Drain pineapple, reserving 2 tablespoons juice. Combine reserved juice, marmalade, mustard, and cloves; stir well with a wire whisk.
• Alternately thread ham, cheese, ham, and pineapple chunks onto 6 (12-inch) skewers. (Cheese cubes must be between and touching ham to prevent rapid melting.) Place kabobs on grill rack. Brush with marmalade mixture.
• Grill, without grill lid, over medium-high heat (350° to 400°) 3 to 4 minutes or until cheese is partially melted and ham is lightly browned, brushing often with marmalade mixture. Serve kabobs immediately. Yield: 6 servings.

Grilled Citrus-Ginger Chicken

Prep: 10 minutes • **Cook:** 30 minutes

¼ cup low-sugar orange marmalade
1 tablespoon prepared mustard
¾ teaspoon ground ginger
⅛ teaspoon ground red pepper
4 bone-in skinned chicken breast
  halves

3 tablespoons butter or margarine,
  softened
½ teaspoon grated orange rind
¼ teaspoon ground ginger

No Fuss Entertaining

Secret Ingredient Savvy
Be sure to use low-sugar orange marmalade in this glaze. The full sugar kind tends to brown too much while the chicken grills.

• Whisk together first 4 ingredients in a small bowl.
• Coat food rack with cooking spray; place rack on grill over medium-high heat (350° to 400°). Brush half of marmalade mixture over chicken. Grill chicken, covered with grill lid, 30 minutes or until done, basting twice with remaining marmalade mixture.
• Stir together butter, orange rind, and ¼ teaspoon ginger. Spoon about 1 tablespoon butter mixture on top of each chicken breast. Yield: 4 servings.

Garlic-Lime Chicken

(pictured on page 48)
Prep: 3 minutes • **Cook:** 12 minutes • **Other:** 20 minutes

A short soak in a zingy marinade infuses this grilled chicken with flavor.

½ cup lite soy sauce
¼ cup fresh lime juice
1 tablespoon Worcestershire sauce
½ teaspoon dry mustard
½ teaspoon coarsely ground pepper

2 garlic cloves, minced
4 skinned and boned chicken
   breast halves
Garnish: lime wedges

• Combine first 6 ingredients in a large zip-top freezer bag; add chicken. Seal bag; marinate in refrigerator 20 minutes, turning bag once.
• Remove chicken from marinade, discarding marinade. Coat grill rack with cooking spray; place rack on grill over medium-high heat (350° to 400°). Place chicken on rack, and grill, covered with grill lid, 6 minutes on each side or until done. Garnish, if desired. Yield: 4 servings.

No Fuss Entertaining

Menu Makings
Layer this zesty chicken atop black beans and yellow saffron rice mix, such as Mahatma.

Teriyaki Grilled Chicken Thighs

Prep: 10 minutes • **Cook:** 20 minutes • **Other:** 8 hours

8 large chicken thighs, skinned if
   desired (about 2 pounds)
½ cup soy sauce
5 green onions, chopped
¼ cup lime juice

2 tablespoons dark brown sugar
1 tablespoon honey
1 teaspoon dried crushed red
   pepper
1 garlic clove, pressed

• Place chicken in an 11- x 7-inch baking dish. Combine soy sauce and next 6 ingredients; pour over chicken. Cover and marinate in refrigerator 8 hours, turning occasionally.
• Drain chicken, reserving marinade. Bring reserved marinade to a boil in a small saucepan; reserve for basting.
• Cook chicken, without grill lid, over medium heat (300° to 350°) 10 minutes on each side or until done, basting often with reserved marinade. Yield: 4 servings.

Make Ahead

Swordfish Steaks with Basil Butter

Prep: 5 minutes • **Cook:** 16 minutes • **Other:** 8 to 24 hours

Basil gives an accented herb punch to this mild-flavored fish. Team leftover butter with any fish, shellfish, or veggies within three days.

Make Ahead ▶

Menu Makings
Round out this
meal with
steamed green
beans and roasted
new potatoes. The
basil butter
compliments
them as well as
the steaks.

½ cup butter, softened
¼ cup loosely packed fresh basil leaves
¼ cup Dijon mustard
1½ teaspoons capers
8 (8-ounce) swordfish steaks
(about 1 inch thick)

½ teaspoon salt
¼ teaspoon freshly ground pepper
Garnishes: basil sprigs and lemon
wedges

• Combine first 4 ingredients in a blender or food processor, and process until blended, stopping once to scrape down sides. Cover and chill 8 to 24 hours.
• Sprinkle steaks with salt and pepper. Grill steaks, covered with grill lid, over medium-high heat (350° to 400°) about 8 minutes on each side or until fish flakes easily when tested with a fork.
• Serve with basil butter. Garnish, if desired. Yield: 8 servings.

Savory Salmon Steaks

Prep: 5 minutes • **Cook:** 10 minutes • **Other:** 8 hours

Make Ahead ▶

Gadget Magic
We recommend
using a grill basket
for these flavorful
salmon steaks. We
found the steaks
stuck when
cooked directly on
the grill rack,
even though we
used vegetable
cooking spray.

4 (8-ounce) salmon steaks
(1 inch thick)
3 tablespoons dark brown sugar
3 tablespoons prepared horseradish

3 tablespoons Dijon mustard
3 tablespoons vegetable oil
3 tablespoons lite soy sauce

• Place steaks in a large shallow dish. Combine brown sugar and next 4 ingredients; brush half of mixture over steaks, reserving remaining half. Cover and marinate steaks in refrigerator up to 8 hours. Cover and chill remaining marinade.
• Remove steaks from dish, discarding marinade in dish; place steaks in a lightly greased grill basket. Grill, covered with grill lid, over medium-high heat (350° to 400°) 5 minutes on each side or until fish flakes easily when tested with a fork, basting often with reserved marinade. Yield: 4 servings.

Swordfish Steaks
with Basil Butter

Grilled Trout

Prep: 10 minutes • **Cook:** 12 minutes

*Lemon slices are stuffed into each trout during grilling, and lemon juice is cooked in
the sauce, lending a citrus flavor to the fish and the sauce drizzled over each fillet.*

3 (1-pound) whole trout, dressed
   (heads and fins removed)
3 tablespoons butter or margarine,
   melted

2 medium lemons, thinly sliced
3 tablespoons butter or margarine
2 tablespoons fresh lemon juice
¼ teaspoon pepper

• Brush cavity of each fish evenly with 3 tablespoons melted butter; stuff each fish
evenly with lemon slices.
• Place fish in a lightly greased grill basket. Place grill basket on food rack, and
grill, covered with grill lid, over medium-high heat (350° to 400°) about 3 to 4
minutes on each side or until fish flakes easily when tested with a fork.
• Melt 3 tablespoons butter in a small saucepan over medium heat; cook 3
minutes or until golden. Stir in lemon juice and pepper.
• Separate each trout into 2 fillets; discard lemon slices. Place trout, skin side
down, on a serving platter. Drizzle butter sauce evenly over fillets. Yield:
6 servings.

Honey-Macadamia Mahimahi

Prep: 9 minutes • **Cook:** 11 minutes

*Mahimahi and macadamia nuts blend deliciously because they both hail from the
tropics. If you need a substitute for the mahimahi, any firm white fish will do.*

**Secret
Ingredient
Savvy**
Toasting nuts
really brings out
their flavor. To
toast macadamias,
toss them in a dry
skillet over
medium heat for a
few minutes.
When you detect
their aroma,
they're done.

2 (8-ounce) mahimahi fillets
½ teaspoon vegetable oil
¼ teaspoon salt
⅛ teaspoon pepper

3 tablespoons honey, divided
¼ cup macadamia nuts, finely
   chopped and toasted

• Rub fillets with oil; sprinkle both sides evenly with salt and pepper. Brush 1 side
of fillets with 1½ tablespoons honey; place fillets in a lightly greased grill basket,
brushed side up.
• Grill, covered with grill lid, over medium-high heat (350° to 400°) 7 minutes;
turn basket. Baste fillets with remaining 1½ tablespoons honey, and sprinkle with
nuts. Grill, covered, 3 to 4 additional minutes or until fish flakes easily when tested
with a fork. Serve immediately. Yield: 2 servings.

20 Minutes or less

Tuna Steaks with Green Peppercorn Sauce

Prep: 3 minutes • **Cook:** 10 minutes

Green peppercorns in brine create a pleasant pepper flavor for this grilled fish. Look for them bottled in the condiment section of the grocery store.

3 tablespoons butter or margarine, melted
1 tablespoon chopped garlic
1 tablespoon lemon juice
6 (8-ounce) tuna steaks
¼ cup Dijon mustard

¼ cup dry red wine
3 tablespoons green peppercorns in brine, drained
2 tablespoons low-sodium teriyaki sauce
1 tablespoon butter or margarine

• Combine first 3 ingredients in a small bowl. Brush mixture evenly over both sides of tuna steaks. Grill steaks, covered with grill lid, over medium-high heat (350° to 400°) about 5 minutes on each side or until fish flakes easily when tested with a fork.
• Meanwhile, combine mustard and remaining 4 ingredients in a small saucepan, stirring well; cook over medium heat until butter melts and sauce is thoroughly heated. To serve, spoon sauce over tuna steaks. Yield: 6 servings.

Secret Ingredient Savvy

If you can't find bottled green peppercorns, substitute 3 tablespoons drained capers plus ¼ teaspoon freshly ground pepper instead.

Pacific Rim Tuna Steaks

Prep: 7 minutes • **Cook:** 12 minutes • **Other:** 15 minutes

¼ cup soy sauce
¼ cup fresh lime juice
1 tablespoon dried crushed red pepper
2 tablespoons sweet rice wine
2 tablespoons dark sesame oil

1 tablespoon grated fresh ginger
1 garlic clove, minced
6 (4-ounce) tuna steaks (1 inch thick)
Garnish: fresh cilantro sprigs

• Combine first 7 ingredients in a large zip-top freezer bag; add fish. Seal bag, and chill 15 minutes, turning occasionally.
• Remove fish from marinade, reserving marinade. Grill, covered with grill lid, over medium heat (300° to 350°) 5 to 6 minutes on each side or until fish flakes easily when tested with a fork, basting twice with reserved marinade. Remove fish to a serving platter. Garnish, if desired. Yield: 6 servings.

Kitchen Timesavers

You can make the ginger marinade for these tuna steaks ahead and store it in the refrigerator up to a week.

Grilled Vegetable Sandwiches

Prep: 18 minutes • **Cook:** 18 minutes • **Other:** 10 minutes

Secret Ingredient Savvy

Focaccia comes in all shapes and sizes and can be found in the bakery section of the grocery store. If the exact dimensions can't be found, use the closest in size possible.

¼ cup soy sauce
¼ cup lemon juice
1 tablespoon honey
½ teaspoon ground red pepper
2 small zucchini, cut diagonally into ½-inch-thick slices
1 medium-size red onion, cut into ¼-inch-thick slices

2 red bell peppers, cut into 1-inch-wide strips
1 (12- x 7-inch) focaccia (Italian flatbread)
2 (4-ounce) packages garlic-and-herb-flavored goat cheese

• Stir together first 4 ingredients in a large bowl; add vegetables, tossing gently to coat. Let mixture stand at room temperature 10 minutes, stirring occasionally.

• Remove vegetables with a slotted spoon, reserving marinade, and place in a large lightly greased grill basket. Cut focaccia in half horizontally.

• Place grill basket on grill rack. Grill, covered with grill lid, over medium-high heat (350° to 400°) 8 minutes on each side or until vegetables are tender. Set aside. Place focaccia halves, cut sides down, on grill rack. Grill, without grill lid, 2 minutes or until toasted.

• Toss grilled vegetables in reserved marinade. Spread goat cheese evenly over cut sides of focaccia; spoon grilled vegetable mixture evenly on bottom half of focaccia. Top with remaining focaccia half. Cut sandwich into 4 slices; serve immediately. Yield: 4 servings.

Grilled Portobello Pizzas

Prep: 3 minutes • **Cook:** 8 minutes

*Grilled portobellos lend a smoky,
meaty flavor to this vegetarian delight.*

1 cup roasted garlic pasta sauce
½ cup chopped fresh basil, divided
8 large portobello mushroom caps

1 (8-ounce) bottle Italian dressing
1 cup (4 ounces) shredded Italian
   three-cheese blend

• Stir together pasta sauce and ¼ cup basil. Set aside.
• Combine half of mushroom caps and half of Italian dressing evenly in each of two large zip-top freezer bags turning to coat. Seal and let stand 2 to 3 minutes. Remove mushrooms from marinade, discarding marinade.
• Place mushrooms, stem side up, on grill rack coated with cooking spray. Grill, covered with grill lid, over medium-high heat (350° to 400°) 3 minutes on each side. Turn mushrooms, stem side up, and spoon sauce mixture evenly into each. Grill 2 more minutes or until thoroughly heated. Sprinkle evenly with shredded cheese and remaining basil; serve immediately. Yield: 8 servings.

**5 Ingredients
or Less**

**Super Fast
and Fresh**

Grilled Okra and Tomatoes

Prep: 8 minutes • **Cook:** 10 minutes

*This recipe pairs two Southern foods
with a favorite style of Southern cooking.*

6 large tomatoes (about 3 pounds)
2 pounds small fresh okra
2 tablespoons olive oil

¾ teaspoon salt
¼ teaspoon freshly ground pepper

• Toss tomatoes and okra with oil. Place okra in a grill wok or basket.
• Grill okra, covered with grill lid, over medium heat (300° to 350°) 3 minutes, stirring or turning occasionally. Place tomatoes on grill rack beside wok; grill tomatoes and okra 5 to 7 minutes, turning tomatoes and okra occasionally.
• Peel tomatoes, if desired, and cut into large chunks; toss gently with okra, salt, and ground pepper. Arrange on a platter, and serve immediately. Yield: 8 servings.

**5 Ingredients
or Less**

**Super Fast
and Fresh**

**Simply
Southern**

How-To Hints
Toss the veggies
on the grill the last
10 minutes that
your entrée grills.

Grilled Corn with
Jalapeño–Lime Butter

Grilled Corn with Jalapeño-Lime Butter

Prep: 7 minutes • **Cook:** 20 minutes

Minced jalapeño mixed into butter adds a twinge of spice to this corn.
Use any leftover butter for steamed vegetables within 5 days.

½ cup butter, softened
2 jalapeño peppers, seeded and minced
2 tablespoons grated lime rind
1 teaspoon fresh lime juice

6 ears fresh corn
1 tablespoon olive oil
2 teaspoons kosher salt
1 teaspoon freshly ground black pepper

• Combine first 4 ingredients, and shape into a 6-inch log; wrap in wax paper, and chill while grilling corn.
• Rub corn with olive oil; sprinkle evenly with salt and black pepper.
• Grill corn, covered with grill lid, over high heat (400° to 500°), turning often, 15 to 20 minutes or until tender. Serve with flavored butter. Yield: 6 servings.

◀ **Editor's Favorite**

◀ **No Fuss Entertaining**

Menu Makings
Spice up traditional fried fish or chicken by serving it alongside this corn with a kick.

Grilled Tomatoes

Prep: 5 minutes • **Cook:** 4 minutes

A quick sizzle on the grill heats these Italian-inspired tomatoes
just enough to serve alongside a deserving grilled entrée.

4 large tomatoes, cut in half crosswise
2 tablespoons olive oil
2 garlic cloves, minced

¼ cup chopped fresh basil
½ teaspoon salt
½ teaspoon pepper

• Brush cut sides of tomato halves with oil, and sprinkle evenly with garlic and remaining ingredients.
• Grill, covered with grill lid, over medium-high heat (350° to 400°) about 2 minutes on each side. Serve immediately. Yield: 8 servings.

◀ **Super Fast and Fresh**

Macaroni and
Cheese, page 74

chapter three

Healthy
Homestyle

Who knew healthy could taste so good? Whether you're cutting back on calories or just want to cook healthier for your family, you can still enjoy your favorites. It's easy to please with this selection of recipes on the lighter side.

Vegetable-Cheese Melts

20 Minutes *or less*

Prep: 10 minutes • **Cook:** 7 minutes

*Nothing tastes better than homegrown vegetables
from the garden. Give them a unique twist in this sandwich.*

Double Delight
This recipe is
easily doubled if
you're having
company.

1 teaspoon vegetable oil
1 small zucchini, cut into
  ¼-inch-thick slices
1 large red bell pepper, cut into
  ¼-inch strips
1 small onion, thinly sliced and
  separated into rings

¼ teaspoon ground cumin
2 tablespoons creamy mustard-
  mayonnaise blend
4 (1.1-ounce) rye bread slices,
  toasted
¼ cup (1 ounce) shredded
  colby-Jack cheese blend

• Heat oil in a large nonstick skillet over medium-high heat. Add zucchini, bell pepper, and onion; cook 6 minutes or until tender. Stir in cumin.
• Spread 1½ teaspoons mustard-mayonnaise blend on each of 4 toast slices. Place 2 slices, mustard side up, on a baking sheet. Arrange 1 cup vegetable mixture on top of each. Sprinkle evenly with cheese. Broil 3 inches from heat 40 seconds or until cheese melts. Top with remaining toast, mustard side down. Serve immediately. Yield: 2 servings (serving size: 1 sandwich).

Per serving: Calories 292 (27% from fat); Fat 8.7g (sat 3.6g, mono 2.2g, poly 1.3g); Protein 10.2g; Carb 43.7g; Fiber 6.7g; Chol 13mg; Iron 2.6mg; Sodium 712mg; Calc 146mg

Spinach-and-Cheese Calzones

Prep: 19 minutes • **Cook:** 24 minutes

1 (10-ounce) package frozen
    chopped spinach, thawed and
    well drained
½ cup chopped onion
½ (6-ounce) package Canadian-style
    bacon, chopped
1 tablespoon garlic powder
½ teaspoon salt
1 (15-ounce) container part-skim
    ricotta cheese

1¼ cups (5 ounces) shredded light
    pizza cheese blend
1 teaspoon dried Italian seasoning
2 (11-ounce) cans refrigerated
    crusty French loaf
1 (26-ounce) jar fat-free garlic-
    and-herb pasta sauce (we used
    Healthy Choice)

• Sauté first 5 ingredients in a large nonstick skillet coated with cooking spray 6 minutes or until bacon is browned. Remove from heat. Combine ricotta cheese, pizza cheese blend, and Italian seasoning; stir into spinach mixture.

• Unroll each bread loaf on a lightly floured surface, and cut each into 4 rectangles. Spoon a heaping ⅓ cup spinach mixture onto half of each rectangle. Fold dough over spinach filling, pressing edges to seal. Crimp edges with a fork dipped in flour.

• Place calzones on baking sheets coated with cooking spray. Coat each calzone with cooking spray.

• Bake at 400° for 18 minutes or until golden. Serve with pasta sauce. Yield: 8 servings (serving size: 1 calzone and ¼ cup pasta sauce).

Per serving: Calories 378 (22% from fat); Fat 9.3g (sat 4.8g, mono 2.3g, poly 0.6g); Protein 23.6g; Carb 50.4g; Fiber 3.6g; Chol 28mg; Iron 3.6mg; Sodium 1,249mg; Calc 332mg

Kid Friendly

Fix it Faster
To save time preparing this recipe, place frozen spinach in refrigerator overnight to thaw.

Vegetable
Pasta

30 Minutes or less

Vegetable Pasta

Prep: 8 minutes • **Cook:** 16 minutes

Ridged penne pasta makes a sturdy base for this chunky tomato-vegetable sauce, but you can substitute an equal amount of another favorite pasta if you'd like.

8 ounces uncooked penne pasta
4 teaspoons olive oil, divided
2 medium zucchini, cut into ¼-inch-thick slices (about 3 cups)
1 medium onion, cut into ¼-inch-thick slices (about 1¼ cups)
2 garlic cloves, minced

2 (14½-ounce) cans Italian-style stewed tomatoes, undrained
¼ teaspoon salt
¼ teaspoon freshly ground pepper
½ cup chopped fresh basil
¼ cup freshly grated Parmesan cheese

• Cook pasta according to package directions, omitting salt and fat; drain. Add 2 teaspoons olive oil; keep warm.
• Meanwhile, heat remaining olive oil in a large nonstick skillet over medium-high heat. Add zucchini, onion, and garlic. Sauté 4 minutes or until lightly browned. Remove vegetables from skillet; keep warm.
• Add tomatoes, salt, and pepper to skillet. Cook over medium-high heat 12 minutes or until thickened, stirring occasionally. Stir in vegetables and basil. Serve over pasta; sprinkle with cheese. Yield: 4 servings (serving size: 1 cup pasta, 1 cup vegetable mixture, and 1 tablespoon cheese).

Per serving: Calories 350 (18% from fat); Fat 7.1g (sat 1.7g, mono 3.9g, poly 0.9g); Protein 12.7g; Carb 61.6g; Fiber 6.6g; Chol 4mg; Iron 2.1mg; Sodium 933mg; Calc 143mg

Stovetop Solution

Secret Ingredient Savvy
Preseasoned canned tomatoes add great flavor to your home-made pasta sauce without wasting time or money.

Mediterranean Ravioli

Prep: 9 minutes • **Cook:** 11 minutes

Frozen ravioli and commercial tomato sauce speed up preparation of this trendy one-dish meal.

1 (14.5-ounce) package light cheese
   ravioli (we used Buitoni Light
   Four-Cheese Ravioli)
2 teaspoons olive oil
1 small eggplant, peeled and cut into
   1-inch cubes

1 cup chopped onion
2 garlic cloves, minced
2 cups chunky tomato sauce (we
   used Classico Tomato and Basil)
3 tablespoons freshly grated
   Parmesan cheese

• Cook ravioli according to package directions, omitting salt and fat. Rinse and drain; set aside.

• Meanwhile, coat a large nonstick skillet with cooking spray. Add oil; place over medium-high heat until hot. Add eggplant, onion, and garlic; cook, stirring constantly, 5 minutes or until tender. Stir in tomato sauce; cook 1 minute or until thoroughly heated.

• Combine ravioli and eggplant mixture in a large bowl; toss gently to coat. Sprinkle evenly with Parmesan cheese. Yield: 6 servings (serving size: 1 cup).

Per serving: Calories 269 (20% from fat); Fat 6.2g (sat 2.3g, mono 1.3g, poly 0.2g); Protein 12.9g; Carb 42.2g; Fiber 5.3g; Chol 29mg; Iron 1.9mg; Sodium 613mg; Calc 178mg

30 Minutes *or less*

Fettuccine Primavera

Prep: 9 minutes • **Cook:** 14 minutes

Enjoy the bounty of vegetables with each bite of this creamy pasta classic.

1 small onion, chopped
1 red bell pepper, cut into thin strips
1 cup fresh broccoli florets
1 cup sliced fresh mushrooms
8 ounces fresh sugar snap peas
1 (9-ounce) package refrigerated
    fettuccine
1 (1.6-ounce) package Alfredo sauce
    mix (we used Knorr)
1½ cups 1% low-fat milk
1 tablespoon butter
½ cup (2 ounces) shredded Parmesan
    cheese, divided
¼ teaspoon freshly ground pepper

• Cook onion in a large nonstick skillet coated with cooking spray over medium heat, stirring constantly, 3 minutes or until tender. Add bell pepper strips, broccoli, and mushrooms. Cook, stirring constantly, until vegetables are crisp-tender. Stir in peas, and cook 2 minutes.
• Meanwhile, prepare pasta according to package directions, omitting salt and fat. Rinse and drain; set aside.
• Prepare sauce mix according to package directions, using 1% low-fat milk and 1 tablespoon butter. Stir in ¼ cup cheese.
• Combine vegetables, pasta, and sauce, tossing gently.
• Sprinkle remaining cheese over top of pasta. Sprinkle with pepper. Serve immediately. Yield: 6 servings (serving size: 1 cup).

Per serving: Calories 266 (25% from fat); Fat 7g (sat 3.7g, mono 1.8g, poly 0.3g); Protein 12.7g; Carb 35.2g; Fiber 3.4g; Chol 16mg; Iron 0.8mg; Sodium 636mg; Calc 197mg

Stovetop Solution

Secret Ingredient Savvy
We found that Knorr's Alfredo sauce mix offered the most abundant creaminess. We made it extra creamy by adding Parmesan cheese.

Macaroni and Cheese

Editor's Favorite

Kid Friendly

Menu Makings
Mac 'n' cheese goes with virtually anything. Serve it with your favorite veggies for a meatless meal.

Prep: 10 minutes • **Cook:** 25 minutes

1 (12-ounce) container 1% low-fat cottage cheese
1 (8-ounce) container light sour cream
4 cups cooked elbow macaroni (cooked without salt or fat)
2 cups (8 ounces) shredded 2% reduced-fat sharp Cheddar cheese
½ cup fat-free milk

1 green onion, chopped
½ teaspoon salt
½ teaspoon pepper
1 large egg
Butter-flavored cooking spray
¼ cup fine, dry breadcrumbs (commercial)
¼ teaspoon paprika

• Process cottage cheese and sour cream in a blender until smooth, stopping to scrape down sides.
• Combine cottage cheese mixture, macaroni, and next 6 ingredients; spoon into a 2-quart deep baking dish coated with butter-flavored cooking spray. Sprinkle with breadcrumbs and paprika; coat with cooking spray.
• Cover and bake at 400° for 20 minutes. Uncover and bake 5 more minutes. Yield: 8 servings.

Per serving: Calories 289 (35% from fat); Fat 10.8g (sat 6.7g, mono 0.4g, poly 0.2g); Protein 20g; Carb 24.9g; Fiber 0.3g; Chol 63mg; Iron 0.8mg; Sodium 697mg; Calc 306mg

Macaroni and Cheese

Broccoli-Ginger Stir-Fry

Prep: 6 minutes • **Cook:** 12 minutes

**Stovetop
Solution**

6 ounces uncooked angel hair pasta
¾ cup vegetable broth
⅓ cup lite soy sauce
3 tablespoons dry white wine
1 tablespoon cornstarch

2 teaspoons minced fresh ginger
3 large garlic cloves, minced
1 teaspoon olive oil
1 (16-ounce) package broccoli stir-
    fry blend (we used Birds Eye)

• Cook pasta according to package directions, omitting salt and fat. Drain pasta, and keep warm.
• Meanwhile, stir together broth and next 5 ingredients; set aside.
• Heat oil in a large nonstick skillet or wok at medium-high heat. Add vegetables; stir-fry 8 minutes.
• Stir in broth mixture, and cook 2 minutes or until slightly thickened. Serve over pasta. Yield: 4 servings.

Per serving: Calories 233 (9% from fat); Fat 2.4g (sat 0.3g, mono 0.9g, poly 0.4g); Protein 9.4g; Carb 42.7g; Fiber 3.4g; Chol 0mg; Iron 1mg; Sodium 1,028mg; Calc 31mg

Garlic-and-Herb Cheese Grits

Prep: 3 minutes • **Cook:** 7 minutes

**Stovetop
Solution**

**5 Ingredients
or Less**

4 cups low-sodium, fat-free chicken
    broth
1 cup quick-cooking grits, uncooked
¼ teaspoon freshly ground pepper

1 (5-ounce) package light garlic-
    and-herb spreadable cheese

• Bring chicken broth to a boil in a medium saucepan over high heat; gradually stir in grits. Cook, stirring constantly, 5 to 7 minutes or until thickened.
• Remove from heat; stir in pepper and cheese. Serve immediately. Yield: 5 cups (serving size: 1 cup).

Per serving: Calories 128 (37% from fat); Fat 5.3g (sat 3.8g, mono 0.1g, poly 0.2g); Protein 7.6g; Carb 26.9g; Fiber 0.5g; Chol 25mg; Iron 1.3mg; Sodium 644mg; Calc 4mg

Menu Makings
Serve these grits as a side dish with grilled or broiled beef or chicken, or serve them as a main dish for breakfast.

Pesto-Crusted Orange Roughy

Prep: 5 minutes • **Cook:** 15 minutes

2 tablespoons pesto
½ cup fine, dry breadcrumbs

¼ teaspoon pepper
4 (4-ounce) orange roughy fillets

• Combine pesto, breadcrumbs, and pepper in a shallow dish. Dredge fillets in breadcrumb mixture, and place in an 11- x 7-inch baking dish coated with cooking spray. Coat fillets with cooking spray.
• Bake at 400° for 15 minutes or until fish flakes easily when tested with a fork. Yield: 4 servings.

Per serving: Calories 172 (25% from fat); Fat 4.7g (sat 1.1g, mono 2.9g, poly 0.4g); Protein 20.2g; Carb 11.2g; Fiber 0.9g; Chol 25mg; Iron 1mg; Sodium 529mg; Calc 105mg

Sautéed Shrimp and Linguine

Stovetop Solution

No Fuss Entertaining

Kitchen Timesavers

If you don't see peeled shrimp at the seafood counter, ask the attendant to peel it for you. If you'd rather peel it yourself, you'll need to purchase 2 pounds in the shell.

Prep: 10 minutes • **Cook:** 14 minutes

8 ounces uncooked linguine
1 tablespoon dark sesame oil
1 small onion, chopped
2 garlic cloves, minced
6 plum tomatoes, coarsely chopped
1 (2¼-ounce) can sliced ripe olives, drained

¼ cup lemon juice
1½ teaspoons dried Italian seasoning
½ teaspoon salt
½ teaspoon freshly ground pepper
1½ pounds peeled, medium-size fresh shrimp
2 ounces crumbled feta cheese

• Cook pasta according to package directions, omitting salt and fat. Drain.
• Meanwhile, heat oil in a large nonstick skillet over medium-high heat. Add onion and garlic; sauté 3 minutes or until tender. Add tomato and next 5 ingredients; cook 6 minutes, stirring constantly. Add shrimp; cook 5 minutes or just until shrimp turn pink, stirring occasionally.
• Serve over pasta; sprinkle with cheese. Yield: 6 servings (serving size: 1 cup shrimp mixture and ⅔ cup pasta).

Per serving: Calories 378 (21% from fat); Fat 8.7g (sat 2.6g, mono 2.5g, poly 2.2g); Protein 38.3g; Carb 36.1g; Fiber 2.8g; Chol 238mg; Iron 6mg; Sodium 618mg; Calc 162mg

Baked Hush Puppies

Prep: 11 minutes • **Cook:** 13 minutes per batch

2 cups self-rising cornmeal mix
⅛ teaspoon ground red pepper
2 large eggs, lightly beaten
¾ cup 1% low-fat milk
¼ cup vegetable oil
½ cup finely chopped onion

• Combine cornmeal mix and red pepper in a large bowl; make a well in center of mixture.
• Combine eggs and next 3 ingredients in a large bowl; stir well. Add egg mixture to cornmeal mixture, stirring just until dry ingredients are moistened. Spoon about 1 tablespoon batter into miniature (1¾-inch) muffin pans coated with cooking spray.
• Bake at 425° for 13 minutes or until golden. Remove from pans, and serve immediately. Yield: about 3 dozen (serving size: 1 hush puppy).

Per serving: Calories 69 (30% from fat); Fat 2.4g (sat 0.3g, mono 1.2g, poly 0.7g); Protein 1.6g; Carb 10.7g; Fiber 0g; Chol 12mg; Iron 0.9mg; Sodium 229mg; Calc 19mg

Big Batch

Menu Makings
Serve these crisp "puppies" with Oven-Fried Catfish (page 78).

Jalapeño Cornbread

Prep: 11 minutes • **Cook:** 21 minutes

1 tablespoon vegetable oil
1 cup self-rising yellow cornmeal
2 teaspoons baking powder
2 large eggs
3 tablespoons nonfat sour cream
1 (8¾-ounce) can cream-style corn
¼ cup sliced pickled jalapeño pepper, chopped

• Heat oil in an 8-inch cast-iron skillet in a 450° oven 5 minutes or until hot.
• Combine cornmeal and baking powder in a large bowl; make a well in the center of mixture. Combine eggs and next 3 ingredients; add to cornmeal mixture, stirring just until dry ingredients are moistened.
• Remove pan from oven. Stir hot oil into batter. Pour batter into hot skillet. Bake at 450° for 21 minutes or until golden. Remove from pan immediately. Cut into wedges. Yield: 8 servings.

Per serving: Calories 137 (26% from fat); Fat 3.9g (sat 0.6g, mono 1.5g, poly 0.7g); Protein 3.7g; Carb 21.6g; Fiber 1.6g; Chol 54mg; Iron 1.2mg; Sodium 526mg; Calc 102mg

Simply Southern

Gadget Magic
For the quickest way to chop jalapeños, snip them in a small cup using kitchen shears.

Hummus

Prep: 10 minutes

No Cook Creation

Super Fast and Fresh

Two Meals in One

Use ½ cup of this creamy bean spread inside a pita to make a sandwich. Or serve it as a dip with pita chips or vegetables.

1 (19-ounce) can chickpeas (garbanzo beans), rinsed and drained
¼ cup tahini
1 tablespooon chopped fresh parsley
1 garlic clove

⅓ cup fresh lemon juice
1½ teaspoons ground cumin
¼ teaspoon ground red pepper
1 shallot, quartered
1 tablespoon lite soy sauce

• Process all ingredients in a food processor until smooth, stopping to scrape down sides. Yield: 1¾ cups (serving size: ¼ cup).

Per serving: Calories 137 (39% from fat); Fat 5.9g (sat 0.8g, mono 2g, poly 2.6g); Protein 6g; Carb 16.9g; Fiber 4.3g; Chol 0mg; Iron 2mg; Sodium 8mg; Calc 41mg

Roasted Garlic-Potato Soup

Prep: 10 minutes • **Cook:** 3 minutes

5 Ingredients or Less

2 cups fat-free milk
1½ cups water
½ (7.6-ounce) package roasted garlic instant mashed potatoes

1 cup (4 ounces) shredded 2% reduced-fat sharp Cheddar cheese, divided
¼ teaspoon freshly ground pepper

• Combine milk and 1½ cups water in a large saucepan; bring to a boil. Remove from heat; add potatoes, and stir with a wire whisk until well blended. Add ¾ cup cheese, stirring until cheese melts. Spoon evenly into 4 bowls; sprinkle evenly with remaining ¼ cup cheese and pepper. Yield: 4 servings (serving size: 1 cup).

Per serving: Calories 146 (40% from fat); Fat 6.5g (sat 3.9g, mono 0.1g, poly 0g); Protein 12.7g; Carb 11g; Fiber 0.2g; Chol 20mg; Iron 0.2mg; Sodium 299mg; Calc 354mg

Stewed Okra, Corn, and Tomatoes

Prep: 5 minutes • **Cook:** 15 minutes

1½ cups frozen sliced okra
1 cup frozen whole kernel corn
¼ cup diced cooked ham
1 teaspoon dried basil

¼ teaspoon salt
¼ teaspoon pepper
1 (14½-ounce) can no-salt-added
    stewed tomatoes, undrained

• Combine all ingredients in a large saucepan coated with cooking spray.
• Bring to a boil; cover, reduce heat, and simmer 15 minutes, stirring occasionally.
Yield: 4 servings (serving size: ¾ cup).

Per serving: Calories 99 (8% from fat); Fat 0.9g (sat 0.3g, mono 0.1g, poly 0.2g);
Protein 5.2g; Carb 19.6g; Fiber 4.9g; Chol 5mg; Iron 2.2mg; Sodium 252mg; Calc 107mg

Stovetop Solution

Simply Southern

Menu Makings
Pair this side dish with your favorite Southern entrée.

Oatmeal-Raisin Cookies

Prep: 8 minutes • **Cook:** 12 minutes per batch

¼ cup margarine, softened
½ cup granulated sugar
½ cup firmly packed brown sugar
½ cup egg substitute
2 teaspoons vanilla extract
¾ cup all-purpose flour

¼ teaspoon baking soda
⅛ teaspoon salt
1½ cups quick-cooking oats,
    uncooked
½ cup raisins

• Beat margarine at medium speed with an electric mixer. Gradually add sugars, beating well. Add egg substitute and vanilla; mix well.
• Combine flour and next 3 ingredients. Gradually add to margarine mixture, mixing well. Stir in raisins.
• Drop dough by 2 teaspoonfuls onto baking sheets coated with cooking spray. Bake at 350° for 10 to 12 minutes or until lightly browned. Remove to wire racks to cool. Yield: 3 dozen (serving size: 1 cookie).

Per serving: Calories 64 (21% from fat); Fat 1.5g (sat 0.3g, mono 0.7g, poly 0.5g);
Protein 1.2g; Carb 11.8g; Fiber 0.5g; Chol 0mg; Iron 0.4mg; Sodium 40mg; Calc 7mg

Kid Friendly

Make Ahead

Pears with
Raspberry
Sherbet

Pears with Raspberry Sherbet

Prep: 15 minutes

5 tablespoons fat-free chocolate
    sundae syrup, divided (we used
    Smucker's)
1 (29-ounce) can pear halves in
    extra light syrup, drained

1¼ cups raspberry sherbet
1¼ cups fresh raspberries
    Garnish: fresh mint sprigs

No Fuss
Entertaining

5 Ingredients
or Less

No-Cook
Creation

• Drizzle 2 tablespoons chocolate syrup evenly over 5 dessert plates. Place pear halves on syrup, using a slotted spoon. Top each serving with ¼ cup sherbet; drizzle evenly with remaining chocolate syrup. Sprinkle raspberries over pear halves. Garnish, if desired. Serve immediately. Yield: 5 servings (serving size: 1 pear half, ¼ cup sherbet, 1 tablespoon chocolate syrup, and ¼ cup raspberries.)

Per serving: Calories 175 (3% from fat); Fat 0.7g (sat 0.3g, mono 0g, poly 0.1g); Protein 1.8g; Carb 41.8g; Fiber 4g; Chol 3mg; Iron 0.5mg; Sodium 72mg; Calc 47mg

Sautéed Pineapple

Prep: 3 minutes • **Cook:** 7 minutes

*Brown sugar and butter add a sweetness
to this pineapple you won't be able to resist.*

2 (20-ounce) cans pineapple chunks
    in juice
1 tablespoon reduced-calorie
    margarine

2 tablespoons brown sugar
1 tablespoon rum or ½ teaspoon
    rum extract
½ teaspoon ground cinnamon

5 Ingredients
or Less

No Fuss
Entertaining

• Drain pineapple chunks, reserving ¼ cup juice.
• Melt margarine in a large nonstick skillet over medium heat; add pineapple chunks, reserved juice, brown sugar, rum, and cinnamon. Bring to a boil; reduce heat, and simmer 5 minutes, stirring frequently. Serve warm. Yield: 6 servings.

Per serving: Calories 91 (9% from fat); Fat 0.9g (sat 0.2g, mono 0.4g, poly 0.3g); Protein 0g; Carb 18.9g; Fiber 1g; Chol 0mg; Iron 0.4mg; Sodium 33mg; Calc 5mg

Greek Spinach
Quiche, page 107

chapter four

One-Dish
Family Favorites

Looking for a new weeknight solution that will get dinner on the table fast? Spend less time in the kitchen and more time relaxing with your family with these one-dish wonders. Select an entrée from this chapter to satisfy any appetite.

Breakfast Burritos

Prep: 8 minutes • **Cook:** 12 minutes

*Have a Southwest-style breakfast with this blend of
potatoes, onions, and eggs wrapped in warm flour tortillas.*

1 (10-ounce) baking potato
8 bacon slices
4 green onions, sliced
3 large eggs, lightly beaten
⅓ cup milk

¼ teaspoon salt
¼ teaspoon pepper
4 flour tortillas (we used
    7-inch)
Toppings: sour cream, picante sauce

• Prick potato with a sharp knife. Microwave at HIGH 5 minutes; let stand
5 minutes. Peel and dice potato.
• While potato cooks, cook bacon in a large skillet until crisp; drain bacon on
paper towels, reserving drippings in skillet. Crumble bacon, and set aside.
• Sauté potato in drippings over medium-high heat 3 minutes or until potato
begins to brown. Remove from skillet, using a slotted spoon; drain on paper
towels. Sauté green onions in drippings 1 minute.
• Combine eggs and next 3 ingredients; pour over green onions. Cook over
medium heat 2 minutes or until set, stirring gently. Stir in bacon and potato.
Remove from heat.
• Place tortillas in a zip-top freezer bag; do not seal. Microwave at HIGH
1 minute or until warm.
• Working with 1 tortilla at a time, spoon one-fourth of egg mixture down center
of tortilla. Fold bottom third of tortilla over filling; fold opposite sides over filling,
leaving top open. Repeat procedure with remaining tortillas and egg mixture.
Serve with desired toppings. Yield: 4 servings.

Green Eggs and Ham

Prep: 15 minutes • **Cook:** 5 minutes

*Guacamole-stuffed eggs are topped with country
ham in this storybook-inspired recipe.*

6 ounces thinly sliced country ham
12 large hard-cooked eggs
1 ripe avocado, peeled and mashed
2 tablespoons finely chopped onion
1 garlic clove, minced
2 tablespoons mayonnaise or salad
   dressing

1½ to 2 tablespoons fresh lime juice
1 teaspoon hot sauce
1 small tomato, peeled, seeded, and
   finely chopped

• Cook ham in a nonstick skillet over medium heat 5 minutes or until lightly
browned, turning once. Drain and finely chop.
• Cut eggs in half lengthwise, and carefully remove yolks. Mash yolks with a fork;
add avocado and next 5 ingredients, stirring well. Fold in tomato, and spoon into
egg whites. Top with ham. Yield: 2 dozen.

◀ **Kid Friendly**

Veggie Scramble

Prep: 10 minutes • **Cook:** 10 minutes

½ small red bell pepper
½ small green bell pepper
¼ small sweet onion
8 large eggs, lightly beaten
½ teaspoon freshly ground black
   pepper

¼ teaspoon salt
½ cup (2 ounces) shredded sharp
   Cheddar cheese

• Chop bell peppers and onion. Cook in a large skillet coated with cooking spray
over medium-high heat 5 minutes or until vegetables are tender.
• Whisk together eggs, black pepper, and salt. Add mixture to vegetables in skillet,
and cook, without stirring, until eggs begin to set on bottom. Draw a spatula
across bottom of skillet to form large curds. Sprinkle with cheese, and continue
cooking until eggs are thickened but still moist. (Do not stir constantly.) Remove
from heat. Serve immediately. Yield: 4 servings.

◀ **Super Fast
and Fresh**

Menu Makings
Serve these
veggie-filled eggs
with whole grain
toast for a healthy
breakfast.

Breakfast Pizza

30 Minutes or less

Gadget Magic
Quickly snip fresh basil in a small cup using kitchen shears.

Prep: 8 minutes • **Cook:** 20 minutes

1 (16-ounce) prebaked Italian pizza crust
1 (8-ounce) package shredded Italian cheese blend, divided
8 bacon slices, cooked and crumbled
4 plum tomatoes, sliced

½ teaspoon freshly ground pepper
2 large eggs
½ cup milk
¼ cup chopped fresh basil

• Place pizza crust on a pizza pan or jellyroll pan. Sprinkle half of cheese over bread shell; top with bacon, tomato, and pepper. Whisk together eggs, milk, and basil; pour in center of pizza (it will spread to edges). Sprinkle with remaining cheese.
• Bake at 425° for 20 minutes or until egg mixture is set. Yield: 4 to 6 servings.

Weeknight Pizza Casserole

Kid Friendly

Prep: 10 minutes • **Cook:** 35 minutes • **Other:** 5 minutes

1 pound ground beef
1 (3.5-ounce) package sliced pepperoni
1 (2¼-ounce) can sliced ripe olives, drained
1 medium-size green bell pepper, chopped (optional)

1 (14-ounce) jar pizza sauce
1 (8-ounce) package shredded mozzarella cheese
¾ cup biscuit mix
1 cup milk
2 large eggs, lightly beaten

• Cook ground beef in a large skillet over medium-high heat, stirring until meat crumbles and is no longer pink; drain. Stir in pepperoni, olives, and bell pepper. Spoon into a lightly greased 8-inch square baking dish. Top with pizza sauce and cheese.
• Combine biscuit mix, milk, and eggs, stirring until smooth. Pour over cheese, spreading evenly.
• Bake, uncovered, at 400° for 30 to 35 minutes or until golden. Let stand 5 minutes before serving. Yield: 4 servings.

Deep-Dish Taco Squares

Prep: 7 minutes • **Cook:** 34 minutes • **Other:** 5 minutes

Kid Friendly

2 cups all-purpose baking mix
½ cup water
1 pound ground chuck
1 small green bell pepper, chopped
1 (8-ounce) jar picante sauce
⅓ cup mayonnaise

1 (8-ounce) container sour cream
1 cup (4 ounces) shredded sharp
    Cheddar cheese
Paprika
Picante sauce (optional)

Secret Ingredient Savvy
Use hot picante sauce to pack a punch in this Tex-Mex creation.

• Combine baking mix and ½ cup water in a medium bowl, stirring with a fork until blended. Press mixture in a lightly greased 11-x 7-inch baking dish. Bake at 375° for 9 minutes.

• While crust bakes, cook beef and bell pepper in a large skillet over medium-high heat, stirring until meat crumbles and is no longer pink; drain. Stir in jar of picante sauce; spoon over crust.

• Stir together mayonnaise, sour cream, and cheese; spoon over meat mixture, spreading to within ½ inch of edges. Sprinkle with paprika.

• Bake, uncovered, at 375° for 25 minutes or until thoroughly heated. Let stand 5 minutes; cut into squares. Serve taco squares with additional picante sauce, if desired. Yield: 4 servings.

20 Minutes or less   Quick Mexican Dinner

Prep: 7 minutes • **Cook:** 12 minutes

1 pound ground beef
1 (15-ounce) can Spanish rice
1 (15-ounce) can Ranch-style
    beans, undrained

10 (10-inch) flour tortillas
Toppings: shredded cheese, shredded
    lettuce, chopped tomato, sour
    cream, sliced jalapeño peppers

Stovetop Solution
5 Ingredients or Less

• Cook beef in a large skillet over medium heat, stirring until it crumbles and is no longer pink; drain. Add rice and beans, and cook until thoroughly heated. Spoon evenly onto half of each tortilla; fold tortillas over. Serve with desired toppings. Yield: 5 servings.

Beefy Noodle
Casserole

Beefy Noodle Casserole

Prep: 7 minutes • **Cook:** 17 minutes

4 ounces uncooked wide egg noodles
1 pound ground chuck
1 (14-ounce) jar pasta sauce
1 (8-ounce) package cream cheese,
    cubed

1 cup cottage cheese
½ cup sour cream
½ cup shredded Parmesan cheese

• Cook noodles according to package directions; drain. Place noodles in a lightly greased 11-x 7-inch baking dish. Set aside.
• Meanwhile, cook beef in a large skillet, stirring until it crumbles and is no longer pink; drain. Stir in pasta sauce; set aside.
• Place cream cheese in a 1-quart glass bowl; microwave at HIGH 1 minute or until softened. Stir in cottage cheese and sour cream. Spread mixture over noodles. Spoon beef mixture over cream cheese mixture. Sprinkle with Parmesan cheese. Cover tightly with heavy-duty plastic wrap; fold back a small corner to allow steam to escape. Microwave at HIGH 6 to 8 minutes or until mixture is thoroughly heated, giving dish a half-turn after 4 minutes. Yield: 4 servings.

Kid Friendly

Menu Makings
Serve this cheesy casserole with a garden salad for a well-rounded meal.

Corn Chip Chili Pie

Prep: 4 minutes • **Cook:** 13 minutes

1 pound ground chuck
1 medium onion, chopped
1 (16-ounce) can kidney beans,
    drained
1 (11-ounce) can sweet whole
    kernel corn, drained
1 (8-ounce) can tomato sauce

1 (2¼-ounce) can sliced ripe
    olives
1 (1.25-ounce) package chili
    seasoning
1 cup (4 ounces) shredded sharp
    Cheddar cheese
1 cup coarsely crushed corn chips

• Combine beef and onion in a 2½-quart baking dish. Cover with wax paper. Microwave at HIGH 5 to 6 minutes or until meat is no longer pink, stirring at 2-minute intervals to crumble meat; drain.
• Stir in beans and next 4 ingredients. Cover and microwave at HIGH 4 to 5 minutes or until thoroughly heated, giving dish a half-turn after 2 minutes. Sprinkle with cheese and corn chips.
• Microwave at MEDIUM HIGH (70% power), uncovered, 2 minutes or until cheese melts. Yield: 6 servings.

Super Fast and Fresh

Kid Friendly

Microwave Miracle

Speedy Shepherd's Pie

Prep: 8 minutes • **Cook:** 14 minutes • **Other:** 5 minutes

½ (22-ounce) package frozen mashed potatoes (about 3 cups)
1⅓ cups milk
1 pound ground round
1 cup fresh or frozen chopped onion

1 cup frozen peas and carrots
½ teaspoon pepper
1 (12-ounce) jar beef gravy
½ cup (2 ounces) shredded Cheddar cheese

• Combine potatoes and milk in a microwave-safe bowl. Microwave at HIGH, uncovered, 8 minutes, stirring once; set aside.
• Meanwhile, cook ground round and onion in a 10-inch ovenproof skillet over medium heat, stirring until meat crumbles and is no longer pink. Add peas and carrots, pepper, and gravy. Cook over medium heat 3 minutes or until thoroughly heated, stirring often; remove mixture from heat.
• Spoon potatoes evenly over meat mixture, leaving a 1-inch border around edge of skillet. Broil 5½ inches from heat 3 minutes or until bubbly. Sprinkle with cheese; let stand 5 minutes. Yield: 6 servings.

Pronto Enchiladas

Prep: 10 minutes • **Cook:** 30 minutes

1 pound ground chuck
1 small onion, chopped
1 (10¾-ounce) can cream of mushroom soup, undiluted
2 (4.5-ounce) cans chopped green chiles

8 (8-inch) flour tortillas
1 (8-ounce) package shredded colby-Jack cheese blend
1 (10¾-ounce) can Cheddar cheese soup, undiluted
Salsa

• Cook beef and onion in a large skillet, stirring until meat crumbles and is no longer pink; drain. Stir in mushroom soup and 1 can green chiles.
• Spoon ½ cup beef mixture down center of each tortilla; sprinkle each with 2½ tablespoons cheese blend. Roll up tortillas, and place each, seam side down, in a lightly greased 13- x 9-inch baking dish. Pour Cheddar cheese soup over tortillas.
• Drain remaining can green chiles; sprinkle chiles and remaining cheese blend over soup.
• Bake, covered, at 350° for 20 minutes; uncover and bake 5 additional minutes. Serve with salsa. Yield: 4 servings.

Skillet Sausage and Cabbage

Prep: 15 minutes • **Cook:** 25 minutes

1 (16-ounce) package kielbasa
   sausage, cut into 1-inch pieces
1 medium onion, thinly sliced
1 green bell pepper, cut into strips
6 cups coarsely chopped cabbage

1 cup dry white wine or chicken
   broth
½ teaspoon caraway seeds
½ teaspoon salt
½ teaspoon pepper

• Sauté sausage in a large heavy nonstick skillet over medium heat until browned; drain on paper towels.

• Add onion and bell pepper to skillet, and sauté 2 to 3 minutes. Add cabbage, and cook, stirring often, 8 minutes. Add sausage, wine, and remaining ingredients. Reduce heat to medium-low, and cook 10 minutes or until cabbage is tender. Serve immediately. Yield: 4 servings.

Stovetop Solution

Menu Makings
Add buttered baby carrots and a hard roll to accompany this dish.

30 Minutes or less Ham-Broccoli Pot Pie

Prep: 8 minutes • **Cook:** 19 minutes

1 (10-ounce) package frozen
   chopped broccoli, thawed
1 (11-ounce) can sweet whole
   kernel corn, drained
1 (10¾-ounce) can cream of
   mushroom soup, undiluted
2 cups chopped cooked ham

1 (8-ounce) package shredded
   colby-Jack cheese blend
1 (8-ounce) container sour cream
½ teaspoon pepper
½ teaspoon dried mustard
½ (15-ounce) package refrigerated
   piecrusts

• Arrange broccoli in a lightly greased 10-inch pieplate or 1½–quart round baking dish.

• Stir together corn and next 6 ingredients; spoon over broccoli. Cover loosely with plastic wrap. Microwave at HIGH 3 to 4 minutes or until heated.

• Meanwhile, unfold piecrust, and roll into a 12-inch circle. Place over warm ham mixture. Fold edges under, and crimp; cut slits in top for steam to escape.

• Bake at 425° for 15 minutes or until golden. Yield: 6 servings.

Kid Friendly

Secret Ingredient Savvy
Look for already chopped ham packaged in the meat department of the supermarket.

20 Minutes or less

Shrimp and Tortellini

Prep: 5 minutes • **Cook:** 7 minutes

Super Fast and Fresh

Secret Ingredient Savvy

It's faster to purchase peeled shrimp for this dish, but if you'd rather, purchase one pound in the shell.

1 (9-ounce) package refrigerated cheese-filled tortellini
¾ pound peeled, medium-size fresh shrimp
1 shallot, minced

2 tablespoons chopped fresh basil or 2 teaspoons dried basil
⅓ cup butter or margarine, melted
½ cup grated Parmesan cheese
Garnish: fresh basil sprigs

• Cook tortellini according to package directions; drain.
• Meanwhile, cook shrimp, shallot, and chopped basil in butter in a large skillet over medium-high heat, stirring constantly, 5 minutes or just until shrimp turn pink. Add tortellini and Parmesan cheese; toss gently. Garnish, if desired. Yield: 4 servings.

Crawfish Étouffée

Prep: 3 minutes • **Cook:** 33 minutes

Stovetop Solution

Simply Southern

This speedy version of the classic gets high flavor from a quick simmer with frozen seasoning blend.

1 pound fresh or frozen peeled crawfish tails, thawed
½ teaspoon ground red pepper
¼ cup vegetable oil
¼ cup all-purpose flour
1 (10-ounce) package frozen seasoning blend, thawed

4 green onions, chopped
1 teaspoon salt
½ teaspoon black pepper
1 cup chicken broth
Hot cooked rice

• Sprinkle crawfish with red pepper; set aside.
• Cook oil and flour in a Dutch oven over medium-low heat, stirring constantly, 20 minutes or until roux is copper penny-colored.
• Stir in seasoning blend and green onions; cook, stirring constantly, until vegetables are tender. Add crawfish tails, salt, black pepper, and broth; cook, uncovered, over low heat 10 minutes, stirring occasionally. Serve over rice. Yield: 4½ cups.

Fish and Vegetable Dinner

Prep: 10 minutes • **Cook:** 15 minutes

Microwave Miracle

4 (6-ounce) orange roughy fillets	2 cups broccoli florets
½ teaspoon salt	1 medium-size red bell pepper, seeded and cut into strips
¼ teaspoon black pepper	1 small onion, cut into strips
½ cup buttermilk dressing	

• Place fish in an 11- x 7-inch baking dish; sprinkle with salt and black pepper. Spread 2 tablespoons dressing over each fillet. Arrange broccoli, pepper strips, and onion evenly over fish.
• Cover with heavy-duty plastic wrap; fold back a small corner to allow steam to escape. Microwave at HIGH 13 to 15 minutes or until fish flakes easily when tested with a fork, giving dish a half-turn after 7 minutes. Yield: 4 servings.

Vegetable Quesadillas

Prep: 10 minutes • **Cook:** 15 minutes

Stovetop Solution

Ideas for Two

1 cup sliced frozen or fresh yellow squash, thawed	½ teaspoon hot sauce
½ cup sliced fresh mushrooms	2 tablespoons olive oil
½ cup chopped onion	1 cup (4 ounces) shredded mozzarella cheese
½ teaspoon salt	2 (8-inch) flour tortillas
¼ teaspoon pepper	Salsa

• Sauté first 6 ingredients in hot oil in a large skillet until vegetables are crisp-tender; remove from skillet, and reserve oil in skillet.
• Place ¼ cup mozzarella cheese on half of each tortilla; top evenly with vegetable mixture and remaining ½ cup cheese. Fold tortillas over filling.
• Cook quesadillas in hot oil in skillet over medium heat 3 to 5 minutes on each side or until lightly browned. Serve immediately with salsa. Yield: 2 servings.

Veggie Sausage Pizzas

Prep: 12 minutes • **Cook:** 15 minutes

Kid Friendly

8 (1-inch-thick) French bread slices
1 sweet onion, sliced
1 medium-size green bell pepper, sliced
1 cup tomato-and-basil pasta sauce
1 cup (4 ounces) shredded mozzarella cheese

1 (8-ounce) package meatless breakfast patties, thawed and crumbled
½ cup shredded Parmesan cheese

• Bake bread slices on a baking sheet at 425° for 5 minutes. Set aside.
• Meanwhile, sauté sliced onion and bell pepper in a large nonstick skillet coated with cooking spray over medium-high heat 5 minutes.
• Spread pasta sauce evenly on one side of each bread slice. Top evenly with mozzarella cheese, onion mixture, crumbled patties, and Parmesan cheese.
• Bake at 425° for 8 to 10 minutes or until thoroughly heated. Yield: 4 servings.

Mediterranean Garlic Pizza

Prep: 5 minutes • **Cook:** 17 minutes

5 Ingredients or Less

How-To Hints
Be careful not to burn the garlic in this recipe, or it will taste bitter.

1 (10-ounce) can refrigerated pizza crust
6 tablespoons dried tomato spread or dried tomato paste (we used California Sun Dry)

4 garlic cloves, thinly sliced
¾ cup crumbled feta cheese with garlic and herbs
¼ cup chopped ripe olives

• Preheat oven to 450°.
• Unroll pizza crust on baking sheet coated with cooking spray; pat dough into a 10- x 8-inch rectangle. Spread dried tomato spread evenly over dough, leaving a ½-inch border.
• Coat a small nonstick skillet with cooking spray; place over medium heat until hot. Add garlic; sauté 5 minutes or until browned. Sprinkle garlic, feta, and olives evenly over tomato spread. Bake pizza at 450° for 12 minutes or until crust is lightly browned. Yield: 4 servings.

Greek Spinach Quiche

Prep: 10 minutes • **Cook:** 33 minutes • **Other:** 10 minutes

½ (15-ounce) package refrigerated
    piecrusts
3 large eggs, lightly beaten
1 cup milk
¼ cup butter or margarine, melted
2 tablespoons all-purpose flour
½ teaspoon salt

¼ teaspoon ground white pepper
1 (10-ounce) package frozen
    chopped spinach, thawed and
    well drained
1 (4-ounce) package crumbled feta
    cheese

• Fit piecrust into a 9-inch pieplate or quiche dish according to package directions. Prick bottom and sides of piecrust with a fork.
• Bake at 400° for 8 minutes. Set aside. Reduce oven temperature to 375°.
• Combine eggs and next 5 ingredients; stir with a wire whisk. Stir in spinach and feta cheese; pour into piecrust.
• Bake at 375° for 25 minutes or until set. Let stand 10 minutes. Yield: 4 servings.

Greek Spinach
Quiche

Slow Cooker Tips and Tricks

- **The beauty of slow cooker cuisine** is that you can change recipe cooking times to accommodate your schedule. For all-day cooking, use the LOW setting. For part-of-the-day cooking, use the HIGH setting. There's no need to preheat a slow cooker.
- **One hour on HIGH** generally equals 2 hours on LOW. When cooking on the LOW setting, don't worry if the food cooks 30 minutes to 1 hour longer than intended— you have a bit of a cushion.
- **Generally, cook with the cover on**, and don't peek inside until it's time to stir. (There are exceptions for uncovering when thickening some sauces briefly at the end of cooking.)
- **For roasts or poultry larger than 2 pounds,** be sure to cut in half to ensure thorough cooking.
- **Place vegetables in the slow cooker first**, and then add the meat. The vegetables will take longer to cook than meat. There's no need to thaw frozen vegetables for most slow cooker recipes.

- **Liquids don't boil away during slow cooking** as they do during conventional cooking methods, so don't be alarmed by the small amounts of liquid called for in slow cooker recipes. Liquids will accumulate from the meat and other ingredients as well as from moisture that condenses inside the cooker. In fact, you may even end up with more liquid than you desire. If that occurs, simply drain excess liquid before serving.
- **Use lean cuts of meat,** and trim visible fat to avoid a finished dish with excess grease floating on top.
- **For roasts and stews,** pour any liquid in recipe over meat to moisten it.
- **After preparing a recipe in a slow cooker**, allow the insert to cool completely before washing it. Running cold water over the insert to cool it may cause it to crack.
- **Never immerse the electric unit in water**; unplug it, and wipe it clean with a damp cloth.

Peppered Beef Brisket in Beer

Prep: 15 minutes • **Cook:** 4 to 10 hours

No Fuss Entertaining

Big Batch

Secret Ingredient Savvy
Beer adds an earthy essence to this tender brisket.

1 large onion, sliced and separated into rings	½ cup chili sauce
1 (4-pound) beef brisket, trimmed	3 tablespoons brown sugar
¾ teaspoon pepper	2 garlic cloves, crushed
¾ cup beer	3 tablespoons all-purpose flour
	3 tablespoons water

• Place onion rings in a 4-quart electric slow cooker. Cut brisket in half to ensure even cooking. Sprinkle brisket with pepper. Place over onion rings in slow cooker. Combine beer and next 3 ingredients; pour over brisket. Cover and cook on HIGH 4 to 6 hours or on HIGH 1 hour and then LOW 7 to 9 hours.
• Remove brisket to a serving platter, reserving juices in slow cooker. Combine flour and water, stirring well; slowly whisk into juices in slow cooker. Cook, uncovered, on HIGH 5 minutes or until thickened, stirring often. Serve sauce over brisket. Yield: 10 servings.

Chuck Roast Barbecue

Prep: 25 minutes • **Cook:** 6 hours

2   medium onions, chopped
1   (2- to 2½-pound) boneless chuck
    roast, trimmed
¾   cup cola soft drink
¼   cup Worcestershire sauce

1   tablespoon cider vinegar
2   garlic cloves, minced
½   cup spicy barbecue sauce
6   hamburger buns

• Place onion in a 4-quart electric slow cooker. Cut roast in half to ensure even cooking. Place roast on top of onion. Combine cola and next 3 ingredients; reserve ½ cup cola mixture. Pour remaining cola mixture over roast and onion.
• Cover and cook on HIGH 6 hours or until roast is very tender. Remove meat and onion to a platter, using a slotted spoon. Discard juices.
• Add reserved cola mixture and barbecue sauce to slow cooker; stir well, and cook, uncovered, on HIGH 10 minutes.
• Meanwhile, shred meat with 2 forks; return meat and onion to slow cooker until sauce is heated, stirring occasionally. Spoon barbecue onto buns. Yield: 6 servings.

Simply Southern

Freeze It
Spoon leftovers into serving size freezer containers, and freeze up to 3 months.

Zippy Barbecue Pot Roast

Prep: 23 minutes • **Cook:** 5 to 9 hours

1½   teaspoons garlic salt
½   teaspoon pepper
1   (4- to 5-pound) boneless chuck
    roast, trimmed
2   tablespoons vegetable oil
1   (12-ounce) can cola soft drink

1   (12-ounce) bottle chili sauce
2   tablespoons Worcestershire sauce
2   tablespoons hot sauce
3   tablespoons cornstarch
¼   cup water

• Combine garlic salt and pepper; rub over roast. Brown roast on all sides in hot oil in a large skillet. Transfer roast to a 4-quart electric slow cooker. Cut roast in half to ensure even cooking. Combine cola and next 3 ingredients; pour over roast. Cover and cook on HIGH 5 to 6 hours or on HIGH 1 hour and then LOW 7 to 8 hours. Remove roast, reserving juices in slow cooker; keep roast warm.
• Combine cornstarch and ¼ cup water, stirring well; stir into juices in slow cooker. Cook, uncovered, on HIGH 15 minutes or until thickened, stirring occasionally. Serve gravy over roast. Yield: 10 to 12 servings.

No Fuss Entertaining

Big Batch

Menu Makings
Grill some Texas toast to serve with this roast and gravy.

Company Pot Roast

No Fuss
Entertaining

Editor's
Favorite

How-To Hints

If you have the time, and you don't want to dirty another dish, simply thicken your gravy 10 minutes on the HIGH setting of your slow cooker, stirring occasionally.

Prep: 25 minutes • **Cook:** 10 hours

1 (2-pound) boneless chuck roast, trimmed
1½ tablespoons freshly ground pepper
1 tablespoon vegetable oil
14 small red potatoes, quartered (about 2 pounds)
3 small onions, quartered

1 (16-ounce) package baby carrots
2 (10½-ounce) cans French onion soup
1 (2.8-ounce) tube dried tomato paste
¼ cup all-purpose flour
½ cup water

• Rub both sides of roast with pepper. Brown roast on all sides in hot oil in a large nonstick skillet over medium-high heat. Place roast in a 6-quart electric slow cooker.
• Arrange vegetables around roast. Combine soup and tomato paste in a small bowl, stirring with a wire whisk; pour evenly over roast and vegetables.
• Cover and cook on HIGH 1 hour. Reduce to LOW, and cook 9 more hours or until roast and vegetables are tender. Remove roast and vegetables to a platter; cover and keep warm.
• Pour drippings into a large skillet. Combine flour and water in a small bowl, whisking until smooth; gradually add to drippings in skillet. Bring to a boil; cook, stirring constantly, 10 minutes or until gravy is slightly thickened and bubbly. Serve gravy with roast and vegetables. Yield: 8 servings.

Company
Pot Roast

Sauerbraten

Prep: 27 minutes • **Cook:** 9 hours • **Other:** 24 to 36 hours

The twang of white vinegar is softened by the spicy sweetness
of crumbled gingersnaps in this classic German dish.

1 (3-pound) rump roast	1 lemon, sliced
1½ cups sliced onion	10 whole cloves
1 cup water	6 peppercorns
1 cup white vinegar	3 bay leaves
2 tablespoons salt	15 crisp gingersnaps, crumbled (we
2 tablespoons sugar	used Nabisco)

• Trim fat from roast; cut roast in half crosswise. Place roast halves in a deep glass bowl. Combine onion and next 8 ingredients; stir well. Pour mixture over meat; cover and marinate in refrigerator 24 to 36 hours, turning meat occasionally.

• Remove roast from marinade, reserving 1½ cups marinade. Discard remaining marinade. Place roast in a 6-quart electric slow cooker; pour reserved 1½ cups marinade over meat. Cover and cook on HIGH 1 hour; reduce to LOW, and cook 7 to 8 hours or until roast is tender.

• Remove roast from slow cooker; set aside, and keep warm. Increase to HIGH. Pour cooking liquid through a sieve into a bowl; discard solids. Return liquid to slow cooker. Add gingersnaps; cover and cook 12 minutes. Serve with roast. Yield: 6 servings.

Menu Makings
Serve the tender marinated beef and sauce over spaetzle (tiny noodles or dumplings) for authenticity.

Peppery Flank Barbecue

Prep: 5 minutes • **Cook:** 7 hours

2 (1¼-pound) flank steaks, cut in	2 tablespoons molasses
half crosswise	1 (28-ounce) bottle original-
1¼ teaspoons pepper	flavored barbecue sauce (we
1 cup chopped onion	used Kraft Original)

• Rub steak evenly with pepper. Place steak in a 4-quart electric slow cooker; top with onion, molasses, and barbecue sauce. Turn steak to coat.

• Cover and cook on HIGH 1 hour; reduce to LOW, and cook 6 hours. Remove steak, reserving sauce in slow cooker.

• Shred steak with 2 forks. Return shredded steak to slow cooker; stir well to coat with sauce. Yield: 8 servings.

5 Ingredients or Less

Simply Southern

Country Steak
with Gravy

Country Steak with Gravy

Prep: 5 minutes • **Cook:** 7 hours

1 (1½ pound) boneless top round
    steak (½ inch thick), trimmed
1 (12-ounce) jar beef gravy (we
    used Heinz)
2 tablespoons tomato paste

½ teaspoon salt
½ teaspoon garlic powder
½ teaspoon pepper
½ teaspoon dried thyme

• Cut steak into 6 equal pieces; place in a lightly greased 4-quart electric slow cooker. Combine gravy and remaining ingredients; pour over steak. Cover and cook on HIGH 1 hour; reduce to LOW and cook 5½ to 6 hours or until meat is tender. Yield: 6 servings.

Simply Southern

Menu Makings
Serve with hot cooked rice or mashed potatoes.

Beef Burgundy

Prep: 14 minutes • **Cook:** 6 hours

1 (2-pound) boneless top round
    steak, trimmed and cut into
    1½-inch cubes
⅓ cup all-purpose flour
1 (10½-ounce) can beef broth,
    undiluted
½ cup dry red wine
2 garlic cloves, minced
2 tablespoons tomato paste

½ teaspoon dried thyme
½ teaspoon salt
¼ teaspoon pepper
2 (16-ounce) packages frozen small
    whole onions, thawed and
    drained
1 (8-ounce) package sliced fresh
    mushrooms
Hot cooked medium egg noodles

• Place a lightly greased nonstick skillet over high heat until hot. Add steak; sauté 2 minutes. Reduce heat to medium-high; cook steak 5 more minutes or until browned. Drain.
• Meanwhile, whisk together flour and next 7 ingredients in a 3½-quart electric slow cooker, stirring until smooth. Add steak, onions, and mushrooms, stirring well. Cover and cook on HIGH 1 hour; reduce to LOW, and cook 5 hours or until meat is tender. Serve over noodles. Yield: 6 servings.

No Fuss Entertaining

Fix It Faster
Thaw your onions in the refrigerator overnight to make your prep in the kitchen even shorter.

Beefy Pasta Sauce

Prep: 11 minutes • **Cook:** 7 hours

Kid Friendly

Secret Ingredient Savvy
A little red wine fools you into thinking this spaghetti sauce is homemade.

1½ pounds ground round
1 cup chopped onion
2 (25-ounce) jars roasted garlic and onion pasta sauce (we used Da Vinci)
¼ cup dry red wine

½ teaspoon dried Italian seasoning
½ teaspoon salt
1 (8-ounce) package sliced fresh mushrooms
Hot cooked pasta

• Cook ground beef and onion in a large skillet, stirring until beef crumbles and is no longer pink. Drain well. Place beef mixture in a 5-quart electric slow cooker. Add pasta sauce and next 4 ingredients to slow cooker. Cover and cook on LOW 7 hours. Serve over hot cooked pasta. Yield: 9 cups.

Chill-Breaker Chili

Prep: 20 minutes • **Cook:** 7 hours

Kid Friendly

Freeze It
Spoon leftovers into serving size containers, and freeze for meals in minutes up to 3 months later.

The mild flavors in this low-fat chili make it suitable for even the youngest family member.

1 pound ground round
1 cup chopped onion
1 cup water
1 (27-ounce) can chili beans, undrained

1 (8-ounce) can tomato sauce
1 (1.25-ounce) package mild chili seasoning
Salt to taste (optional)

• Cook beef and onion in a large skillet, stirring until meat crumbles and is no longer pink; drain.
• Place meat mixture in a 3½-quart electric slow cooker. Stir in 1 cup water and next 3 ingredients. Cover and cook on HIGH 1 hour; reduce to LOW, and cook 6 hours. Add salt, if desired. Yield: 7½ cups.

Caribbean-Style
Pork

Pork Chops and Gravy

Prep: 20 minutes • **Cook:** 5 hours

The slow cooker simmers these chops up nice and tender.

**Simply
Southern**

Menu Makings
Serve pork chops
with mashed
potatoes and
gravy. Try Ore-Ida
frozen mashed
potatoes to
save time.

6 (6-ounce) bone-in center-cut pork   ½ teaspoon salt
loin chops (about ½ inch thick)   ¼ teaspoon garlic powder
1 tablespoon vegetable oil   ⅔ cup all-purpose flour
1 (14-ounce) can chicken broth   Freshly ground pepper (optional)
1½ teaspoons dry mustard

• Trim fat from chops. Brown chops, in batches, in hot oil in a large nonstick
skillet over medium-high heat. Place chops in a 4½-quart electric slow cooker.
• Combine broth, mustard, salt, and garlic powder; stir well. Pour broth mixture
over pork chops in slow cooker. Cover with lid; cook on HIGH 1 hour. Reduce
to LOW; cook 4 hours or until pork chops are tender. Remove pork chops from
slow cooker, reserving cooking liquid. Set chops aside, and keep warm. Increase
to HIGH.
• Place flour in a small bowl. Gradually add 1 cup cooking liquid to flour, stirring
with a wire whisk until well blended. Stir flour mixture into cooking liquid in
slow cooker. Cook, uncovered, 10 minutes or until thickened, stirring occasionally.
Spoon gravy over chops; sprinkle with pepper, if desired. Yield: 6 servings.

Caribbean-Style Pork

Prep: 30 minutes • **Cook:** 7 hours

Cumin seeds and peanut butter
create a sweetly spiced sauce for this tender pork.

**Editor's
Favorite**

Menu Makings
Serve this savory
pork with rice
for soaking up
the sauce.

2 pounds boneless pork chops
1 tablespoon olive oil, divided
2 cups chopped red bell pepper
1 bunch green onions, cut into
    1-inch pieces
2 tablespoons hoisin sauce
2 tablespoons soy sauce

1 tablespoon fresh lime juice
2 tablespoons creamy peanut
    butter
1 teaspoon cumin seeds, crushed
1 teaspoon dried crushed red
    pepper
1 teaspoon bottled minced garlic

• Cut pork into 1-inch pieces. Heat 1½ teaspoons oil in a large nonstick skillet over medium-high heat. Add half of pork; sauté 10 minutes or until browned. Remove from skillet with a slotted spoon, and drain on paper towels. Repeat procedure with remaining oil and pork.
• Place pork, bell pepper, and green onions in a 4-quart electric slow cooker coated with cooking spray; stir well.
• Add hoisin sauce and remaining ingredients to slow cooker; stir well.
• Cover and cook on HIGH 1 hour. Reduce to LOW, and cook 5 to 6 hours. Yield: 6 servings.

Spicy-Sweet Ribs and Beans

Prep: 30 minutes • **Cook:** 5 to 10 hours

Slow cookers don't brown food, so we broil
these ribs for extra flavor before adding them to the pot.

Menu Makings
Serve with
cornbread and a
simple green salad
with creamy
Italian or Ranch
dressing.

2 (16-ounce) cans pinto beans,
    drained
4 pounds country-style pork ribs,
    trimmed
1 teaspoon garlic powder
½ teaspoon salt
½ teaspoon pepper

1 medium onion, chopped
1 (10.5-ounce) jar red jalapeño jelly
1 (18-ounce) bottle hickory-flavored
    barbecue sauce (we used Kraft
    Thick 'n Spicy Hickory Smoke)
1 teaspoon green hot sauce (we
    used Tabasco)

• Place beans in a 5-quart electric slow cooker; set aside.
• Cut ribs apart; sprinkle with garlic powder, salt, and pepper. Place ribs on a broiling pan.
• Broil 5½ inches from heat 18 to 20 minutes or until browned, turning once. Add ribs to slow cooker, and sprinkle with onion.
• Meanwhile, combine jelly, barbecue sauce, and hot sauce in a saucepan; cook over low heat until jelly melts. Pour over ribs; stir gently.
• Cover and cook on HIGH 5 to 6 hours or on LOW 9 to 10 hours. Remove ribs. Drain bean mixture, reserving sauce. Skim fat from sauce. Arrange ribs over bean mixture; serve with sauce. Yield: 8 servings.

Pinto Beans with Ham

Prep: 6 minutes • **Cook:** 10 hours • **Other:** 8 hours

*Just like Mama used to make! Some may remember this recipe served
with a little more liquid; others remember it less saucy.*

1 (16-ounce) package dried pinto
   beans
5½ cups water
1 large onion, chopped
1 (8-ounce) package diced cooked
   ham (we used Cumberland Gap)

1 tablespoon chili powder
2 teaspoons salt
1 teaspoon pepper
¼ teaspoon dried oregano
¼ teaspoon ground cumin
2 garlic cloves, minced

• Sort and wash beans; place in a 3½ to 5-quart electric slow cooker. Cover with
water 2 inches above beans; soak at least 8 hours. Drain; add 5½ cups water and
remaining ingredients.
• Cover and cook on LOW 10 hours or until beans are tender. Serve with French
bread or cornbread. Yield: 8 servings.

Lamb Meatballs with Chutney Sauce

Prep: 25 minutes • **Cook:** 3 hours

1½ pounds ground lean boneless leg
   of lamb
½ cup fine, dry breadcrumbs
   (commercial)
2 green onions, finely chopped
3 tablespoons minced seeded
   pickled jalapeño peppers
½ teaspoon salt

1 large egg
2 garlic cloves, minced
½ cup mango chutney
¼ cup tomato paste
3 tablespoons soy sauce
2 tablespoons pickled jalapeño
   pepper liquid

• Combine ground lamb and next 6 ingredients in a bowl; stir well. Shape into 42
(1-inch) meatballs. Place meatballs in a 3½- to 4-quart electric slow cooker.
• Combine chutney and next 3 ingredients in a bowl; stir well. Pour over meatballs. Cover and cook on HIGH 1 hour; reduce to LOW, and cook 2 hours or
until done. Yield: 6 servings.

How-To Hints
The size of your slow
cooker will make all
the difference. Use a
5-quart slow cooker
to allow more liquid
to evaporate from
this dish, or use a
3½-quart slow
cooker if you want
more yummy broth
for dipping freshly
baked cornbread.

Menu Makings
Serve these juicy
meatballs and
sweet sauce
over couscous.

Provençale
Chicken Supper

Provençale Chicken Supper

Prep: 10 minutes • **Cook:** 6 hours

4 (6-ounce) skinned, bone-in
  chicken breast halves
2 teaspoons dried basil
¼ teaspoon salt, divided
¼ teaspoon black pepper, divided

1 cup diced yellow bell pepper
1 (16-ounce) can navy beans, rinsed
  and drained
1 (14½-ounce) can pasta-style
  chunky tomatoes, undrained

• Place chicken in a 4½-quart electric slow cooker; sprinkle with dried basil, ⅛ teaspoon salt, and ⅛ teaspoon black pepper.
• Combine remaining ⅛ teaspoon salt, remaining ⅛ teaspoon black pepper, bell pepper, beans, and tomatoes in a bowl; stir well. Spoon over chicken. Cover and cook on HIGH 1 hour; reduce to LOW, and cook 5 hours.
• To serve, place 1 chicken breast into each of 4 shallow bowls; top each with bean mixture. Yield: 4 servings.

Saucy Drumsticks and Thighs

Prep: 5 minutes • **Cook:** 6 hours

After simmering in a well-seasoned sauce,
this chicken is fall-off-the-bone tender.

6 chicken drumsticks (about
  1½ pounds), skinned
6 chicken thighs (about 1½
  pounds), skinned
1 (14½-ounce) can diced tomatoes
  with roasted garlic, undrained
1 (6-ounce) can tomato paste

¼ cup dried onion flakes
2 teaspoons chicken bouillon
  granules
1 teaspoon dried Italian seasoning
½ teaspoon garlic powder
½ teaspoon dried crushed red pepper

• Place chicken in a 4-quart electric slow cooker. Combine tomatoes and remaining ingredients; stir well. Pour over chicken. Cover and cook on HIGH 1 hour; reduce to LOW, and cook 4 to 5 hours or until chicken is tender. Yield: 6 servings.

Menu Makings
Serve this saucy
chicken over rice
or egg noodles.

Braised Chicken Thighs with Rosemary and Potatoes

Editor's
Favorite

Prep: 20 minutes • **Cook:** 5 hours

8   chicken thighs (about 2½ pounds)
¾   teaspoon salt, divided
½   teaspoon pepper, divided
1   tablespoon vegetable oil
1   medium onion, halved lengthwise
     and sliced

2   large baking potatoes (about 1½
     pounds), peeled and sliced
⅔   cup chicken broth
1½   teaspoons dried rosemary
4   garlic cloves, minced

• Sprinkle chicken evenly with ¼ teaspoon salt and ¼ teaspoon pepper. Heat oil in a large nonstick skillet over medium-high heat; add chicken, and cook 3 to 4 minutes on each side or until browned.
• Place onion in a 4-quart electric slow cooker; top with potato. Arrange chicken on top of potato.
• Combine remaining ½ teaspoon salt, ¼ teaspoon pepper, broth, rosemary, and garlic in a small bowl; pour over chicken. Cover and cook on HIGH 1 hour; reduce to LOW, and cook 4 hours or until chicken is done and vegetables are tender. Yield: 4 servings.

Chicken Pepper Pot

5 Ingredients
or Less

Kitchen
Timesavers
There's no need to
thaw the frozen
vegetables in this
recipe—simply let
your slow cooker
do the work.

Prep: 5 minutes • **Cook:** 8 hours

2   (16-ounce) packages frozen
     pepper stir-fry
4   (6-ounce) skinned chicken breast
     halves
1   (10¾-ounce) can low-fat, reduced-
     sodium tomato soup with garden
     herbs and peppercorns

1   tablespoon white wine
     Worcestershire sauce
½   teaspoon garlic salt

• Place all ingredients in a 4- or 5-quart electric slow cooker. Cover and cook on HIGH 1 hour; reduce to LOW, and cook 7 hours. Yield: 4 servings.

Chicken Lasagna Florentine

Prep: 16 minutes • **Cook:** 6 hours

*This is the simplest lasagna ever! There's no need to boil
the noodles beforehand—just layer them with the creamy spinach mixture
and cheese, and let the slowcooker do the rest.*

2 (10¾-ounce) cans cream of
    chicken soup, undiluted
1 (10-ounce) package frozen
    chopped spinach, thawed,
    drained, and squeezed dry
1 (9-ounce) package frozen diced
    cooked chicken (we used Tyson)

1 (8-ounce) container sour cream
1 cup milk
½ cup shredded Parmesan cheese
⅓ cup chopped onion
9 uncooked lasagna noodles
2 cups (8 ounces) shredded
    mozzarella cheese

• Combine first 7 ingredients in a large bowl; stir well.
• Place 3 uncooked lasagna noodles in a 5-quart electric slow cooker coated with cooking spray, breaking noodles in half, as necessary, to fit in slow cooker. Spread one-third of spinach mixture over noodles; sprinkle with ⅔ cup mozzarella cheese. Layer 3 more noodles, half of remaining spinach mixture, and ⅔ cup mozzarella cheese. Top with remaining 3 noodles and spinach mixture; sprinkle with remaining ⅔ cup mozzarella cheese.
• Cover and cook on HIGH 1 hour; reduce to LOW, and cook 5 hours or until pasta is done. Yield: 6 servings.

No Fuss
Entertaining

How-To Hints
It's easy to drain and squeeze dry frozen spinach. Place the spinach in a colander to thaw and drain, then press with paper towels to remove excess moisture.

Apricot-Glazed Turkey and Sweet Potatoes

5 Ingredients or Less

Prep: 5 minutes • **Cook:** 8 hours

6 cups (1-inch) cubed peeled sweet potato (about 1¾ pounds)
1 cup apricot preserves, divided
1 teaspoon salt, divided
2 bay leaves
2 (¾-pound) turkey tenderloins

• Place sweet potato, ½ cup preserves, and ½ teaspoon salt in a 4½- to 5-quart electric slow cooker; toss well. Add bay leaves. Arrange tenderloins over sweet potato, and sprinkle with remaining ½ teaspoon salt. Spread remaining ½ cup preserves over tenderloins.
• Cover and cook on HIGH 1 hour; reduce to LOW, and cook 7 hours or until turkey and sweet potato are tender. Remove turkey from slow cooker, and slice. Discard bay leaves. Serve turkey with sweet potato and cooking liquid. Yield: 6 servings.

Thai Coconut Shrimp and Rice

No Fuss Entertaining

Prep: 17 minutes • **Cook:** 4 hours and 50 minutes

Friends will hardly believe this shrimp and fresh snow pea sensation cooked in your slow cooker.

Secret Ingredient Savvy
If you want to buy shrimp in the shell instead of peeled, purchase 2 pounds.

2 red bell peppers, cut into strips
1 (32-ounce) container chicken broth
1½ cups uncooked converted rice (we used Uncle Ben's)
1 tablespoon garlic-chili sauce
1 (14-ounce) can coconut milk
10 (⅛-inch-thick) slices peeled fresh ginger
5 garlic cloves, minced
1½ pounds peeled, medium-size fresh shrimp
2 cups fresh sugar snap peas, trimmed
½ cup (1-inch) sliced green onion tops
⅓ cup fresh lime juice

• Place first 7 ingredients in a 5-quart electric slow cooker; stir well. Cover and cook on LOW 4 hours.
• Increase to HIGH. Add shrimp and remaining 3 ingredients; cover and cook 50 minutes or just until shrimp turn pink. Spoon into bowls. Yield: 8 servings.

Thai Coconut
Shrimp and Rice

Black Bean Soup

Prep: 10 minutes • **Cook:** 5 to 6 hours

Big Batch

Secret
Ingredient
Savvy

Black beans are
the base for this
traditional
Mexican soup. Our
kitchen prefers
Bush's brand
because they hold
their shape best.

2 (15-ounce) cans black beans,
   rinsed and drained
2 (4.5-ounce) cans chopped green
   chiles
1 (14½-ounce) can Mexican-style
   stewed tomatoes, undrained
1 (14½-ounce) can diced
   tomatoes, undrained

1 (11-ounce) can sweet whole
   kernel corn, drained
4 green onions, sliced
2 to 3 tablespoons chili powder
1 teaspoon ground cumin
½ teaspoon dried minced garlic

• Combine all ingredients in a 5-quart electric slow cooker.
• Cover and cook on HIGH 5 to 6 hours. Yield: 8 cups.

Homestyle Potato Soup

Prep: 5 minutes • **Cook:** 5½ hours

Kid Friendly

1 (14-ounce) can chicken broth
1 (1-pound, 4-ounce) package
   refrigerated diced potatoes
   with onion
4 green onions, coarsely chopped
3 tablespoons butter or margarine,
   cut into small pieces

¾ teaspoon salt
½ teaspoon freshly ground pepper
3 garlic cloves, minced
¼ cup all-purpose flour
1½ cups milk
½ cup (2 ounces) shredded sharp
   Cheddar cheese

• Place first 7 ingredients in a 4-quart electric slow cooker; stir well. Cover and
cook on LOW 5 hours or until vegetables are tender. Increase to HIGH.
• Place flour in a bowl; gradually add milk, stirring with a wire whisk until
smooth. Stir into soup. Cover and cook 30 minutes or until thickened, stirring
twice. Ladle into bowls; sprinkle evenly with cheese. Yield: 5½ cups.

Spicy Vegetable Soup

Prep: 5 minutes • **Cook:** 8 hours

2 (16-ounce) packages frozen
    vegetable soup mix
2 (14.5-ounce) cans diced tomatoes
    with basil, garlic, and oregano,
    undrained

1 (10-ounce) can diced tomatoes
    and green chiles
1 (14.5-ounce) can beef broth
1 large onion, chopped
¾ teaspoon salt

• Place all ingredients in a 4-quart electric slow cooker; stir well. Cover and cook on LOW 8 hours or until vegetables are tender. Yield: 8 servings.

Secret Ingredient Savvy

For a not-so-spicy vegetable soup use the mild variety of canned tomatoes and green chiles instead of the regular.

Eggplant and Artichoke Parmigiana

Prep: 20 minutes • **Cook:** 5 to 6 hours

1 (25-ounce) jar roasted garlic pasta
    sauce with Merlot wine (we
    used Sutter Home)
½ teaspoon freshly ground pepper
1 (1-pound) eggplant, cut into
    ¼-inch-thick slices
1 (9-ounce) package frozen artichoke
    hearts, thawed and drained

1 cup (4 ounces) shredded part-skim
    mozzarella cheese
2 tablespoons chopped fresh parsley
1 tablespoon chopped fresh oregano
Hot cooked spaghetti
¼ cup finely shredded fresh
    Parmesan cheese

• Combine pasta sauce and pepper; stir well. Spoon ½ cup pasta sauce into a 4-quart electric slow cooker. Arrange half of eggplant slices over sauce; top with half of artichoke hearts, and sprinkle with half of mozzarella cheese. Spoon ½ cup pasta sauce over mozzarella cheese.
• Repeat layers with remaining eggplant, artichoke hearts, and mozzarella cheese. Top with remaining pasta sauce; sprinkle with parsley and oregano.
• Cover and cook on LOW 5 to 6 hours or until eggplant is tender. Serve over hot cooked spaghetti; sprinkle with Parmesan. Yield: 4 servings.

Make Ahead

Kitchen Timesavers

Assemble these ingredients in the crockery insert the night before you plan to serve it. The next day it can go straight from the fridge to the slow cooker; simply add about one hour to the total cook time to compensate for the chilled ingredients.

Enchilada
Casserole

Enchilada Casserole

Prep: 10 minutes • **Cook:** 5½ hours

3 tablespoons chopped green chiles, divided
¾ cup chunky salsa
¼ cup chopped fresh cilantro
1 (15.5-ounce) can black beans, rinsed and drained
1 (11-ounce) can yellow corn with red and green bell peppers
1 (10-ounce) can enchilada sauce

1 (8½-ounce) package corn muffin mix
2 large eggs, lightly beaten
2 tablespoons chopped roasted red bell peppers
1½ cups (6 ounces) shredded Monterey Jack cheese
Sour cream (optional)

• Stir together 2 tablespoons green chiles and next 5 ingredients in a 3½-quart electric slow cooker. Cover and cook on LOW 4 hours.
• Stir together remaining 1 tablespoon green chiles, muffin mix, eggs, and roasted red bell peppers. Spoon batter evenly over bean mixture in slow cooker. Cover and cook on LOW 1 hour and 20 minutes or until cornbread is done.
• Sprinkle cheese over cornbread. Cover and cook 5 to 10 minutes or until cheese melts. Serve with sour cream, if desired. Yield: 6 servings.

Secret Ingredient Savvy
You control the spice in this Tex-Mex favorite by the type of salsa and enchilada sauce you use.

Hearty Baked Beans

Prep: 30 minutes • **Cook:** 2½ to 6 hours

3 bacon slices, chopped
1 large onion, chopped
2 garlic cloves, minced
3 (16-ounce) cans pinto beans, drained
⅓ cup firmly packed brown sugar

⅓ cup molasses
⅓ cup ketchup
2½ tablespoons prepared mustard
½ medium-size green bell pepper, chopped

• Cook bacon slices in a large skillet until crisp; remove bacon, reserving drippings in skillet.
• Sauté onion and garlic in reserved drippings until tender.
• Combine bacon, onion mixture, beans, and remaining ingredients in an electric slow cooker.
• Cover and cook on HIGH 2½ to 3 hours or on LOW 5 to 6 hours. Yield: 6 to 8 servings.

Simply Southern

Menu Makings
Double your pleasure and ease with two slow cookers and one of our barbecue beefs on page 115 to accompany these beans.

Caramel Pie

Caramel Pie

Prep: 4 minutes • **Cook:** 9 hours • **Other:** 2 hours

Wake up to pie? Indeed! This pie is a great candidate to cook while you sleep.

- 1 (14-ounce) can sweetened condensed milk
- 1 (9-inch) ready-made graham cracker crust
- 1 (8-ounce) container frozen whipped topping, thawed
- 2 (1.4-ounce) chocolate-covered toffee candy bars, coarsely chopped (we used Skor)

• Pour milk into a 2-cup glass measuring cup; cover with aluminum foil.
• Place measuring cup in a 3½-quart electric slow cooker; carefully pour hot water in slow cooker to reach the level of milk in measuring cup. Cover and cook on LOW 9 hours.
• Pour caramelized milk into crust; cool completely. Spread whipped topping over pie; sprinkle with chopped candy bars. Cover and chill 2 hours or until ready to serve. Yield: 1 (9-inch) pie.

5 Ingredients or Less

Secret Ingredient Savvy
If you'd like to make this pie with a twist, slice a couple of bananas onto the crust before pouring the caramel on top.

Apple Grunt

Prep: 20 minutes • **Cook:** 6 hours

This old fashioned fruit dessert is topped with slightly sweet biscuit dough.

- 5 medium-size Golden Delicious apples (about 2 pounds), peeled and cut into ½-inch wedges
- ½ cup sugar
- ⅓ cup all-purpose flour
- ¼ teaspoon apple pie spice
- 2 cups all-purpose baking mix (we used Bisquick)
- ¾ cup milk
- 3 tablespoons sugar
- 3 tablespoons butter or margarine, melted
- 3 cups vanilla ice cream

• Place apple, ½ cup sugar, flour, and apple pie spice in a 4-quart electric slow cooker; stir well.
• Combine baking mix, milk, 3 tablespoons sugar, and butter in a bowl; stir just until moist. Spoon dough over apple mixture.
• Cover and cook on LOW 6 hours. Divide mixture evenly between 9 dessert dishes; top each serving with ice cream. Serve warm. Yield: 9 servings.

Secret Ingredient Savvy
Reduced-fat baking mix works equally well in this classic dessert.

Chicken Won Tons with Hoisin-Peanut Dipping Sauce, page 156

chapter six

Quick

Bites

Family and friends mean gatherings galore. And being a great host or hostess means welcoming guests and loved ones with an offering of yummy fare to nibble on while mingling. Serving up a tasty treat is a cinch with this smorgasbord of appetizers.

Kahlúa-Pecan Brie

Prep: 10 minutes • **Cook:** 5 minutes

Crunchy pecans lend a nice texture contrast to the soft creamy Brie.

1 (15-ounce) round Brie
½ cup chopped pecans, toasted
2½ tablespoons Kahlúa or other
    coffee liqueur

2 tablespoons brown sugar

• Remove rind from top of cheese, cutting to within ½ inch of edge. Place on an oven-safe dish.
• Combine pecans, Kahlúa, and brown sugar; spread over cheese. Bake at 350° for 5 minutes or just until softened. Yield: 8 appetizer servings.

No Fuss Entertaining

5 Ingredients or Less

Menu Makings
Serve this hot from the oven so the cheese is smooth and melty alongside gingersnaps or apple slices.

Mexican Cheese Spread

Prep: 13 minutes

2 cups (8 ounces) shredded sharp
    Cheddar cheese
½ cup sour cream
¼ cup butter or margarine, softened
2 green onions, chopped

1 (2-ounce) jar diced pimiento,
    drained
2 tablespoons chopped green chiles

• Combine first 3 ingredients in a mixing bowl; beat at medium speed with an electric mixer until blended.
• Stir in green onions, pimiento, and chiles. Cover and chill cheese spread, if desired. Yield: 2 cups.

No Fuss Entertaining

No-Cook Creation

Menu Makings
Serve this creamy spread with stone-ground wheat crackers.

One-Minute Salsa

Prep: 1 minute

Super Fast and Fresh

No-Cook Creation

5 Ingredients or less

You control the consistency of this salsa by how long you process the ingredients.

1 (14½-ounce) can stewed
  tomatoes, undrained
1 (10-ounce) can diced tomatoes
  and green chiles, undrained

½ teaspoon garlic salt
½ teaspoon pepper

• Combine all ingredients in container of blender; cover and process 15 seconds or until smooth. Transfer mixture to a bowl; cover and chill, if desired. Serve with tortilla chips. Yield: 2¾ cups.

Black Bean Salsa

Prep: 15 minutes

No-Cook Creation

Make Ahead
Prepare this salsa a day ahead to allow the flavors to mingle.

This tangy salsa is made for Open-Faced Southwestern Chicken Sandwiches (page 278), but it's also great served with chips as an appetizer.

1 plum tomato
1 avocado
⅓ cup chopped red onion
1 (15-ounce) can black beans, rinsed
  and drained

1½ tablespoons chopped fresh cilantro
1 tablespoon olive oil
2 tablespoons lime juice
⅛ teaspoon dried crushed red pepper
⅛ teaspoon salt

• Dice tomato. Peel, seed, and dice avocado. Combine tomato, avocado, onion, beans, and cilantro in a bowl.
• Whisk together oil and remaining 3 ingredients. Toss with bean mixture. Cover and chill, if desired. Yield: about 3 cups.

Avocado-Corn Salsa

Prep: 12 minutes • **Other:** 2 hours

Big Batch
Make Ahead

**Secret
Ingredient
Savvy**

If you prefer
canned corn,
substitute
2 (15.25-ounce)
cans sweet whole
kernel corn for the
frozen kind.

2½ cups frozen whole kernel corn,
    thawed
1 medium tomato, chopped
1 jalapeño pepper, seeded and
    chopped
¼ cup chopped bell pepper
¼ cup chopped red onion

¼ cup chopped fresh cilantro
¼ cup white wine vinegar
2 tablespoons lime juice
½ teaspoon salt
3 small avocados, peeled and
    chopped

• Combine all ingredients except avocado. Gently stir in avocado. Cover and chill at least 2 hours. Serve with tortilla chips or grilled fish or chicken. Yield: about 6 cups.

Carolina Caviar

Prep: 20 minutes • **Other:** 8 to 24 hours

Big Batch
**No-Cook
Creation**
Make Ahead

This isn't a real caviar, but rather a salsa made from black-eyed peas that, for Southerners, rivals the flavor of the ritzier roe. It marinates in Italian dressing, so spoon the spicy blend into a serving bowl using a slotted spoon.

2 (15.8-ounce) cans black-eyed
    peas, rinsed and drained
1 (16-ounce) bottle Italian dressing
1 (11-ounce) can white shoepeg
    corn, drained
1 large firm tomato, chopped
1 green bell pepper, chopped

1 small onion, chopped
1 cup chopped fresh parsley
4 green onions, chopped
1 tablespoon chopped fresh
    cilantro
2 garlic cloves, minced

• Stir together all ingredients in a large bowl. Cover and chill 8 to 24 hours. Spoon mixture into a serving bowl, using a slotted spoon. Serve with tortilla chips. Yield: 8 cups.

Avocado-Corn
Salsa

Vidalia Onion Dip

Prep: 8 minutes • **Cook:** 18 minutes

Editor's
Favorite

Simply
Southern

Big Batch

Fix It Faster

Put your kitchen
shears to use!
Chop the water
chestnuts in the
can after you
drain them.

French baguette slices serve as sturdy dippers for this cheesy appetizer.

2 tablespoons butter or margarine
3 large Vidalia onions, coarsely
  chopped
2 cups (8 ounces) shredded Swiss
  cheese
2 cups mayonnaise

¼ cup dry white wine
2 garlic cloves, minced
½ teaspoon hot sauce
1 (8-ounce) can sliced water
  chestnuts, drained and
  chopped (optional)

• Melt butter in a large skillet over medium-high heat; add onion. Sauté 10
minutes or until tender.
• Combine cheese and next 4 ingredients in a bowl; add water chestnuts, if
desired. Stir in onion. Spoon mixture into a lightly greased shallow 2-quart
baking dish. Microwave at MEDIUM HIGH (70% power) 8 minutes.
Yield: 6 cups.

Layered Nacho Dip

Prep: 15 minutes

No-Cook
Creation

No Fuss
Entertaining

Big Batch

**Kitchen
Timesavers**

This dip can be
made ahead and
chilled up to
4 hours.

This quick version of the classic is the perfect meatless appetizer.
With plentiful veggies, sour cream, and cheese, it's sure to please any crowd.

1 (16-ounce) can refried beans
2 teaspoons taco seasoning mix
1 (6-ounce) container refrigerated
  avocado dip or 1 cup guacamole
1 (8-ounce) container sour cream
1 (4½-ounce) can chopped black
  olives, drained

2 large tomatoes, diced
1 small onion, diced
1 (4-ounce) can chopped green
  chiles
1½ cups (6 ounces) shredded
  Monterey Jack cheese

• Stir together beans and seasoning mix; spread mixture in bottom of an 11- x 7-
inch baking dish. Spread avocado dip and sour cream evenly over bean mixture.
Sprinkle with olives and next 4 ingredients. Serve with corn or tortilla chips.
Yield: 8 cups.

Cinco de Mayo Bean Dip

Prep: 10 minutes • **Cook:** 5 minutes

1 (16-ounce) can refried beans
1 (8-ounce) package shredded
    Mexican four-cheese blend,
    divided
1 cup chunky salsa
1 (4½-ounce) can chopped black
    olives, drained

3 green onions, sliced
¼ teaspoon salt
¼ teaspoon garlic powder
    Chopped fresh cilantro

• Combine beans, 1 cup cheese, and next 5 ingredients. Spoon into a 9-inch pieplate. Top with remaining 1 cup cheese. Cover tightly with heavy-duty plastic wrap; fold back a small edge to allow steam to escape.
• Microwave at HIGH 4 to 5 minutes or until cheese melts, stirring after 3 minutes. Sprinkle with chopped fresh cilantro. Serve with tortilla chips or corn chips. Yield: 4¾ cups.

▶ Microwave
Miracle
▶ No Fuss
Entertaining

▶ Big Batch

Bacon-Blue Cheese Dip

Prep: 20 minutes

½ cup sour cream
1 (4-ounce) package crumbled blue
    cheese
1 (3-ounce) package cream cheese,
    softened

⅛ teaspoon hot sauce
2 tablespoons diced onion
4 bacon slices, cooked and
    crumbled

• Process first 5 ingredients in a blender or food processor until smooth, stopping to scrape down sides. Stir in half of bacon. Place dip in a serving bowl. Sprinkle with remaining bacon. Serve with crackers, raw vegetables, or potato chips. Yield: 1½ cups.

▶ No Fuss
Entertaining

Fix It Faster
To shave a couple of minutes off of this recipe, use precooked bacon slices instead of starting with uncooked.

Pizza Dip

Prep: 12 minutes • **Cook:** 12 minutes

Kid Friendly

Fix It Faster
Cut your cook
time in half by
microwaving this
dip instead of
baking it. It's done
in 6 minutes
on HIGH.

1 (8-ounce) package cream cheese, softened
1 (14-ounce) jar pizza sauce
½ cup chopped green bell pepper
½ cup chopped pepperoni

1 (2¼-ounce) can sliced ripe olives, drained
1 (8-ounce) package shredded mozzarella cheese
2 green onions, chopped

• Spread cream cheese in bottom of a 9-inch pieplate; spread pizza sauce over cream cheese. Sprinkle bell pepper, pepperoni, and olives over sauce. Top with mozzarella cheese.
• Bake at 350° for 10 to 12 minutes or until cheese melts. Sprinkle with green onions. Serve warm with corn chips. Yield: 8 to 10 servings.

Meaty Cheese Dip

Prep: 3 minutes • **Cook:** 12 minutes

No Fuss
Entertaining
5 Ingredients
or Less

**Secret
Ingredient
Savvy**
Want a spicer dip?
Substitute 1
(32-ounce) loaf
Mexican
pasteurized
prepared cheese
product for the
regular loaf
cheese product.

*You'll be amazed at the flavor from these four ingredients.
The hot sausage and salsa keep things lively.*

1 pound ground chuck
½ pound ground hot pork sausage
1 (32-ounce) loaf pasteurized prepared cheese product, cubed

1 (8-ounce) jar medium salsa

• Cook ground chuck and sausage in a large skillet, stirring until meat crumbles and is no longer pink; drain.
• Add cheese and salsa; cook over low heat, stirring constantly, until cheese melts. Serve warm with large corn chips. Yield: 6 cups.

Sweet 'n' Savory Snack Mix

Prep: 5 minutes • **Cook:** 12 minutes

Big Batch

Make Ahead

This is the perfect after-school or in-the-car traveling snack mix.

3 cups crispy corn or rice cereal
    squares
1 cup small pretzels
1 (6-ounce) can roasted almonds
8 ounces salted peanuts
⅓ cup firmly packed light brown
    sugar

1½ tablespoons Worcestershire
    sauce
Butter-flavored cooking spray
1 cup bear-shaped graham
    crackers
½ cup raisins

• Combine first 4 ingredients in a large bowl. Stir together brown sugar and Worcestershire sauce until blended; pour over cereal mixture. Coat a 15- x 10-inch jellyroll pan with butter-flavored cooking spray; spread cereal mixture in a single layer in pan, stirring to coat.
• Bake at 325° for 12 minutes, stirring every 5 minutes. Stir in graham crackers and raisins. Cool completely. Store snack mix in an airtight container. Yield: 8 cups.

Mexicali Snack Mix

Prep: 7 minutes • **Cook:** 20 minutes

Make Ahead

1½ cups bite-size crispy wheat cereal
    squares
1½ cups roasted salted peanuts
1 cup salted sunflower seed kernels
1 cup nutlike toasted-corn snacks
    (we used Cornnuts)

¼ cup butter or margarine, melted
2 teaspoons chili powder
¼ teaspoon ground cumin
¼ teaspoon dried crushed red pepper
⅛ teaspoon garlic powder

How-To Hints
To prevent this snack mix from becoming chewy, cool it completely before sealing in an airtight container.

• Combine first 4 ingredients; spread evenly in an ungreased 15- x 10-inch jellyroll pan. Drizzle butter evenly over cereal mixture; stir well.
• Combine chili powder and remaining ingredients; sprinkle evenly over cereal mixture, and stir gently.
• Bake, uncovered, at 350° for 20 minutes, stirring after 10 minutes. Cool completely. Store in an airtight container at room temperature. Yield: 5 cups.

Balsamic Marinated Olives

Prep: 5 minutes • **Other:** 8½ hours

Make Ahead

Big Batch

Fix It Faster
One cup of commercial balsamic vinaigrette is a great substitute for the olive oil and vinegar in this recipe.

This make-ahead recipe can be easily halved for a smaller crowd.

2 (6-ounce) jars ripe olives, drained
2 (6-ounce) jars kalamata olives, drained
2 (7½-ounce) jars pimiento-stuffed olives, drained
½ cup olive oil
½ cup balsamic vinegar
1 tablespoon Italian seasoning

• Combine all ingredients; cover and chill at least 8 hours. Let stand 30 minutes at room temperature before serving. Serve with a slotted spoon. Yield: 6 cups.

Spiced Pecans

Prep: 3 minutes • **Cook:** 12 minutes

Editor's Favorite

Make Ahead

No Fuss Entertaining

Double Delight
This recipe can be conveniently doubled for gift giving.

These sweet-hot nibbles are addictive.

4 cups pecan halves
¼ cup sugar
4 tablespoons butter, melted
1 teaspoon salt
½ teaspoon ground red pepper
4 teaspoons Worcestershire sauce
1 tablespoon sugar

• Stir together all ingredients; spread in a lightly greased 13- x 9-inch baking pan.
• Bake at 350° for 10 to 12 minutes or until lightly toasted, stirring mixture once.
• Spread nuts on waxed paper to cool. Sprinkle cooled nuts with 1 tablespoon sugar. Yield: 4 cups.

Balsamic
Marinated Olives

Spiced
Pecans

Broccoli-Cauliflower Fritters

Prep: 25 minutes • **Cook:** 4 minutes per batch

Heat the oil while you prepare the rest of your meal.

Simply
Southern

**Kitchen
Timesavers**
Use a sharp pastry
blender to
quickly mash the
cooked veggies.

Peanut oil
1 (16-ounce) package frozen
   broccoli and cauliflower blend
3 egg whites

1 small onion, chopped
½ cup chopped pecans
½ cup self-rising flour
1 teaspoon salt

• Pour oil to a depth of 1 inch into a Dutch oven; heat to 380°.
• Meanwhile, place vegetable blend in a large microwave-safe bowl; microwave according to package directions. Mash vegetables with a pastry blender or fork.
• Place egg whites in a small bowl; whisk with a fork to blend. Stir beaten egg whites, onion, and pecans into mashed vegetables. Add flour and salt, stirring until blended.
• Drop vegetable mixture by heaping tablespoonfuls into hot oil; fry, in batches, 1 to 2 minutes on each side or until golden brown. Drain on paper towels. Yield: 21 fritters.

20 Minutes or less

Stuffed Cherry Tomatoes

Prep: 18 minutes

**No-Cook
Creation**

**Super Fast
and Fresh**

Fix It Faster
Quickly soften
1 (8-ounce) package
of cream cheese
by unwrapping the
block and placing
it on a microwave-
safe plate. Then
microwave at
MEDIUM (50%
power) 1 minute or
just until softened.

1 pint cherry tomatoes
½ (8-ounce) package cream cheese,
   softened
1½ to 2 tablespoons whipping cream

1 tablespoon chopped fresh chives
⅛ teaspoon salt
⅛ teaspoon ground white pepper

• Cut top off each tomato; scoop out pulp, leaving shells intact. Discard pulp. Invert tomato shells onto paper towels to drain.
• Combine cream cheese and remaining 4 ingredients in a small mixing bowl; beat at medium speed with an electric mixer until creamy, adding enough whipping cream to make a slightly soft mixture. Spoon filling into tomato shells. Yield: about 1½ dozen.

Bacon Biscuit Cups

Prep: 10 minutes • **Cook:** 22 minutes

Editor's Favorite

2 (3-ounce) packages cream cheese, softened
1 large egg
2 tablespoons milk
½ cup (2 ounces) shredded Swiss cheese
1 green onion, chopped

1 (10-ounce) can refrigerated flaky biscuits (we used Pillsbury)
5 fully-cooked bacon slices, chopped (we used Oscar Mayer Ready to Serve Bacon)
Sliced green onions

• Place cream cheese and egg in a mixing bowl. Beat at medium speed with an electric mixer; add milk, beating until smooth. Stir in Swiss cheese and chopped green onion.

• Separate biscuits into 10 portions. Pat each portion into a 5-inch circle; press onto bottom and up sides of greased muffin cups, forming a ¼-inch edge. Sprinkle evenly with bacon; spoon cream cheese mixture into cups over bacon.

• Bake at 375° for 22 minutes or until set. Sprinkle evenly with sliced green onions, lightly pressing into filling. Remove immediately from pan, and serve warm. Yield: 10 biscuit cups.

Chicken Won Tons with Hoisin-Peanut Dipping Sauce

Prep: 25 minutes • **Cook:** 1½ minutes per batch

You can stir up the chicken mixture and fill the won ton wrappers while the frying oil heats. The dipping sauce that follows is great with these crispy won tons, but if you'd prefer, use one of the many bottled Asian sauces on the market.

Editor's Favorite

Make Ahead

Kitchen Timesavers

If you're running short on time, you can easily prepare these won tons the day before, and refrigerate overnight. The next day, simply heat the oil, and fry your won tons for an Asian appetizer that's sure to please.

Pinching Won Tons

Bring 2 opposite points of wrapper to center over filling; pinch points gently to seal. Bring remaining points to center, and pinch gently to seal.

Peanut oil
1 cup chopped cooked chicken
1 cup finely shredded cabbage (prepackaged)
4 green onions, finely chopped
2 tablespoons finely chopped fresh cilantro
1 tablespoon hoisin sauce
2 teaspoons light brown sugar
1 teaspoon sesame oil
24 won ton wrappers
Hoisin-Peanut Dipping Sauce

• Pour peanut oil to a depth of 3 inches into a large Dutch oven; heat to 375° (about 25 minutes).
• While oil heats, combine chicken and next 6 ingredients in a medium bowl. Spoon 1 heaping teaspoonful of meat mixture in center of each won ton wrapper; moisten edges with water.
• Carefully bring 2 opposite points of wrapper to center over filling; pinch points gently to seal. Bring remaining opposite points to center, and pinch gently to seal.
• Fry won tons, in batches, 1½ minutes or until golden, turning once. Drain well on paper towels. Serve with Hoisin-Peanut Dipping Sauce. Yield: 2 dozen.

Hoisin-Peanut Dipping Sauce

Prep: 3 minutes • **Cook:** 3 minutes

½ cup chicken broth
2 tablespoons hoisin sauce
2 tablespoons sesame oil
2 tablespoons soy sauce
1 tablespoon creamy peanut butter
1 teaspoon cornstarch

• Combine all ingredients in a small saucepan; bring to a boil. Cook, stirring constantly, 1 minute. Serve with Chicken Won Tons or other Asian dippers. Yield: ¾ cup.

Chicken Won Tons
with Hoisin-Peanut
Dipping Sauce

Cocktail Meatballs

Prep: 20 minutes • **Cook:** 25 minutes

*These tangy meatballs, covered with sauerkraut, cranberry sauce,
and chili sauce, are delicious served alone or on sandwich rolls with melted Swiss.*

2 pounds lean ground beef
1 cup fine, dry breadcrumbs
1 (1.4-ounce) envelope onion soup
   and recipe mix
3 large eggs
1 (14.5-ounce) can sauerkraut,
   drained

1 (16-ounce) can whole-berry
   cranberry sauce
1 (12-ounce) bottle chili sauce
½ cup water
1 cup firmly packed light brown
   sugar

• Combine ground beef, breadcrumbs, onion soup mix, and eggs in a large bowl;
stir until blended. Shape into 1-inch meatballs. Place meatballs in a greased 13- x
9-inch baking dish.
• Stir together sauerkraut and remaining 4 ingredients. Spoon over meatballs.
• Bake, uncovered, at 450° for 25 minutes. Yield: 3 dozen.

Bourbon Meatballs

Prep: 5 minutes • **Cook:** 19 minutes

No Fuss
Entertaining

Big Batch

1 (32-ounce) package frozen cooked Italian-style meatballs (about 60 meatballs)
2 cups barbecue sauce (we used KC Masterpiece Original)

1 cup bourbon
1 cup honey
¾ cup prepared mustard
1 teaspoon Worcestershire sauce

• Partially open package of meatballs; place package in a large microwave-safe bowl. Microwave at HIGH 3 to 4 minutes or until meatballs are thawed.
• Meanwhile, combine barbecue sauce and remaining ingredients in a Dutch oven. Bring to a boil over medium heat.
• As soon as meatballs are thawed, add them to sauce, and simmer, stirring occasionally, 15 minutes or until heated. Yield: 12 to 14 appetizer servings.

Santa Fe Chicken Quesadillas

Prep: 10 minutes • **Cook:** 8 minutes

Kid Friendly

Fix It Faster
If you have two skillets handy, heat both at the same time so the quesadillas will be hot off the griddle twice as fast.

½ cup salsa
1 cup chopped cooked chicken
2 tablespoons chopped fresh cilantro
1 teaspoon ground cumin
1 (4-ounce) can chopped green chiles, drained

4 (7-inch) flour tortillas
1 cup (4 ounces) shredded sharp Cheddar cheese
Butter-flavored cooking spray
Salsa

• Combine ½ cup salsa, chicken, and next 3 ingredients. Spoon mixture evenly onto half of each tortilla. Sprinkle evenly with cheese.
• Coat a nonstick skillet with butter-flavored cooking spray; place over medium-high heat until hot. Add one tortilla; cook 1 minute. Fold in half; cook 30 seconds. Turn; cook other side 30 seconds. Repeat with remaining tortillas. Cut each into 4 wedges. Serve with salsa. Yield: 1¼ dozen appetizers.

Santa Fe Chicken
Quesadillas

Savory Tomato-Bacon Biscuits

Prep: 20 minutes • **Cook:** 10 minutes

A little red pepper pumps up the flavor in these Parmesan biscuits. They're yummy alone or made into these little sandwiches.

Fit It Faster
These little Parmesan biscuits make a yummy bacon and tomato appetizer, but you can substitute any small ready-made or frozen biscuits if you'd like.

2 cups all-purpose baking mix (we used Bisquick)
⅓ cup grated Parmesan cheese
1 tablespoon sugar
1 teaspoon Italian seasoning
¼ teaspoon ground red pepper

⅔ cup mayonnaise, divided
¼ cup milk
4 large plum tomatoes, each cut into 8 slices
10 bacon slices, cooked and crumbled

• Combine first 5 ingredients in a medium bowl; stir in ⅓ cup mayonnaise and milk with a fork until moistened. Turn dough out onto a lightly floured surface, and knead 5 or 6 times.

• Pat or roll dough to ¼-inch thickness; cut with a 1¾-inch round cutter, and place on a lightly greased baking sheet.

• Bake at 425° for 8 to 10 minutes or until golden brown. Cool slightly.

• Spread each biscuit evenly with half of remaining ⅓ cup mayonnaise; top with a tomato slice. Spread tomato slices with remaining mayonnaise; sprinkle with bacon. Yield: 32 appetizer servings.

Blue Cheese Crisps

Prep: 8 minutes • **Cook:** 8 minutes

5 Ingredients
or Less

Editor's
Favorite

*These nutty snacks are sure to entice taste buds with the
flavor combination of blue cheese and pecans.*

½ cup butter or margarine, softened
1 (4-ounce) package crumbled blue
 cheese, softened

½ cup chopped pecans or walnuts
1 (12-ounce) French baguette, cut
 in ½-inch slices

• Stir together butter and blue cheese until blended; stir in pecans. Set aside.
• Place baguette slices in a single layer on baking sheets.
• Bake at 350° for 3 minutes. Turn slices, and spread evenly with blue cheese mixture. Bake 5 more minutes. Serve immediately. Yield: 28 appetizers.

Tomato Crostini

Prep: 20 minutes

Super Fast
and Fresh

5 Ingredients
or Less

No Fuss
Entertaining

Double Delight
This recipe easily
doubles or
quadruples for
a crowd.

Try these light and airy wedges as a simple savory appetizer.

¼ cup goat cheese
¼ cup cream cheese, softened
1 (6-inch) prebaked Italian pizza
 crust

5 plum tomatoes, chopped
1 tablespoon chopped fresh
 herbs (parsley, thyme, basil,
 or rosemary)

• Stir together goat cheese and cream cheese; spread on pizza crust. Cut into
wedges; top evenly with tomato and herbs. Yield: 4 servings.

Campagne Blossom
Punch, page 174

chapter seven

Drinks

In a Blink

Let your drinks be in the limelight! Beverages are an ideal way to liven up weeknight dinners and holiday parties. With this selection of quick drink solutions, you're sure to find a thirst quencher to please young and old alike.

Berry Mint Iced Tea

Prep: 5 minutes • **Other:** 5 minutes

Lemon lime soft drink adds refreshing carbonation to this strawberry-mint tea.
Stir it in just before serving to maximize the effect.

2 cups boiling water
2 family-size tea bags
¼ cup firmly packed fresh mint
   leaves

10 ounces frozen whole strawberries,
   partially thawed
3 tablespoons sugar
4 cups lemon lime soft drink, chilled

• Pour 2 cups boiling water over tea bags and mint leaves; cover and steep 5 minutes. Remove tea bags from water, squeezing gently. Pour tea mixture through a wire-mesh strainer into a blender or food processor; add strawberries and sugar. Process until strawberries are pureed, stopping to scrape down sides. Pour tea mixture through a wire-mesh strainer, discarding solids. Stir in soft drink just before serving. Serve over ice. Yield: 6½ cups.

Almond-Lemonade Tea

Prep: 3 minutes • **Other:** 1 hour and 5 minutes

2 family-size tea bags
3 cups boiling water
¼ cup sugar
1 (6-ounce) can frozen lemonade
   concentrate, undiluted

2¼ cups cold water
1 teaspoon almond extract

• Warm a 2-quart pitcher by rinsing with boiling water. Place tea bags in pitcher. Pour 3 cups boiling water over tea bags. Cover and steep 5 minutes. Remove tea bags, squeezing gently. Stir in sugar and lemonade concentrate until sugar dissolves. Stir in 2¼ cups cold water and almond extract. Cover and chill 1 hour. Serve over ice. Yield: 6 cups.

Cayenne Lemonade

Prep: 5 minutes

Pepper in lemonade? Surprisingly, yes. The zing actually heightens the sweetness and fresh lemon flavor.

1 cup fresh lemon juice (about 4 to 6 lemons)
1 cup pure maple syrup

4 cups water
⅛ to ¼ teaspoon ground red pepper

• Stir together all ingredients. Serve over ice. Yield: 6 cups.

5 Ingredients or Less

Super Fast and Fresh

Fix It Faster
Substitute one 7.5-ounce bottle of frozen lemon juice for the 1 cup fresh juice.

Blackberry Lemonade

Prep: 10 minutes

3 cups fresh blackberries
7 cups water
¼ cup sugar
¼ (1.9-ounce) package sugar-free pink lemonade drink mix (we used Crystal Light)

Garnishes: fresh mint sprigs, lemon slices

• Process blackberries in a blender until smooth, stopping to scrape down sides.
• Pour through a fine wire-mesh strainer into a 2-quart pitcher, discarding solids.
• Stir in 7 cups water, sugar, and drink mix. Serve over ice; garnish, if desired. Yield: 2 quarts.

5 Ingredients or Less

Secret Ingredient Savvy
Freeze fresh blackberries when they're in season to make this refresher year-round. Just pop the pint-size containers into freezer bags, and freeze. It's easy to separate and measure what you need and leave the rest frozen.

No-Squeeze Lemonade

Prep: 6 minutes

You'll be amazed how "fresh" lemonade can taste when you try this recipe using frozen lemon juice.

1 cup sugar
⅓ cup boiling water
1 (7.5-ounce) bottle frozen pure
lemon juice, thawed (we used
Minute Maid)

3⅓ cups cold water
Garnishes: lemon slices

• Stir together sugar and ⅓ cup boiling water in a large saucepan. Stir in lemon juice and 3⅓ cups cold water until sugar dissolves. Garnish, if desired. Yield: 5 cups.

Fresh Limeade: Substitute fresh lime juice for lemon juice. (This is not a "No-Squeeze" option.)

Southern Breeze

Prep: 10 minutes • **Other:** 8 hours

1 cup sugar
1 (0.22-ounce) envelope unsweetened blue raspberry lemonade
drink mix (we used Kool-Aid)
7 cups water
1 (6-ounce) can frozen lemonade
concentrate, thawed and
undiluted

1 (46-ounce) can unsweetened
pineapple juice, chilled
1 (2-liter) bottle ginger ale, chilled

• Stir together first 4 ingredients in a 2-quart pitcher; pour evenly into 5 ice cube trays, and freeze at least 8 hours.
• Combine pineapple juice and ginger ale; serve over raspberry ice cubes. Yield: 12 servings.

No-Squeeze
Lemonade

Apricot Coolers

Prep: 3 minutes

2 cups apricot nectar, chilled

2 cups unsweetened pineapple juice, chilled

⅓ cup lemon juice

1 (12-ounce) can ginger ale, chilled

• Stir together all ingredients. Serve immediately over ice. Yield: 6 cups.

5 Ingredients or Less

Super Fast and Fresh

Cranberry Cooler

Prep: 10 minutes

This fizzy, wine-spiked cooler gets its ruby red hue from cranberry juice.

3 cups seltzer water, chilled

2 cups dry white or rosé wine, chilled

1 (12-ounce) can frozen cranberry juice concentrate, thawed and undiluted

1 tablespoon lemon juice

• Stir together all ingredients; serve over ice. Yield: 6½ cups.

No Fuss Entertaining

5 Ingredients or Less

Secret Ingredient Savvy
To make a nonalcoholic version of this cooler, substitute 2 cups orange juice for the white wine.

Cherry Sparkler

Prep: 5 minutes • **Other:** 8 hours

*There's a cherry surprise in each of these ice cubes. They make a
fun presentation in a light pink hue of Cherry 7 Up.*

4 (6-ounce) jars red or green
    maraschino cherries, drained
½ gallon distilled water

1 (2-liter) bottle cherry-flavored,
    lemon lime soft drink, chilled
    (we used Cherry 7 Up)

• Place 1 cherry in each compartment of 4 ice cube trays. Fill trays with distilled
water; freeze 8 hours. Serve soft drink over ice cubes. Yield: 8½ cups.

Kid Friendly

Make Ahead

5 Ingredients
or Less

**Secret
Ingredient
Savvy**
Use red cherries
for Valentine's Day
or July 4th and
green cherries for
Christmas.

Banana Shake

Prep: 6 minutes

2 large ripe bananas, sliced
¾ cup milk

2 cups vanilla ice cream
½ teaspoon vanilla extract

• Process all ingredients in a blender until smooth, stopping to scrape down sides.
(Mixture will be thick). Yield: 4 cups.

Kid Friendly

5 Ingredients
or Less

**Secret
Ingredient
Savvy**
Slice and freeze
the banana a day
ahead for an extra
frosty shake.

Choco-nana
Smoothie

Pineapple Smoothie

Prep: 3 minutes

1 quart pineapple sherbet
1 (6-ounce) can pineapple juice
¼ cup fresh lemon juice

½ teaspoon grated lemon rind (optional)

• Process all ingredients in a blender until smooth, stopping once to scrape down sides. Serve immediately. Yield: 4 cups.

▸ Kid Friendly

▸ 5 Ingredients or Less

Choco-nana Smoothie

Prep: 10 minutes

*Ice cream and bananas combine to make
this smoothie extra thick and creamy.*

2 cups chocolate ice cream
2 bananas, sliced
½ cup milk

¼ cup chocolate syrup
Garnish: shaved chocolate

• Process first 4 ingredients in a blender until smooth. Add ice to 4½-cup level; process until smooth, stopping once to scrape down sides. Garnish, if desired; serve immediately. Yield: 4½ cups.

▸ Kid Friendly

▸ 5 Ingredients or Less

Gadget Magic
Using a vegetable peeler, scrape down the edge of a milk chocolate bar to create perfect chocolate curls. Be sure your chocolate is the correct temperature—too cold, the curls will break; too warm, the chocolate won't curl as much.

Dreamy Creamy Fruit Punch

Prep: 10 minutes

*You can mix up the juices a day or two ahead if you'd like,
and stir in the ice cream when ready to serve.*

Kid Friendly

**5 Ingredients
or Less**

Big Batch

**Secret
Ingredient
Savvy**

Thaw the juice
concentrates in the
fridge overnight,
and stir everything
in just before
serving.

9 cups water
1 (12-ounce) can frozen lemonade
   concentrate, thawed and
   undiluted
1 (6-ounce) can frozen orange juice
   concentrate, thawed and
   undiluted

½ gallon orange sherbet, softened
½ gallon vanilla ice cream, softened

• Combine first 3 ingredients in a punch bowl. Add sherbet and ice cream, stirring until creamy. Yield: 20 cups.

Minted Fruit Punch

Prep: 8 minutes • **Other:** 8 hours and 10 minutes

Kid Friendly

Make Ahead

Big Batch

1 cup loosely packed fresh mint
   leaves
2 cups hot water
2½ cups sugar
2 cups water
2 (7.5-ounce) bottles frozen lemon
   juice, thawed

2 (46-ounce) cans pineapple juice,
   chilled
3 cups orange juice, chilled
1 (1-liter) bottle ginger ale
Garnish: fresh mint sprigs

• Stir together mint leaves and 2 cups hot water in a bowl, pressing mint with the back of a spoon to bruise leaves. Let stand, uncovered, 10 minutes. Pour mixture through a wire-mesh strainer into a 2-quart container, discarding mint.
• Stir in sugar, 2 cups water, and lemon juice. Cover and chill 8 hours. Pour mixture into a large punch bowl. Stir in pineapple juice, orange juice, and ginger ale just before serving. Serve over ice. Garnish, if desired. Yield: 7 quarts.

Aloha Punch

Prep: 5 minutes

*Garnish these tropical drinks with paper
parasols for a Hawaiian-style party.*

2 cups pineapple juice
1 cup strawberry juice
1 cup guava juice

1 cup pear nectar
1 cup orange soft drink (we used
    Orangina)

• Stir together all ingredients; serve over crushed ice. Yield: 6 cups.

Kid Friendly

**No Fuss
Entertaining**

**5 Ingredients
or Less**

Berry-Colada Punch

Prep: 6 minutes

*For a nonalcoholic version of this rosy colada,
substitute additional club soda for the rum.*

1 (16-ounce) package frozen sliced
    strawberries, partially thawed
1 (15-ounce) can cream of coconut

3 cups pineapple juice
3 cups club soda, chilled
2 cups light rum

• Process strawberries and cream of coconut in a blender or food processor until
smooth, stopping to scrape down sides. Pour into a pitcher, and stir in pineapple
juice, club soda, and rum. Serve over crushed ice. Yield: 10 cups.

**No Fuss
Entertaining**

Big Batch

**5 Ingredients
or Less**

Freezer Fresh
Prepare this punch
ahead for your next
party. Simply make
as directed, exclud-
ing the club soda.
Freeze the punch
mixture; thaw it
overnight in the
refrigerator and
add the club soda
when you're ready
to serve.

Champagne Blossom Punch

(pictured on page 162)
Prep: 5 minutes

(pictured on page 162)

⅓ cup frozen orange juice
    concentrate
¼ cup frozen lemonade concentrate
1 (750-milliliter) bottle dry white
    wine, chilled (we used Riesling)

1 (750-milliliter) bottle champagne,
    chilled

• Combine all ingredients, stirring until concentrate dissolves. Serve immediately over ice. Yield: 7 cups.

5 Ingredients or Less
No Fuss Entertaining

How-To Hints
Concentrate usually doesn't freeze hard, so just spoon out the amount you need and refreeze the rest.

Mango Margaritas

Prep: 15 minutes

This fruity drink won our highest rating when taste tested. We created a fiesta of flavor and finesse with colored decorative sugar crystals around the rims of the glasses.

1 (24-ounce) jar sliced mangoes,
    undrained
Colored decorator sugar crystals
1 (6-ounce) can frozen limeade
    concentrate, thawed and
    undiluted

1 cup gold tequila
½ cup Triple Sec or Cointreau
¼ cup Grand Marnier
Crushed ice

• Spoon 3 tablespoons mango liquid into a saucer; pour mangoes and remaining liquid into a blender.
• Place sugar in a saucer; dip rims of glasses into 3 tablespoons mango liquid and then sugar. Set aside.
• Add limeade concentrate and next 3 ingredients to blender; process until smooth, stopping once to scrape down sides.
• Pour half of mixture into a small pitcher, and set aside.
• Add ice to remaining mixture in blender to bring it to 5-cup level; process until slushy, stopping to scrape down sides. Pour into prepared glasses; repeat with remaining mango mixture and ice. Serve immediately. Yield: 10 cups.

Big Batch
No Fuss Entertaining
Make Ahead

Freezer Fresh
Alcohol keeps liquids from freezing solid, so these margaritas are great candidates to freeze ahead for a party. A quick stir before serving creates mango slushiness.

Mango
Margaritas

Frosted Bellinis

Prep: 3 minutes

5 Ingredients or Less

Freeze It

This bellini mixture tastes great simply served over ice or served as a slushy version by freezing in a pan prior to serving.

1 (750-milliliter) bottle champagne   ½ cup peach schnapps
2 (12-ounce) cans peach nectar

• Combine all ingredients in a large pitcher, stirring until well blended. Serve immediately in glasses over crushed ice, or pour mixture into a 13- x 9-inch pan. Cover and freeze until firm. Yield: 6 cups.

 Amaretto-Coffee Freeze

Prep: 10 minutes

No Fuss Entertaining

Freezer Fresh
This "freeze" can be made ahead if you aren't having a large crowd over for dinner. When you process half of the ingredients, freeze that half, and serve the second half you process.

A touch of almond liqueur heightens the vanilla flavor of this freeze.

½ cup almond liqueur   1 quart frozen vanilla yogurt,
¼ cup coffee liqueur   softened

• Process all ingredients in a blender until smooth, stopping to scrape down sides. Serve immediately. Yield: 4¾ cups.

Chocolate-Caramel Royale Coffee

Prep: 4 minutes

3¾ cups hot strongly brewed coffee
2 tablespoons chocolate syrup

2 tablespoons caramel syrup
½ teaspoon vanilla extract

• Combine all ingredients, stirring until syrups dissolve. Serve hot. Yield: 4 cups.

Praline Coffee

Prep: 5 minutes • **Cook:** 5 minutes

Linger over this rich, creamy coffee, and enjoy your favorite shortbread cookie for an after-dinner treat.

3 cups hot brewed coffee
⅔ to ¾ cup firmly packed light
   brown sugar

¾ cup half-and-half
¾ cup praline liqueur
Sweetened whipped cream

• Cook first 3 ingredients in a large saucepan over medium heat, stirring constantly, until thoroughly heated (do not boil). Stir in liqueur, and serve coffee with dollops of sweetened whipped cream. Yield: 5 cups.

White Chocolate-Macadamia Nut Muffins

Prep: 10 minutes • **Cook:** 12 minutes

Chunks of melted white chocolate make little pockets of sweetness in these muffins.

2½ cups all-purpose baking mix
½ cup sugar
¾ cup coarsely chopped white
  chocolate (we used Baker's
  Premium white chocolate)
½ cup coarsely chopped
  macadamia nuts

¾ cup half-and-half
3 tablespoons vegetable oil
2 teaspoons vanilla extract
1 large egg, lightly beaten

• Combine baking mix and sugar in a large bowl; stir in chocolate and nuts. Make a well in center of mixture. Combine half-and-half and remaining 3 ingredients; add to dry ingredients, stirring just until dry ingredients are moistened.
• Spoon into a lightly greased muffin pan, filling two-thirds full. Bake at 400° for 11 to 12 minutes or until a wooden pick inserted into center comes out clean. Remove from pan immediately. Yield: 1 dozen.

Pumpkin Pancakes

Prep: 8 minutes • **Cook:** 4 minutes per batch

These spiced pumpkin pancakes are a true autumn
treat when served with apple butter on top.

1 cup all-purpose flour
2 teaspoons baking powder
½ teaspoon salt
1 tablespoon sugar
½ teaspoon ground cinnamon or
  pumpkin pie spice

2 large eggs, separated
¾ cup milk
½ cup canned pumpkin
¼ cup butter or margarine, melted

- Combine first 5 ingredients in a large bowl; make a well in center of mixture.
- Combine egg yolks, milk, pumpkin, and butter; add to flour mixture, stirring just until dry ingredients are moistened.
- Beat egg whites at high speed with an electric mixer until stiff peaks form. Gently fold beaten whites into pumpkin mixture.
- Pour about ¼ cup batter for each pancake onto a hot, lightly greased griddle. Cook pancakes until tops are covered with bubbles and edges look cooked; turn and cook other side. Yield: 12 (4-inch) pancakes.

Easy Banana Pancakes

Prep: 5 minutes • **Cook:** 4 minutes per batch

These airy cakes come together in a flash, thanks to biscuit mix and mashed bananas.

2 cups biscuit mix
1 cup milk
2 ripe bananas, mashed

2 large eggs, lightly beaten
Maple syrup or fruit topping

- Combine first 4 ingredients in a medium bowl, stirring just until dry ingredients are moistened.
- Pour about ¼ cup batter for each pancake onto a hot, lightly greased griddle. Cook pancakes 2 minutes or until tops are covered with bubbles and edges look cooked; turn and cook other side. Serve immediately with syrup or fruit topping. Yield: 16 pancakes.

5 Ingredients
or Less

Stovetop
Solution

Big Batch

Cornbread Waffles

Prep: 10 minutes • **Cook:** 20 minutes

1½ cups plain white cornmeal
½ cup all-purpose flour
 2 tablespoons sugar
2½ teaspoons baking powder

¾ teaspoon salt
1 large egg
1½ cups milk

• Stir together first 5 ingredients in a large bowl. Stir together egg and milk; add to cornmeal mixture, stirring just until dry ingredients are moistened.
• Cook in a preheated, oiled waffle iron just until crisp. Yield: 12 (4-inch) waffles.

Freeze It

Freezer Fresh
Freeze any leftover waffles up to a month in a zip-top freezer bag. Crisp them up in a toaster oven to reheat them. No need to thaw.

Spicy Breadsticks

Prep: 15 minutes • **Cook:** 12 minutes

Spicy seasoned pepper blend makes these crisp breadsticks perfect for pairing with robust gumbo or stew.

1 (11-ounce) can refrigerated
   soft breadsticks
1 large egg, lightly beaten

2 tablespoons paprika
2 tablespoons seasoned pepper blend
   (we used McCormick)

• Separate breadsticks; working with two at a time, roll each breadstick into a 12-inch rope. Brush ropes with egg. Twist ropes together, pinching ends to seal. Repeat with remaining breadsticks.
• Combine paprika and pepper blend; spread mixture on a paper plate. Roll breadsticks in pepper mixture, pressing gently to coat. (Wash hands between rolling each breadstick, if necessary.)
• Place breadsticks on a lightly greased baking sheet. Bake at 375° for 10 to 12 minutes. Yield: 4 servings.

5 Ingredients or Less

No Fuss Entertaining

Secret Ingredient Savvy
If you can't find seasoned pepper blend, combine equal portions of cracked black pepper, red bell pepper flakes, and salt.

Spicy
Breadsticks

Italian Cheese Breadsticks

Prep: 5 minutes • **Cook:** 12 minutes

5 Ingredients or Less

No Fuss Entertaining

Dip these pizza-flavored sticks into your favorite brand of marinara sauce.

1 (11-ounce) can refrigerated soft breadsticks
1 to 2 tablespoons olive oil
1½ teaspoons garlic powder

1 teaspoon dried Italian seasoning
1 cup (4 ounces) shredded mozzarella cheese

• Unroll breadstick dough; twist breadsticks, and place 1 inch apart on a lightly greased aluminum foil-lined baking sheet. Brush breadsticks with oil. Combine garlic powder and Italian seasoning; sprinkle over breadsticks.
• Bake at 400° for 9 to 10 minutes or until golden. Sprinkle with cheese; bake 1 to 2 minutes or until cheese melts. Serve immediately. Yield: 8 breadsticks.

Buttery Garlic Bread

Prep: 10 minutes • **Cook:** 7 minutes

Super Fast and Fresh

No Fuss Entertaining

Menu Makings
This garlicky treat is the perfect match for spaghetti with meat sauce.

½ cup butter or margarine
4 garlic cloves, pressed
½ teaspoon salt
1 (16-ounce) Italian bread loaf

1½ teaspoons Italian seasoning
¼ cup freshly grated Parmesan cheese

• Melt butter in a skillet over medium-high heat; add garlic and salt, and sauté 2 minutes.
• Cut bread into 1½-inch slices, and dip into butter mixture, coating both sides. Place on a baking sheet.
• Stir together Italian seasoning and Parmesan cheese; sprinkle on 1 side of each bread slice.
• Broil 5 inches from heat 4 minutes or until cheese melts. Yield: 8 slices.

Parmesan-Grilled Garlic Bread

Prep: 10 minutes • **Cook:** 15 minutes

1 (16-ounce) French bread loaf
½ cup butter or margarine, softened
¼ cup grated Parmesan cheese
¼ teaspoon black pepper

1 garlic clove, crushed
Dash of ground red pepper

• Slice bread loaf diagonally into 1-inch slices. Combine butter and remaining 4 ingredients; spread between bread slices. Wrap bread in heavy-duty aluminum foil. Grill, covered with grill lid, over medium-high heat (350° to 400°) 15 minutes, turning once. Yield: 1 loaf.

Herb Bread

Prep: 10 minutes • **Cook:** 25 minutes

This medley of herbs creates a savory bread suitable for any entrée or soup.

1 (16-ounce) French bread loaf
1 cup butter or margarine, softened
1 (2¼-ounce) can chopped ripe
   olives
½ cup chopped fresh parsley

⅓ cup chopped green onions
1½ teaspoons dried basil
½ teaspoon garlic powder
½ teaspoon dried tarragon
¼ teaspoon celery seeds

• Slice bread in half horizontally.
• Combine butter and remaining 7 ingredients; spread evenly over cut sides of bread. Place halves together; wrap in aluminum foil. Store in refrigerator until ready to bake.
• Bake at 350° for 25 minutes or until thoroughly heated. Cut into slices to serve. Yield: 12 servings.

Super Fast and Fresh

No Fuss Entertaining

Make Ahead

How-To Hints
To prepare ahead, spread this bread with its seasoned butter, roll in foil, and chill until ready to put on the grill.

Make Ahead

Big Batch

Fast Rosemary-Dried Tomato Flatbread

Prep: 8 minutes • **Cook:** 16 minutes • **Other:** 15 minutes

This yummy flatbread resembles the famous focaccia bread, but it's laced with pockets of flavorful rosemary, garlic, and tomato.

No Fuss Entertaining

Two Meals in One
The package of frozen bread dough actually comes as two loaves. So use one loaf and leave the second one frozen for the next time you prepare this recipe.

¼ cup chopped fresh rosemary
2 tablespoons dried tomatoes in oil, drained and chopped
1 garlic clove, minced
½ (32-ounce) package frozen bread dough, thawed

1 teaspoon olive oil
1 tablespoon freshly grated Parmesan cheese

• Combine first 3 ingredients. Turn dough out onto a lightly floured surface; knead in rosemary mixture. Place dough on a lightly greased baking sheet. Press into a 9-inch circle.
• Cover and let rise in a warm place (85°), free from drafts, 15 minutes. Brush loaf with oil. Sprinkle with cheese.
• Bake at 400° for 16 minutes or until golden. Yield: 8 servings.

Quick Biscuits

Prep: 10 minutes • **Cook:** 17 minutes

These unbelievably easy biscuits have a buttery, flaky texture like the ones Grandma used to bake.

2¼ cups biscuit mix
 1 (8-ounce) container sour cream
½ cup butter, melted

• Combine all ingredients, stirring well.
• Drop dough by heaping tablespoonfuls into an ungreased muffin pan.
• Bake at 375° for 15 to 17 minutes or until golden. Yield: 1 dozen.

5 Ingredients or Less

No Fuss Entertaining

Mayonnaise Rolls

Prep: 8 minutes • **Cook:** 15 minutes

These moist rolls are a delight thanks to the addition of mayonnaise. Bake for guests, and utilize an entire muffin pan by doubling these four simple ingredients.

 1 cup self-rising flour
½ cup milk
3 tablespoons mayonnaise
¾ teaspoon sugar

• Combine all ingredients in a bowl, stirring just until dry ingredients are moistened. Spoon batter into a lightly greased muffin pan, filling three-fourths full. Bake at 425° for 15 minutes. Yield: 6 rolls.

5 Ingredients or Less

Super Fast and Fresh

Ideas for Two

Miniature Cinnamon Rolls

Editor's Favorite

Kid Friendly

No Fuss Entertaining

Prep: 16 minutes • **Cook:** 18 minutes • **Other:** 10 minutes

This recipe easily doubles for a crowd, and it's so yummy, no one will ever believe you started with crescent roll dough.

2 (8-ounce) cans refrigerated crescent rolls
6 tablespoons butter or margarine, softened
⅓ cup firmly packed light brown sugar

1 tablespoon granulated sugar
1 teaspoon ground cinnamon
¼ cup chopped pecans
1⅓ cups sifted powdered sugar
2 tablespoons milk
¼ teaspoon vanilla extract

• Unroll crescent rolls, and separate each dough portion along center perforation to form 4 rectangles; press diagonal perforations to seal.
• Stir together butter and next 3 ingredients; spread evenly over 1 side of each rectangle. Sprinkle with pecans. Roll up jellyroll fashion, starting at long end. Gently cut each log into 6 slices, using a sharp knife. Place rolls, ¼ inch apart, into 2 (8-inch) round cakepans placing 3 in the center.
• Bake at 375° for 16 to 18 minutes or until golden. Remove from pans. Cool 5 to 10 minutes.
• Stir together powdered sugar, milk, and vanilla. Drizzle evenly over warm rolls. Yield: 2 dozen.

Caramel-Pecan Rolls

Editor's Favorite

Prep: 10 minutes • **Cook:** 14 minutes

¼ cup caramel syrup
1 (8-ounce) can refrigerated crescent rolls

¼ cup firmly packed brown sugar
2 tablespoons finely chopped pecans
½ teaspoon ground cinnamon

• Spoon 1½ teaspoons syrup into each of 8 muffin cups coated with cooking spray; set aside.
• Unroll crescent roll dough, and separate into rectangles. Combine brown sugar, pecans, and cinnamon; sprinkle evenly over each rectangle, pressing gently into dough. Roll up jellyroll fashion, starting at long end. Pinch ends of dough to seal. Gently cut each log into 6 slices. Place 3 slices, cut sides down, in prepared muffin cups. Bake at 375° for 14 minutes. Run a knife around edges of cups; invert onto a platter. Yield: 8 servings.

Easy Caramel-Chocolate Sticky Buns

Prep: 12 minutes • **Cook:** 30 minutes

5 Ingredients
or Less

Big Batch

Kid Friendly

*It's a good thing these sticky buns serve a crowd. Everyone will clamor
for the recipe when they discover hidden chocolate in the center of each bite!*

1 (15-ounce) container ready-to-spread coconut-pecan frosting
1 cup pecan halves

2 (10-ounce) cans refrigerated buttermilk biscuits
20 milk chocolate kisses, unwrapped

• Spread frosting in bottom of a lightly greased 9-inch square pan. Sprinkle pecan halves over frosting.
• Separate biscuits; flatten each to about ¼-inch thickness. Place a chocolate kiss to 1 side of center of each biscuit. Fold biscuit in half, forming a semicircle; press edges of biscuit gently to seal. Repeat procedure with remaining biscuits and chocolate kisses. Arrange biscuits over pecans, placing flat sides down.
• Bake at 375° for 28 to 30 minutes or until lightly browned. Cool in pan on a wire rack 3 minutes; invert onto serving plate, and serve immediately. Yield: 20 servings.

Cinnamon-Apple Breakfast Buns

Prep: 4 minutes • **Cook:** 22 minutes

30 Minutes or less

Kid Friendly

1 (12.4-ounce) can refrigerated cinnamon rolls
1 (1.62-ounce) package of instant cinnamon and spice oatmeal
¼ cup firmly packed brown sugar
¼ cup chopped pecans

¼ teaspoon ground cinnamon
Dash of ground nutmeg
1 tablespoon butter or margarine, melted
1 Granny Smith apple, peeled, cored, and cut into 8 rings

• Separate cinnamon rolls, and place in a lightly greased 8- or 9-inch round cakepan; set icing aside. Bake rolls according to package directions.
• Meanwhile, stir together oatmeal and next 5 ingredients. Place 1 apple ring on each cinnamon roll; sprinkle oatmeal mixture evenly over cinnamon rolls.
• Bake at 400° for 20 to 22 minutes.
• Remove top to icing. Microwave icing at LOW (10% power) for 20 seconds; drizzle evenly over rolls. Yield: 8 rolls.

Beef Fillets with Orange
Cream, page 204

chapter nine

Main Dishes
In Minutes

Sitting down to the same entrées over and over again can take the excitement out of family dinners. It's easier than ever to spice up the night. Find new ideas and quick fixes on these pages of main dishes from land, sea, and garden.

Beef Fillets with Orange Cream

(shown on page 202)
Prep: 5 minutes • **Cook:** 17 minutes

No Fuss
Entertaining

*The slightly orange-colored sauce and orange rind curls make a pretty presentation
and lend a hint to the flavor of these succulent fillets.*

4 (6- to 8-ounce) beef tenderloin
     fillets
½ teaspoon cracked pepper (optional)
1 cup whipping cream

2 tablespoons orange marmalade
1 to 2 tablespoons prepared
     horseradish
Garnish: orange rind curls

• Sprinkle fillets with cracked pepper, if desired.
• Grill, covered with grill lid, over medium-high heat (350° to 400°) 4 to 6
minutes on each side or to desired degree of doneness.
• Bring whipping cream, marmalade, and horseradish to a boil over medium-high
heat, stirring constantly; reduce heat, and simmer, stirring often, 5 minutes or until
thickened. Serve immediately with fillets; garnish, if desired. Yield: 4 servings.

Pan-Seared Steaks with Roasted Red Pepper Sauce

Prep: 4 minutes • **Cook:** 6 minutes

Super Fast
and Fresh

No Fuss
Entertaining

5 Ingredients
or Less

1 teaspoon roasted garlic-pepper
     seasoning
½ teaspoon salt, divided
4 (4-ounce) beef tenderloin fillets
     (1 inch thick)

Olive oil cooking spray
1 (7-ounce) jar roasted red bell
     peppers, drained

**Secret
Ingredient
Savvy**
Can't find garlic-
pepper seasoning?
Use ½ teaspoon
black pepper and
½ teaspoon garlic
powder instead.

• Combine garlic-pepper and ¼ teaspoon salt. Rub both sides of fillets with
pepper mixture.
• Place a large nonstick skillet coated with olive oil cooking spray over medium-
high heat until hot. Add fillets; cook 2 to 3 minutes on each side or to desired
degree of doneness.
• While fillets cook, place bell peppers and remaining ¼ teaspoon salt in a
blender. Cover and process until smooth. Serve fillets with roasted red pepper
sauce. Yield: 4 servings.

Spicy Beef Fillets

Prep: 10 minutes • **Cook:** 20 minutes

A touch of bourbon adds depth of flavor to the juicy beef fillets.

6 (6-ounce) beef tenderloin fillets
   (1½ inches thick)
¼ teaspoon salt
¼ teaspoon pepper
¼ cup butter or margarine
2 garlic cloves, pressed

2 tablespoons all-purpose flour
1 cup beef broth
1 cup dry red wine
¼ cup bourbon
2 tablespoons Dijon mustard
1 teaspoon Worcestershire sauce

• Sprinkle fillets with salt and pepper.
• Melt butter in a skillet over medium heat. Add fillets, and cook 5 to 7 minutes on each side or to desired degree of doneness. Remove fillets from pan, and keep warm.
• Add garlic and flour to pan drippings; cook over medium heat, stirring constantly, 1 minute. Gradually add broth, wine, and bourbon, stirring to loosen particles from bottom of pan; bring to a boil. Stir in mustard and Worcestershire sauce; reduce heat, and simmer 5 minutes. Top steaks with sauce. Yield: 6 servings.

Stovetop Solution

No Fuss Entertaining

Secret Ingredient Savvy
1¼ cups beef broth or cranberry juice may be substituted for red wine and bourbon.

Fillets with Tarragon Butter

Prep: 3 minutes • **Cook:** 15 minutes

*A candlelight dinner for two is the perfect occasion
to serve these elegant, yet simple, herbed fillets.*

2 (6-ounce) beef tenderloin fillets
   (1 inch thick)
¼ teaspoon salt
¼ teaspoon pepper
1 teaspoon olive oil

1 shallot, finely chopped
¼ cup butter, softened
⅛ teaspoon salt
2 tablespoons finely chopped fresh
   tarragon

• Sprinkle fillets evenly with ¼ teaspoon salt and pepper. Place a 10-inch cast-iron skillet over medium-high heat until hot; add oil. Cook fillets in hot oil 2 minutes on each side. Place pan in oven, and bake, uncovered, at 400° for 10 minutes or to desired degree of doneness.
• Meanwhile, cook shallot in 1 teaspoon butter in a small skillet over medium-high heat until tender, stirring often; cool 2 minutes. Combine shallot, remaining butter, ⅛ teaspoon salt, and tarragon in a small bowl. Top each fillet evenly with tarragon butter before serving. Yield: 2 servings.

Ideas for Two

Menu Makings
Steamed asparagus is a great accompaniment to these beef fillets. Simply double the butter mixture to serve with the asparagus, if you'd like.

Filet Mignon with Horseradish Gravy

Prep: 3 minutes • **Cook:** 30 minutes

No Fuss
Entertaining

Menu Makings
Serve this zippy
entrée and its
mushroom gravy
with mashed
potatoes.

1 (¾-ounce) package brown
   gravy mix
2 tablespoons prepared horseradish
4 (5-ounce) beef tenderloin fillets
¼ teaspoon salt

¼ teaspoon pepper
2 tablespoons butter
1 (8-ounce) package sliced fresh
   mushrooms

• Prepare gravy according to package directions; stir in horseradish. Set aside.
• Coat a large nonstick skillet with cooking spray. Place skillet over medium-high heat until hot; add fillets, and cook 1 minute on each side. (Fillets will be rare.) Place in a lightly greased 1-quart baking dish; sprinkle with salt and pepper.
• Melt butter in skillet over medium heat. Add mushrooms, and cook, stirring constantly, 5 minutes or until tender. Remove from heat, and stir in gravy. Pour gravy over fillets; bake, uncovered, at 350° for 15 minutes or to desired degree of doneness. Yield: 4 servings.

Garlic-Herb Steaks

Prep: 10 minutes • **Cook:** 20 minutes • **Other:** 1 hour

5 Ingredients
or Less

**Secret
Ingredient
Savvy**
Minced garlic in
a jar can be
found in the
produce area
of your grocery
store.

4 (4-ounce) beef tenderloin fillets
¼ teaspoon salt
¼ teaspoon freshly ground pepper

¼ cup jarred minced garlic
1 tablespoon minced fresh rosemary

• Sprinkle fillets with salt and pepper; coat with garlic and rosemary. Chill 1 hour.
• Prepare a hot fire by piling charcoal or lava rocks on 1 side of grill, leaving other side empty; place rack on grill. Arrange fillets over empty side, and grill, covered with grill lid, over high heat (400° to 500°) 10 minutes on each side or to desired degree of doneness. Yield: 4 servings.

Filet Mignon with
Horseradish Gravy

Sirloin Steaks with Thyme Pesto

Prep: 3 minutes • **Cook:** 19 minutes

No Fuss Entertaining

Secret Ingredient Savvy

Traditional pesto is made from basil. Using thyme gives this recipe an herbal twist.

2 tablespoons pine nuts
2 (12-ounce) boneless beef top loin
   steaks, trimmed
¾ teaspoon salt, divided
½ teaspoon coarsely ground pepper
⅓ cup fresh thyme leaves

½ cup chopped fresh parsley
1 garlic clove, chopped
¼ cup freshly grated Parmesan
   cheese
2 tablespoons olive oil

• Bake pine nuts in a shallow pan at 350°, stirring occasionally, 5 minutes or until toasted; cool.
• Coat steaks evenly with ½ teaspoon salt and pepper.
• Grill, covered with grill lid, over medium–high heat (350° to 400°) 7 minutes on each side or to desired degree of doneness. Keep warm.
• Process pine nuts, remaining ¼ teaspoon salt, thyme, and next 4 ingredients in a blender until smooth. Serve with steaks. Yield: 6 servings.

Grecian Skillet Rib-Eyes

Prep: 5 minutes • **Cook:** 14 minutes

Ideas for Two

Stovetop Solution

You'll find that this olive-feta-herb topping works great on chicken and lamb, too.

1½ teaspoons garlic powder
1½ teaspoons dried basil, crushed
1½ teaspoons dried oregano, crushed
½ teaspoon salt
⅛ teaspoon pepper
2 (1-inch-thick) rib-eye steaks
   (1¾ to 2 pounds)

1 tablespoon olive oil
1 tablespoon fresh lemon juice
2 tablespoons crumbled feta cheese
1 tablespoon chopped kalamata or
   ripe olives

• Combine first 5 ingredients; rub evenly onto all sides of steaks.
• Add oil to a large nonstick skillet; place over medium heat until hot. Add steaks, and cook 10 to 14 minutes or to desired degree of doneness, turning once. Sprinkle with lemon juice; top with cheese and olives. Yield: 2 to 4 servings.

30 Minutes or less

Teriyaki Burgers

Prep: 5 minutes • **Cook:** 20 minutes

1½ pounds ground beef
3 tablespoons teriyaki or soy sauce
1 tablespoon honey
1 teaspoon salt
¾ teaspoon ground ginger
2 garlic cloves, minced

4 sesame seed hamburger buns, toasted
Lettuce leaves
Red onion slices
Chinese sweet-hot mustard

• Combine first 6 ingredients; shape into 4 patties. Cook patties in a large skillet over medium-low heat 20 minutes, turning once.
• Place patties on buns with lettuce and onion; serve with Chinese mustard. Yield: 4 servings.

Beef and Kraut Skillet Dinner

Prep: 5 minutes • **Cook:** 35 minutes

Tangy sauerkraut gives this beefy skillet entrée a German flair.

1 tablespoon butter or margarine
1 (14.5-ounce) can sauerkraut, undrained
½ cup uncooked long-grain rice
½ cup water

1 medium onion, chopped
1 pound ground round, crumbled
½ teaspoon salt
¼ teaspoon pepper
1 (8-ounce) can tomato sauce

• Melt butter in a large skillet over medium heat. Spread sauerkraut evenly in bottom of skillet; layer rice, ½ cup water, onion, and ground round over sauerkraut. Sprinkle evenly with salt and pepper; top with tomato sauce. Cover and cook over medium heat 35 minutes. Serve from skillet. Yield: 7 cups.

Kid Friendly

No Fuss Entertaining

How-To Hints
Cooking the burgers over medium-low heat keeps the honey in them from burning.

Stovetop Solution

Menu Makings
Serve a stout brew to complete this meal's German theme.

Veal Parmesan

**No Fuss
Entertaining**

Prep: 12 minutes • **Cook:** 33 minutes

1 pound veal scaloppine	2 large eggs, lightly beaten
1½ cups soft white breadcrumbs	1 (26-ounce) can chunky garlic and
¾ cup grated Parmesan cheese,	herb pasta sauce
divided	¼ cup olive oil, divided
¼ cup chopped fresh parsley	2 (6-ounce) packages mozzarella
½ teaspoon salt	cheese slices
¼ teaspoon pepper	

• Cut scaloppine into serving size pieces. Place between 2 sheets of heavy-duty plastic wrap; flatten to ⅛-inch thickness, using a meat mallet or rolling pin.
• Combine breadcrumbs, ½ cup Parmesan cheese, and next 3 ingredients. Dip veal into beaten egg, draining excess; dredge in breadcrumb mixture.
• Spread ½ cup pasta sauce in a lightly greased 11- x 7-inch baking dish.
• Sauté half of veal in 2 tablespoons hot oil in a large skillet over medium-high heat 2 minutes on each side or until golden. Remove from skillet; place in baking dish. Repeat procedure with remaining oil and veal; top with remaining sauce.
• Sprinkle with remaining ¼ cup Parmesan cheese. Bake, uncovered, at 400° for 20 minutes. Top with mozzarella cheese. Bake 5 more minutes or until cheese melts. Yield: 4 servings.

30 Minutes or less — Veal in Lime Sauce

Menu Makings
Complement these
succulent cutlets
by pairing with
roasted aspargus
drizzled with a bit
of lime juice.

Prep: 13 minutes • **Cook:** 10 minutes

1 pound veal cutlets (¼ inch thick)	2 tablespoons dry white wine
¼ teaspoon salt	4 teaspoons all-purpose flour
¼ teaspoon freshly ground pepper	½ cup chicken broth
Butter-flavored cooking spray	⅔ cup fat-free evaporated milk
2 tablespoons fresh lime juice	

• Sprinkle veal cutlets with salt and pepper. Coat a large nonstick skillet with butter-flavored cooking spray; place over medium-high heat until hot. Add cutlets; cook 1 minute on each side or until browned. Remove from skillet; set aside, and keep warm.
• Add lime juice and wine to skillet; cook over high heat 1 minute or until mixture is reduced by half. Combine flour, broth, and milk; stir well. Add to lime juice mixture. Cook over medium heat, stirring constantly, 5 minutes or until thickened and bubbly. Return cutlets to skillet; cook until thoroughly heated. Transfer to a serving platter, and serve immediately. Yield: 4 servings.

Lamb and Vegetable Stir-Fry

Prep: 10 minutes • **Cook:** 8 minutes

1½ pounds boneless leg of lamb top
    cutlets (½ inch thick)
2 tablespoons olive oil, divided
1 medium onion, sliced
1 red bell pepper, cut into thin strips
1 yellow bell pepper, cut into
    thin strips
1 teaspoon minced garlic

1 (6-ounce) package fresh baby
    spinach
¾ teaspoon salt
¾ teaspoon black pepper
¼ to ½ teaspoon dried crushed red
    pepper
Hot cooked rice

• Cut lamb diagonally across the grain into wafer-thin slices.
• Heat 1 tablespoon oil in a wok or Dutch oven over medium-high heat 1 minute. Add lamb; stir-fry 3 minutes. Remove from wok, and drain well.
• Wipe wok with paper towels. Add remaining 1 tablespoon oil to wok, and heat over medium-high heat. Add onion and next 3 ingredients; stir-fry 2 minutes. Add spinach and lamb, and stir-fry 1 minute or until spinach wilts. Stir in salt, black pepper, and crushed red pepper. Serve over hot rice. Yield: 4 servings.

Mustard-Garlic Lamb Chops

Prep: 7 minutes • **Cook:** 14 minutes

2 garlic cloves, minced
½ teaspoon pepper
¼ teaspoon dried thyme
⅛ teaspoon salt

2 teaspoons fresh lemon juice
2 teaspoons Dijon mustard
1 teaspoon olive oil
4 (5-ounce) lean lamb loin chops

• Combine garlic, pepper, thyme, and salt in a small bowl; mash with back of a spoon until mixture forms a paste. Stir in lemon juice, mustard, and olive oil.
• Trim fat from chops. Spread garlic mixture over both sides of chops. Place chops on rack of a broiler pan coated with cooking spray. Broil 6 to 7 minutes on each side or to desired degree of doneness. Yield: 4 servings.

Chicken Cutlets with Artichoke Cream Sauce

30 Minutes *or less*

Prep: 7 minutes • **Cook:** 15 minutes

The combination of fresh garlic and the marinade from the artichoke hearts gives this cream sauce its rich flavor.

Stovetop Solution

Secret Ingredient Savvy

Using boneless pork chops in place of chicken breasts is an easy way to create a variation on this recipe. Be sure to pound the pork chops to tenderize the meat and keep the cooking time low.

4 skinned and boned chicken breast halves
3 tablespoons all-purpose flour, divided
½ teaspoon salt
½ teaspoon pepper
¼ cup butter or margarine, divided

1 cup milk
1 (6-ounce) jar marinated quartered artichoke hearts, undrained
2 garlic cloves, minced
¼ teaspoon salt
¼ teaspoon pepper

• Place chicken between 2 sheets of heavy-duty plastic wrap; flatten to ¼-inch thickness, using a meat mallet or rolling pin.
• Combine 2 tablespoons flour and ½ teaspoon each of salt and pepper in a large zip-top freezer bag; add chicken. Seal bag, and shake to coat.
• Melt 2 tablespoons butter in a large nonstick skillet over medium-high heat. Add chicken; cook 4 minutes on each side or until done. Remove chicken from skillet, and keep warm.
• Meanwhile, melt remaining butter in a small, heavy saucepan over low heat; whisk in remaining flour until smooth. Cook 1 minute, whisking constantly. Gradually whisk in milk. Cook over medium heat, whisking constantly, until mixture is thickened and bubbly. Stir in artichoke hearts and garlic. Cook 1 minute. Stir in ¼ teaspoon each of salt and pepper. Serve over chicken. Yield: 4 servings.

Tarragon Cream Chicken

Prep: 9 minutes • **Cook:** 16 minutes

Calling all tarragon lovers! With a rich tarragon-garlic sauce, this simple chicken dish is sure to make all mouths happy at the dinner table.

4 skinned and boned chicken breast halves
½ teaspoon salt
½ teaspoon ground white pepper
3 tablespoons butter or margarine
2 tablespoons lemon juice
1 cup whipping cream
⅓ cup minced green onions
2 tablespoons chopped fresh tarragon
½ teaspoon minced garlic
¼ teaspoon salt
¼ teaspoon ground white pepper
Garnishes: lemon slices, fresh tarragon sprigs

• Place chicken between 2 sheets of heavy-duty plastic wrap; flatten to ¼-inch thickness, using a meat mallet or rolling pin.
• Combine ½ teaspoon each of salt and white pepper; sprinkle over both sides of chicken.
• Melt butter in a large nonstick skillet over medium-high heat. Add chicken; cook 5 minutes on each side or until done. Remove from skillet, and keep warm.
• Add lemon juice to skillet, and cook over high heat 30 seconds, stirring to loosen particles from bottom of skillet.
• Add cream and next 5 ingredients; bring to a boil. Cook, stirring constantly, 4 minutes or until slightly thickened. Pour over chicken. Garnish, if desired. Yield: 4 servings.

Stovetop Solution

Super Fast and Fresh

No Fuss Entertaining

Kitchen Timesavers
To save time, use bottled minced garlic instead of mincing fresh.

Mediterranean Chicken Breasts on Eggplant

Prep: 8 minutes • **Cook:** 37 minutes

We like to leave the skin on the eggplant
for texture and fiber, but you can peel it if you'd prefer.

**Secret
Ingredient
Savvy**
For more flavor,
substitute basil-
and-tomato-
flavored feta
cheese for regular
feta cheese.

1 small eggplant	1 teaspoon minced garlic
¾ teaspoon salt, divided	1½ cups tomato and basil pasta sauce
½ teaspoon pepper, divided	(we used Classico)
¼ cup all-purpose flour	½ cup crumbled feta cheese
6 tablespoons olive oil, divided	
4 skinned and boned chicken breast halves	

• Cut eggplant into ¾-inch-thick slices.
• Combine ¼ teaspoon each of salt and pepper with flour in a shallow dish. Dredge eggplant slices in flour mixture, shaking off excess flour mixture.
• Heat 4 tablespoons olive oil in a large skillet over medium-high heat; add eggplant slices, and cook 2 to 3 minutes on each side or until golden. Drain on paper towels. Arrange in a single layer in a lightly greased 13- x 9-inch baking dish.
• Sprinkle chicken with remaining ½ teaspoon salt and ¼ teaspoon pepper.
• Brown chicken in remaining 2 tablespoons oil in a large skillet over medium-high heat 5 minutes on each side. Remove chicken, reserving drippings in skillet. Place chicken breast halves on top of eggplant slices.
• Cook garlic in pan drippings over medium-high heat 1 minute, stirring constantly. Add pasta sauce; cook 5 minutes, stirring often. Spoon over chicken; sprinkle with cheese. Bake, uncovered, at 425° for 15 minutes. Serve immediately. Yield: 4 servings.

Chicken Piccata

Prep: 7 minutes • **Cook:** 14 minutes

1 large egg, lightly beaten
1 tablespoon lemon juice
4 skinned and boned chicken breast
   halves
⅓ cup all-purpose flour
¼ teaspoon salt
¼ teaspoon pepper

⅛ teaspoon garlic powder
¼ cup butter or margarine
½ cup hot water
2 teaspoons chicken bouillon
   granules
2 tablespoon lemon juice
Garnish: lemon slices

• Combine egg and 1 tablespoon lemon juice. Dip chicken in egg mixture.
• Combine flour and next 3 ingredients in a zip-top freezer bag. Add chicken; seal bag, and shake to coat.
• Melt butter in a large nonstick skillet over medium-high heat. Add chicken; cook 5 minutes on each side or until done. Remove from pan, and keep warm.
• Combine ½ cup hot water, bouillon, and 2 tablespoons lemon juice, stirring until bouillon dissolves. Add bouillon mixture to skillet. Bring to boil, and cook over high heat 3 minutes or until mixture reduces to ¼ cup. Spoon sauce over chicken. Garnish, if desired. Yield: 4 servings.

Chicken Breasts Dijon

Prep: 10 minutes • **Cook:** 16 minutes

⅓ cup fine, dry breadcrumbs
1 tablespoon Parmesan cheese
1 teaspoon dried Italian seasoning
½ teaspoon dried thyme
¼ teaspoon salt
¼ teaspoon freshly ground pepper

4 (4-ounce) skinned and boned
   chicken breast halves
2 tablespoons Dijon mustard
1 teaspoon olive oil
1 teaspoon margarine

• Combine first 6 ingredients in a small bowl, stirring well. Brush both sides of each chicken breast half with mustard; dredge in breadcrumb mixture.
• Heat olive oil and margarine in a large nonstick skillet over medium-high heat until margarine melts. Add chicken breasts, and saute 6 to 8 minutes on each side or until chicken is done. Yield: 4 servings.

Stovetop Solution

Kitchen Timesavers
Make less mess in the kitchen, and save time in cleanup by dredging the chicken in a freezer bag.

Menu Makings
For a super-quick supper, serve this entrée with steamed sugar snap peas, instant brown rice, and orange wedges.

Chicken-Veggie Kabobs

Prep: 16 minutes • **Cook:** 14 minutes

Super Fast
and Fresh

No Fuss
Entertaining

How-To Hints
If you use wooden
skewers, soak
them in water for
30 minutes to
help prevent them
from burning
while on the grill.

1 pound Italian-seasoned skinned
    and boned chicken breast halves,
    cut into 1-inch pieces (we used
    Butterball)
1 medium-size green bell pepper,
    cut into 1-inch pieces
1 medium-size red bell pepper, cut
    into 1-inch pieces

1 medium-size red onion, cut into
    1-inch pieces
16 fresh pineapple chunks
8 small fresh mushrooms
8 cherry tomatoes
½ cup Italian dressing, divided

• Thread first 7 ingredients alternately onto 8 (12-inch) skewers. Brush with ¼
cup dressing.
• Broil 5½ inches from heat 7 minutes. Turn and baste with remaining dressing;
broil 7 more minutes or until chicken is done. Yield: 8 servings.

Lemon Chicken Stir-Fry

Prep: 10 minutes • **Cook:** 10 minutes

Super Fast
and Fresh

Ideas for Two

The lemon zing of this dish is sure to make you pucker a little.

2 tablespoons soy sauce
¼ cup water
1 tablespoon cornstarch
½ cup lemon juice
2 tablespoons sugar
2 tablespoons vegetable oil
1 pound chicken breast strips,
    cut into chunks

3 green onions, sliced
1 large carrot, sliced
1 large green bell pepper,
    cut into strips
2 garlic cloves, minced
Hot cooked rice

• Combine soy sauce and next 4 ingredients in a small bowl. Set aside.
• Heat oil in a large skillet over medium heat; add chicken, and stir-fry 3 to 4
minutes or until browned. Add onion and next 3 ingredients to chicken; cook,
stirring often, 2 to 3 minutes or until vegetables are tender. Stir in soy sauce
mixture; cook 2 minutes or until sauce begins to thicken. Serve over hot cooked
rice. Yield: 2 to 3 servings.

Parmesan-Pecan Turkey Cutlets

Prep: 13 minutes • **Cook:** 6 minutes

The nutty layer covering these cutlets seals the moisture inside.

1 cup shredded Parmesan cheese	1 teaspoon salt
¼ teaspoon salt	½ teaspoon pepper
1 cup all-purpose flour	3 tablespoons olive oil
⅔ cup chopped pecans	¼ cup chopped fresh parsley
½ cup milk	1 cup jarred marinara sauce,
1 pound turkey cutlets	warmed

• Process first 4 ingredients in a blender or food processor until pecans are finely chopped; transfer to a shallow dish.
• Pour milk into a shallow bowl.
• Sprinkle turkey cutlets evenly with 1 teaspoon salt and pepper. Dredge cutlets in cheese mixture. Dip in milk, and dredge in cheese mixture again, coating well.
• Heat oil in a large nonstick skillet over medium-high heat until hot; add cutlets, and cook 2 to 3 minutes on each side or until lightly browned. Sprinkle with parsley, and serve with warm marinara sauce. Yield: 4 servings.

Parmesan-Crusted Orange Roughy

Prep: 5 minutes • **Cook:** 9 minutes

4 (6-ounce) orange roughy fillets (1 inch thick)	1 teaspoon dried dillweed
3 tablespoons freshly shredded Parmesan cheese	

• Arrange fillets in a single layer in a lightly greased 15- x 10-inch jellyroll pan. Combine Parmesan cheese and dillweed. Sprinkle evenly over fillets.
• Bake at 450° for 7 to 9 minutes or until fish flakes easily when tested with a fork. Yield: 4 servings.

Kid Friendly

Menu Makings
These cutlets are great served with marinara sauce for dunking. Sautéed Fennel and Carrots (page 334) make a great side.

5 Ingredients or Less

No Fuss Entertaining

Coconut Shrimp with Mustard Sauce

Editor's Favorite

No Fuss Entertaining

Fix It Faster
Feel free to substitute ⅔ cups commerial mustard sauce instead of making your own.

Prep: 20 minutes • **Cook:** 2 minutes per batch

The crunchy coating on these shrimp serves as the perfect surface for soaking up the tangy mustard sauce.

1½ pounds unpeeled, jumbo fresh shrimp
2 cups all-purpose baking mix, divided
1 cup beer

½ teaspoon salt
⅛ to ¼ teaspoon ground red pepper
3 cups sweetened flaked coconut
Vegetable oil
Mustard Sauce

• Peel shrimp, leaving tails intact; devein, if desired. Set aside.
• Stir together 1 cup baking mix and 1 cup beer until smooth.
• Stir together remaining 1 cup baking mix, salt, and ground red pepper. Dredge shrimp in dry mixture, and dip in beer mixture, allowing excess coating to drip off. Gently roll shrimp in coconut.
• Pour vegetable oil to a depth of 3 inches into a Dutch oven or heavy saucepan, and heat to 350°. Cook shrimp, in batches, 1 to 2 minutes or until golden; remove shrimp, and drain on paper towels. Serve immediately with Mustard Sauce. Yield: 4 servings.

Mustard Sauce
Prep: 5 minutes

½ cup Dijon mustard
2 tablespoons light brown sugar

2 tablespoons beer
⅛ to ¼ teaspoon ground red pepper

• Stir together all ingredients. Yield: ⅔ cup.

Shrimp with Roasted Red Pepper Cream

Prep: 15 minutes • **Cook:** 10 minutes

1 (7-ounce) package vermicelli
1 (12-ounce) jar roasted red bell peppers, drained (we used Alessi Sweet Pimento Italian-Style, Fire-Roasted Peppers)
1 (8-ounce) package ⅓-less-fat cream cheese, softened
½ cup low-sodium, fat-free chicken broth

3 garlic cloves, chopped
½ teaspoon ground red pepper
2 pounds cooked peeled, large fresh shrimp
¼ cup chopped fresh basil
Garnish: fresh basil sprigs

• Prepare pasta according to package directions, omitting salt and fat. Keep warm.
• Meanwhile, process bell peppers and next 4 ingredients in a blender or food processor until smooth, stopping to scrape down sides. Pour into a large skillet.
• Cook over medium heat 5 minutes, stirring often, until thoroughly heated. Add shrimp, and cook, stirring occasionally, 2 minutes or until thoroughly heated. Remove from heat. Serve over hot cooked pasta. Sprinkle with basil. Garnish, if desired. Yield: 6 servings.

Super Fast and Fresh

Secret Ingredient Savvy
If you'd rather buy raw shrimp, purchase 4 pounds large in the shell, and peel it yourself. You may need to cook it a minute or two longer.

Lime Shrimp in Tortillas

Prep: 15 minutes • **Cook:** 9 minutes

8 (6-inch) flour tortillas
1 small onion, sliced
½ green bell pepper, cut into strips
1 tablespoon olive oil
¾ pound cooked peeled, medium-size fresh shrimp
¼ cup fresh lime juice

2 teaspoons minced garlic
1 tablespoon minced fresh cilantro
½ teaspoon pepper
¼ teaspoon salt
Toppings: salsa, shredded Cheddar cheese, sour cream, lime wedges

• Heat tortillas according to package directions; keep warm.
• Cook onion and bell pepper in hot oil in a large skillet over medium-high heat, stirring constantly, 3 minutes or until tender. Add shrimp and next 5 ingredients to pan. Cook 3 minutes or just until shrimp are thoroughly heated.
• Spoon mixture into warmed tortillas using a slotted spoon. Serve with desired toppings. Yield: 4 servings.

Super Fast and Fresh

Secret Ingredient Savvy
If you prefer to buy raw shrimp in the shell, purchase 1½ pounds shrimp, and cook 5 minutes instead of 3, or just until shrimp turn pink.

Mexican Lasagna

Prep: 15 minutes • **Cook:** 20 minutes • **Other:** 5 minutes

*Corn tortillas take the place of classic lasagna noodles
in this Southwestern "lasagna."*

**Microwave
Miracle**

**Secret
Ingredient
Savvy**
Montery Jack
cheese with
peppers punches
up this
lasagna's flavor.

1 medium onion, chopped (about
   1½ cups)
1 medium-size green bell pepper,
   chopped (about 1¼ cups)
2 garlic cloves, minced
1½ teaspoons olive oil
1 teaspoon ground cumin
1 (16-ounce) can pinto beans,
   drained

1 (8-ounce) can tomato sauce
1 cup frozen whole kernel corn
6 (6-inch) corn tortillas
1 cup cottage cheese
1 cup (4 ounces) shredded Cheddar
   cheese

• Cook first 3 ingredients in oil in a large skillet over medium-high heat, stirring
constantly, until vegetables are tender. Stir in cumin; cook 1 minute. Remove from
heat; stir in beans, tomato sauce, and corn.
• Place 3 tortillas in bottom of a lightly greased 11- x 7-inch baking dish. Spread
half of bean mixture over tortillas. Spread half of cottage cheese over bean mixture; sprinkle with half of Cheddar cheese. Layer remaining 3 tortillas over cheese.
Repeat layers with remaining bean mixture and cheeses.
• Microwave, uncovered, at HIGH 12 minutes or until thoroughly heated, turning
one-quarter turn after 6 minutes. Let lasagna stand 5 minutes before serving.
Yield: 6 servings.

Curried Chickpeas in Coconut-Cilantro Broth

Prep: 10 minutes • **Cook:** 23 minutes

Stovetop
Solution

Regular coconut milk (rather than light) provides a rich, full flavor to this dish.

1 teaspoon butter or margarine
1 cup chopped onion
1 garlic clove, minced
1 (14½-ounce) can diced tomatoes, undrained
⅔ cup canned coconut milk
1 tablespoon seeded minced jalapeño pepper

1 to 2 teaspoons curry powder
1 (19-ounce) can chickpeas (garbanzo beans), drained
⅓ cup chopped fresh cilantro
5 cups hot cooked basmati rice

• Heat butter in a large skillet over medium-high heat. Add onion and garlic; sauté 3 minutes or until tender. Stir in tomatoes and next 3 ingredients; reduce heat, and simmer 5 minutes. Add chickpeas; partially cover, and simmer 15 minutes. Remove from heat; stir in cilantro. Serve over hot cooked rice. Yield: 5 servings.

Bean-and-Cheese Chimichangas

Prep: 10 minutes • **Cook:** 20 minutes

Ideas for Two

1 (16-ounce) can refried beans
1 cup (4 ounces) shredded Monterey Jack cheese
⅓ cup medium salsa
1 tablespoon taco seasoning mix
½ (5-ounce) package yellow rice mix, cooked (optional)

5 (10-inch) flour tortillas
2 cups vegetable oil
Shredded lettuce
Toppings: salsa, guacamole, sour cream

• Stir together first 4 ingredients. Stir in rice, if desired. Place ⅓ cup mixture just below center of each tortilla. Fold opposite sides of tortillas over filling, forming rectangles; secure with wooden picks.
• Pour oil into a large skillet; heat to 325°. Fry, in batches, 4 to 5 minutes on each side or until lightly browned. Drain on paper towels. Remove picks; arrange on lettuce. Serve with desired toppings. Yield: 5 chimichangas.

How-To Hints
To bake instead of frying, coat both sides of chimichangas with cooking spray, and place on a baking sheet. Bake at 425° for 8 minutes; turn chimichangas, and bake 5 more minutes.

Cheeseburger Pizza

20 Minutes or less

(pictured on page 242)
Prep: 4 minutes • **Cook:** 16 minutes

*This fun twist on the traditional cheeseburger
lends excitement to the dinner doldrums.*

**Editor's
Favorite**

Kid Friendly

**Super Fast
and Fresh**

1 pound ground beef
1 medium onion, chopped (about
   1 cup)
2 garlic cloves, pressed
1 tablespoon Worcestershire sauce
2 tablespoons ketchup
2 tablespoons prepared mustard

1 (10-ounce) package prebaked
   Italian pizza crust
1 (8-ounce) package shredded pizza
   cheese blend, divided
Toppings: shredded lettuce, chopped
   tomato, pickle slices

• Cook first 3 ingredients in a large skillet over medium heat 6 to 8 minutes,
stirring until beef crumbles and is no longer pink; drain mixture well. Stir in
Worcestershire sauce.
• Combine ketchup and mustard; spread over pizza crust. Sprinkle with 1 cup
cheese. Top with beef mixture and remaining cheese.
• Bake at 450° for 8 minutes. Sprinkle with desired toppings. Yield: 4 servings.

One-Skillet Spaghetti

30 Minutes or less

Prep: 5 minutes • **Cook:** 23 minutes

**Stovetop
Solution**

Kid Friendly

**No Fuss
Entertaining**

How-To Hints
Want to make this
easy one-dish an
adventure for kids?
Use wagon wheel
pasta instead of
spaghetti noodles.

1 pound ground chuck
1 small onion, chopped
2 (14-ounce) cans beef broth
1 (6-ounce) can tomato paste
¾ teaspoon garlic salt

1 teaspoon dried Italian seasoning
¼ teaspoon pepper
7 ounces uncooked spaghetti,
   broken into 3-inch pieces
Grated Parmesan cheese

• Cook ground chuck and onion in a large skillet over medium-high heat, stirring
until meat crumbles and is no longer pink; drain. Return to skillet. Stir in broth
and next 4 ingredients. Bring to a boil; add pasta. Reduce heat, and simmer,
uncovered, 15 minutes or until pasta is tender, stirring often. Sprinkle with cheese.
Yield: 4 servings.

20 Minutes or less
Creamy Tomato-Sausage Sauce with Shells

Prep: 3 minutes • **Cook:** 17 minutes

A hint of rosemary gives these creamy shells an herby essence,
while a bit of red pepper adds a touch of spice.

8   ounces uncooked medium pasta
    shells
1   tablespoon olive oil
1   pound mild Italian sausage
2   (14½-ounce) cans diced
    tomatoes with green pepper,
    celery, and onions, undrained
    (we used Hunt's)

1   teaspoon chopped fresh rosemary
½   teaspoon salt
¼   teaspoon freshly ground black
    pepper
¼   teaspoon dried crushed red pepper
¾   cup heavy whipping cream
½   cup grated Parmesan cheese

• Cook pasta according to package directions, including salt. Drain and keep warm.
• Meanwhile, heat oil in a large nonstick skillet. Remove casings from sausage, and crumble sausage into skillet; cook, stirring often, over medium-high heat 8 minutes or until sausage is no longer pink.
• Stir in tomatoes, rosemary, salt, black pepper, and crushed red pepper; cook, uncovered, over medium-high heat 6 minutes.
• Add whipping cream; cook, stirring often, 3 minutes or until mixture begins to thicken. Pour sauce over pasta; add cheese, and toss well. Yield: 4 servings.

Stovetop Solution

Secret Ingredient Savvy
Penne pasta substitutes well in this dish. The sauce is thick and chunky and needs a firm pasta to stand up to it.

Fettuccine with Cream, Basil, and Romano

Prep: 10 minutes • **Cook:** 16 minutes

*Crumbled bacon, freshly grated Romano cheese,
and sprigs of basil mingle in the hot cooked fettuccine,
creating a meal-in-one dish for two.*

Super Fast and Fresh

Ideas for Two

Secret Ingredient Savvy
Feel free to use Parmesan cheese instead of Romano, if you prefer. Either one provides the perfect flavor for this dish.

8 ounces uncooked dried fettuccine

4 bacon slices

4 green onions, chopped (about ⅓ cup)

½ cup whipping cream

½ cup freshly grated Romano cheese

⅓ cup chopped fresh basil

Freshly ground pepper

Freshly grated Romano cheese

• Cook fettuccine according to package directions, including salt. Drain and place in a large bowl.

• Meanwhile, cook bacon in a large skillet until crisp; remove bacon, and drain on paper towels, reserving drippings in skillet. Crumble bacon, and set aside. Add green onions to drippings, and cook, stirring constantly, 1 minute.

• Add cream; bring to a boil. Reduce heat, and simmer, uncovered, 1 minute or until slightly thickened. Stir in ½ cup Romano cheese and basil.

• Pour sauce over pasta; add crumbled bacon, and toss well. Sprinkle pasta with pepper and additional Romano cheese. Yield: 2 servings.

Mediterranean Chicken 'n' Linguine

Prep: 18 minutes • **Cook:** 12 minutes

Stovetop
Solution

No Fuss
Entertaining

*Garlic and lemon juice infuse a complementary flavor
to the feta cheese in this chicken pasta.*

8 ounces uncooked linguine
2 garlic cloves, minced
2 tablespoons olive oil
1 pound skinned and boned
    chicken breast halves, cut into
    ½-inch strips
1 (8-ounce) package sliced fresh
    mushrooms

¼ cup fresh lemon juice
½ teaspoon dried oregano
¼ teaspoon freshly ground pepper
2 tablespoons cornstarch
1 (14-ounce) can chicken broth
4 ounces crumbled feta cheese

• Cook pasta according to package directions, including salt; drain and keep warm.
• Meanwhile, cook garlic in hot oil in a large skillet over medium-high heat 30
seconds or until golden. Add chicken, and cook 5 minutes or until browned, stirring constantly. Remove chicken from skillet.
• Cook mushrooms in skillet over medium-high heat 3 minutes or until tender;
stir in chicken, lemon juice, oregano, and pepper.
• Combine cornstarch and chicken broth in a small bowl, whisking until smooth.
Pour over chicken mixture; cook, stirring constantly, 3 minutes or until sauce
thickens. Serve chicken and sauce over pasta, and sprinkle evenly with feta. Yield:
3 to 4 servings.

Fettuccine with Pesto Chicken

20 Minutes or less

5 Ingredients or Less

Super Fast and Fresh

Prep: 5 minutes • **Cook:** 11 minutes

8 ounces uncooked dried fettuccine
1 pound chicken breast strips or
   4 skinned and boned chicken
   breast halves, cut into thin strips

1 red bell pepper, cut into thin strips
1 (7.5-ounce) jar pesto sauce
¼ teaspoon salt

• Cook pasta according to package directions, including salt. Drain well, and keep pasta warm.
• Meanwhile, cook chicken in a large nonstick skillet over medium-high heat, stirring constantly, 5 minutes or until done. Remove chicken from skillet, and keep warm.
• Add bell pepper strips to skillet, and cook over medium heat 3 minutes or until crisp-tender, stirring occasionally. Add pesto sauce and chicken to skillet; cook over medium heat 3 minutes. Add pasta, tossing gently. Sprinkle with salt, and serve immediately. Yield: 4 servings.

Cheesy Chicken Penne

20 Minutes or less

5 Ingredients or Less

Kid Friendly

Secret Ingredient Savvy
Substitute 2 (8-ounce) loaves pasteurized prepared cheese product with peppers for regular prepared cheese product, if you desire a spicy version of this dish.

Prep: 10 minutes • **Cook:** 10 minutes

The combination of sour cream and melted cheese makes this pasta creation incredibly saucy.

8 ounces uncooked penne
1 (16-ounce) loaf pasteurized
   prepared cheese product,
   cubed

1 (8-ounce) container sour cream
½ cup milk
2½ cups prepackaged chopped
   cooked chicken

• Cook pasta according to package directions, including salt; drain.
• Meanwhile, cook cubed cheese, sour cream, and milk over medium-low heat, stirring constantly, 5 minutes or until cheese melts. Stir in pasta and chicken, and cook until thoroughly heated. Yield: 4 to 6 servings

Shrimp-Tomato Fettuccine

Prep: 15 minutes • **Cook:** 10 minutes

10 ounces uncooked lemon-pepper fettuccine
¾ pound peeled and deveined medium-size fresh shrimp
1 (14½-ounce) can diced tomatoes with basil, garlic, and oregano, undrained (we used Hunt's)
1 (8-ounce) package sliced fresh mushrooms

2 green onions, sliced
1 (2¼-ounce) can sliced ripe olives
¼ cup dry white wine
1 tablespoon olive oil
½ teaspoon salt
¼ teaspoon pepper
¼ cup grated Parmesan cheese

• Cook pasta according to package directions, including salt; drain.
• Meanwhile, combine shrimp and next 8 ingredients in a large nonstick skillet; bring to a boil. Reduce heat; simmer, stirring occasionally, 5 minutes or just until shrimp turn pink and sauce is slightly thickened. Serve over pasta; sprinkle with cheese. Yield: 4 servings.

Stovetop Solution

No Fuss Entertaining

Super Fast and Fresh

Secret Ingredient Savvy
If you're buying your shrimp in the shell, purchase 1 pound.

Shrimp and Feta Vermicelli

Prep: 5 minutes • **Cook:** 12 minutes

8 ounces uncooked vermicelli
2 tablespoons olive oil
1 (14½-ounce) can diced tomatoes, undrained
¼ cup dry white wine
1¼ teaspoons dried Italian seasoning
½ teaspoon minced garlic

¼ teaspoon salt
¼ teaspoon black pepper
¼ teaspoon dried crushed red pepper
¾ pound peeled, medium-size fresh shrimp
1 (4-ounce) package crumbled feta cheese

• Cook pasta according to package directions, including salt; drain and keep warm.
• Meanwhile, heat oil in a large skillet over medium heat. Add tomatoes and next 6 ingredients; bring to a boil. Reduce heat, and simmer, uncovered, 7 minutes, stirring occasionally. Add shrimp, and simmer 3 minutes or just until shrimp turn pink. Serve over pasta, and top with feta cheese. Yield: 3 servings.

Stovetop Solution

Menu Makings
A side salad and crusty bread are all you need to round out this meal.

Speedy Scampi

Prep: 10 minutes • **Cook:** 10 minutes

**No Fuss
Entertaining**

**Super Fast
and Fresh**

**Secret
Ingredient
Savvy**

If you're buying
your shrimp in the
shell, purchase
2⅓ pounds.

Have your supermarket's seafood section peel and devein the shrimp for you.

12 ounces uncooked dried angel hair
    pasta
⅓ cup butter or margarine
1¾ pounds peeled and deveined large
    fresh shrimp
2 green onions, sliced

4 large garlic cloves, minced
1 tablespoon grated lemon rind
½ cup fresh lemon juice
½ teaspoon salt
½ cup chopped fresh parsley
½ teaspoon hot sauce

• Cook pasta according to package directions, including salt. Drain and keep
pasta warm.
• Meanwhile, melt butter in a large skillet over medium-high heat; add shrimp,
and cook, stirring constantly, 5 minutes or just until shrimp turn pink. Stir in
green onions and next 6 ingredients. Cook mixture 1 minute or until bubbly.
Serve over hot cooked pasta. Yield: 4 servings.

Saucy Scallop Fettuccine

**No Fuss
Entertaining**

Prep: 5 minutes • **Cook:** 10 minutes

8 ounces uncooked dried fettuccine
1½ pounds bay scallops
2 tablespoons olive oil
½ cup whipping cream
2 tablespoons chopped fresh parsley

1 garlic clove, minced
½ teaspoon salt
¾ cup shredded Parmesan cheese
    Freshly ground pepper

• Cook fettuccine according to package directions, including salt; drain.
• Meanwhile, sauté scallops in hot oil in a large skillet over medium-high heat 2
minutes. Drain scallops, reserving liquid. Return scallops and ½ cup liquid to skillet. Add cream and next 3 ingredients. Bring to a boil; remove from heat. Stir in
fettuccine and cheese. Spoon into a large serving bowl; sprinkle with pepper.
Serve immediately. Yield: 4 servings.

Speedy
Scampi

Linguine with Spicy Tomato Cream Sauce

Prep: 5 minutes • **Cook:** 12 minutes

**Secret
Ingredient
Savvy**
If you can't
find seasoned
tomatoes, simply
buy original diced
tomatoes and
add 1 teaspoon
Italian seasoning.

8 ounces uncooked linguine
1 tablespoon minced onion
2 garlic cloves, crushed
½ teaspoon dried crushed red pepper
2 tablespoons olive oil
1 (14½-ounce) can diced tomatoes
   with basil, garlic, and oregano
   (we used Del Monte)

½ cup whipping cream
¼ cup chopped fresh basil
¼ teaspoon salt
¼ teaspoon freshly ground
   black pepper
Freshly grated Romano cheese

• Cook pasta according to package directions, including salt; drain well.
• Meanwhile, cook onion, garlic, and red pepper in hot oil in a large skillet over medium heat 3 minutes, stirring often. Add tomatoes; cook over medium-high heat 6 minutes or until liquid is absorbed. Stir in whipping cream; bring to a boil over medium-high heat, and cook 1 minute.
• Combine pasta, whipping cream mixture, basil, salt, and black pepper; toss gently. Spoon pasta mixture onto a serving platter. Sprinkle with cheese, and serve immediately. Yield: 4 servings.

Ziti with Mozzarella and Tomato

Prep: 4 minutes • **Cook:** 10 minutes

**Super Fast
and Fresh**

This Italian pasta has a balsamic flair.

12 ounces uncooked ziti
2 (14½-ounce) cans diced tomatoes
   with balsamic vinegar, basil, and
   olive oil (we used Hunt's)
½ cup chopped black olives
⅓ cup diced red onion

¼ cup balsamic vinaigrette (we used
   Kraft)
1 (8-ounce) block mozzarella
   cheese, diced
½ cup grated Parmesan cheese
½ teaspoon pepper

• Cook pasta according to package directions, including salt; drain.
• Meanwhile, combine tomatoes and next 3 ingredients.
• Add pasta, cheeses, and pepper; toss gently. Serve immediately. Yield: 5 servings.

Cheese Tortellini in Jalapeño Tomato Sauce

Prep: 2 minutes • **Cook:** 10 minutes

1 (9-ounce) package refrigerated cheese-filled tortellini
1 (15-ounce) can chunky Italian-style tomato sauce (we used Hunt's)
1 jalapeño pepper, seeded and finely chopped
½ cup freshly grated Parmesan cheese

• Cook pasta according to package directions; drain.
• Meanwhile, combine tomato sauce and chopped pepper in a saucepan; cook over medium heat until thoroughly heated, stirring occasionally. Spoon over pasta; sprinkle with cheese. Yield: 4 servings.

5 Ingredients or Less

Kid Friendly

Secret Ingredient Savvy
If you want this dish to be on the spicy side, don't seed the jalapeño pepper.

One-Pot Pasta Dinner

Prep: 8 minutes • **Cook:** 15 minutes

Hot pasta combined with a savory sauce marries into a warm medley that's incredibly easy to make.

4 cups water
2 cups uncooked rotini or tortellini
2 tablespoons dried minced onion
2 tablespoons dried crushed red pepper
½ teaspoon salt
1 (2.4-ounce) package tomato with basil soup mix (we used Knorr)
1 teaspoon dried oregano
1 teaspoon dried minced garlic
½ cup grated Parmesan cheese
¼ teaspoon ground red pepper

• Bring 4 cups water to a boil in a Dutch oven. Add pasta and next 3 ingredients; cook 10 minutes or until tender. Add soup mix, oregano, and garlic; cook 5 minutes. Stir in cheese and red pepper. Serve immediately. Yield: 2 servings.

Ideas for Two

Two Meals in One
To give this simple pasta a hearty appeal, add 1 cup chopped cooked chicken in with the pasta.

Thai Noodles

Prep: 8 minutes • **Cook:** 10 minutes

This spicy Asian noodle dish gets a wonderful kick from bottled peanut sauce.

Stovetop
Solution

Super Fast
and Fresh

How-To Hints
Create a fun Friday
night dinner by
serving these noo-
dles in Asian-style
takeout boxes—
they also make
cleanup a snap.

8 ounces uncooked dried angel hair
   pasta
¾ cup Bangkok Padang peanut sauce
   (we used House of Tsang)
½ cup chopped unsalted dry-roasted
   peanuts, divided

¼ cup chopped fresh cilantro
½ cup shredded carrot
⅓ cup sliced green onions
3 tablespoons sesame seeds, toasted

• Cook pasta according to package directions, including salt. Drain well, and return to pan. Add peanut sauce and ¼ cup chopped peanuts, tossing well. Divide pasta evenly among 4 takeout boxes. Top each serving evenly with remaining peanuts, cilantro, carrot, green onions, and sesame seeds. Serve immediately. Yield: 4 servings.

Artichoke Pasta

Prep: 5 minutes • **Cook:** 10 minutes

No Fuss
Entertaining

Menu Makings
Serve this pasta
alongside broiled
fish or chicken.

12 ounces uncooked dried angel hair
    pasta
11 large garlic cloves, minced (about
    ⅓ cup)
¼ cup olive oil
 2 (6-ounce) jars marinated quartered
    artichoke hearts, undrained

2 (3-ounce) packages shredded
   Parmesan and Romano cheese
   blend
½ cup chopped fresh basil

• Cook pasta according to package directions, including salt; drain well, and return pasta to pan.
• Meanwhile, cook garlic in olive oil in a large skillet over medium-high heat, stirring constantly, 1 minute or until tender. Add artichoke hearts, and cook 1 minute or until thoroughly heated. Pour artichoke mixture over warm pasta; add cheese, and toss well. Sprinkle with basil, and serve immediately. Yield: 8 servings.

Thai
Noodles

Tomato-Jalapeño Vermicelli

Prep: 10 minutes • **Cook:** 10 minutes

Stovetop Solution

Menu Makings
Serve this spicy pasta side as a main dish or as a side with Chicken Breasts Dijon (page 223).

This recipe offers maximum heat from the jalapeño peppers when you don't seed them.

7 ounces uncooked vermicelli
6 garlic cloves, crushed
2 tablespoons olive oil
4 jalapeño peppers, seeded and minced

8 plum tomatoes, chopped
½ cup shredded fresh basil
Freshly grated Parmesan cheese
½ teaspoon salt
Garnish: fresh basil leaves

• Cook pasta according to package directions, including salt; drain.
• Meanwhile, cook garlic in hot oil in a large skillet over medium-heat heat, stirring constantly, until golden. Add minced pepper, and cook 1 minute. Add tomato; cook 3 minutes or until thoroughly heated, stirring occasionally. Stir in shredded basil. Serve over hot cooked pasta, and sprinkle with cheese and salt. Garnish, if desired. Yield: 4 servings.

Blue Cheese Noodles

Prep: 5 minutes • **Cook:** 12 mintues

No Fuss Entertaining

*Blue cheese afficionados adore this dish.
It has an entire package of the tangy cheese.*

12 ounces uncooked fettuccine
½ teaspoon canola oil
1 tablespoon chicken bouillon granules
½ cup butter or margarine
6 green onions, sliced

1 (4-ounce) package crumbled blue cheese
1 (8-ounce) container sour cream
1 teaspoon seasoned pepper
¼ teaspoon garlic powder

• Cook fettuccine according to package directions, adding oil and bouillon granules to water. Drain and keep warm.
• Meanwhile, melt butter in a large skillet; add green onions, and sauté until tender. Add cheese; reduce heat, and cook, stirring constantly, 5 minutes or until melted. Remove from heat; stir in sour cream, pepper, and garlic powder. Add fettuccine, tossing to coat; serve immediately. Yield: 6 servings.

20 Minutes or less

Cheese Tortellini Pasta Salad

Prep: 4 minutes • **Cook:** 12 minutes

1 (20-ounce) package refrigerated cheese-filled tortellini
¼ cup balsamic vinegar
6 dried tomatoes in oil
1½ tablespoons chopped fresh rosemary

1 tablespoon sugar
¼ teaspoon salt
¼ teaspoon pepper
½ cup olive oil
1 pint cherry tomatoes, halved
3 tablespoons minced red onion

• Cook pasta according to package directions, including salt; drain.
• Meanwhile, process vinegar and next 5 ingredients in a food processor until smooth, stopping to scrape down sides. With processor running, pour oil in a slow, steady stream through food chute.
• Combine tortellini, tomato halves, and onion in a large bowl. Drizzle dressing over pasta mixture; toss gently. Serve immediately, or cover and chill. Yield: 4 to 6 servings.

Make Ahead

Secret Ingredient Savvy
Substitute whole grape tomatoes for cherry tomatoes to save chopping time—grape tomatoes' smaller size means there's no need to half them.

Greek Pasta Salad

Prep: 15 minutes • **Cook:** 10 minutes • **Other:** 30 minutes

This bountiful salad offers a showy presentation at any gathering.

8 ounces uncooked rotini
2 tablespoons olive oil
1 head romaine lettuce, torn into bite-size pieces
½ (16-ounce) package frozen cut green beans, thawed
1 cup chopped celery (about 2 ribs)
2 tablespoons finely chopped red onion

1 (4-ounce) package crumbled feta cheese
⅓ cup pitted kalamata olives, chopped
2 large tomatoes, cut into wedges
¾ cup Greek dressing (we used Ken's Steak House with feta cheese, black olives, and olive oil)

• Cook pasta according to package directions, including salt; drain. Toss together pasta and oil; cover and chill 30 minutes.
• Layer lettuce, pasta, beans, and celery on a serving platter. Sprinkle with red onion, cheese, and olives. Arrange tomato wedges around salad; drizzle with dressing. Serve immediately. Yield: 4 servings.

Make Ahead

No Fuss Entertaining

Secret Ingredient Savvy
If time is not an issue, fresh green beans make a wonderful substitute for frozen. You can cook them while the pasta cooks.

Nutty Raisin Couscous

Prep: 2 minutes • **Cook:** 6 minutes • **Other:** 5 minutes

Super Fast and Fresh

Secret Ingredient Savvy

It's easy to vary this simple side. Use golden raisins or regular raisins—or a combination of both. You can vary the nuts, too.

½ cup pine nuts
2½ cups chicken broth
½ cup orange juice
2 tablespoons butter or margarine
¼ teaspoon salt
¼ teaspoon pepper
10 ounces uncooked couscous (about 1½ cups)
½ cup raisins

• Bake pine nuts in a shallow pan at 350°, stirring occasionally, 5 minutes or until toasted. Set aside.
• Meanwhile, bring chicken broth and the next 4 ingredients to a boil in a medium saucepan.
• Stir in couscous; cover, remove from heat, and let stand 5 minutes. Fluff with a fork; stir in pine nuts and raisins. Serve immediately. Yield: 6 servings.

Mushroom Couscous

Prep: 5 minutes • **Cook:** 8 minutes • **Other:** 5 minutes

Super Fast and Fresh

A mushroom, onion, and garlic sauté turns this simple couscous into a savory side.

Butter-flavored cooking spray
4 cups sliced fresh mushrooms (about ¾ pound)
½ cup chopped onion
2 garlic cloves, minced
1 cup water
¼ teaspoon salt
⅛ teaspoon ground red pepper
⅔ cup uncooked couscous

• Coat a large saucepan with butter-flavored cooking spray; place over medium-high heat until hot. Add mushrooms, onion, and garlic; sauté until tender. Stir in 1 cup water, salt, and red pepper; bring to a boil. Remove saucepan from heat.
• Stir in couscous; cover and let stand 5 minutes or until couscous is tender and liquid is absorbed. Fluff couscous with a fork. Yield: 4 servings.

Spinach-and-Onion Couscous

Prep: 5 minutes • **Cook:** 12 minutes • **Other:** 5 minutes

1 medium onion, chopped
1 garlic clove, pressed
2 tablespoons olive oil
1 (14-ounce) can chicken broth
1 (10-ounce) package frozen
    chopped spinach
10 ounces uncooked couscous
    (about 1½ cups)

¾ cup freshly grated Parmesan
    cheese
2 tablespoons lemon juice
½ teaspoon salt
½ teaspoon freshly ground pepper
½ cup chopped pecans, toasted

• Sauté onion and garlic in hot oil in a large saucepan until tender. Add broth and spinach; cook, stirring occasionally, until spinach thaws. Bring to a boil, stirring occasionally. Stir in couscous; cover, remove from heat, and let stand 5 minutes or until liquid is absorbed.
• Stir in cheese and remaining ingredients. Serve couscous immediately. Yield: 6 to 8 servings.

Hazelnut-Herb Couscous

Prep: 5 minutes • **Cook:** 15 minutes

Sweet hazelnuts offer a nutty texture to this herbed side.

¼ cup hazelnuts (about 1 ounce)
1 (16-ounce) can chicken broth
1 teaspoon chopped fresh thyme
1 teaspoon chopped fresh rosemary

1 teaspoon chopped fresh oregano
⅛ teaspoon pepper
2 garlic cloves, minced
1⅓ cups uncooked couscous

• Place hazelnuts on a baking sheet. Bake at 350° for 15 minutes, stirring once. Turn nuts out onto a towel. Roll up towel, and rub off skins. Chop nuts.
• Meanwhile, bring chicken broth and the next 5 ingredients to a boil in a medium saucepan; gradually stir in couscous. Remove from heat; cover couscous, and let stand 5 minutes. Fluff couscous with a fork. Stir in hazelnuts. Yield: 6 servings.

Stovetop Solution

Menu Makings
Add some greens to your menu of Veal Parmesan (page 212) with spinach-filled couscous.

Super Fast and Fresh

Cheese-Steak Wraps

Prep: 7 minutes • **Cook:** 10 minutes

**Secret
Ingredient
Savvy**
If you want some
pizazz with your
wraps, use flavored
tortillas as your
wrappers. Try
dried tomato or
avocado for
a twist.

*These meaty wraps rival the New England bun version. Wraps are
easier to hold—and they're less messy.*

4 (10-inch) flour tortillas
1 small onion, sliced
1 small green bell pepper, sliced
2 tablespoons vegetable oil
1 (1-pound) flank steak, cut
   diagonally across grain into
   thin slices

1 tablespoon cornstarch
6 ounces pasteurized prepared
   cheese product

• Heat tortillas according to package directions; keep warm.

• Sauté onion and bell pepper in hot oil in a large skillet over medium-high heat
3 to 4 minutes or until tender. Remove from skillet, and set aside; reserve drippings in skillet.

• Toss together steak strips and cornstarch.

• Sauté half of steak in drippings 2 to 3 minutes; remove from skillet, and repeat
procedure with remaining half of steak.

• Meanwhile, microwave cheese in a 1-quart glass bowl at HIGH 2 minutes or
until melted, stirring once.

• Place steak slices evenly down the center of each tortilla. Top with vegetables
and cheese.

• Roll up and serve immediately. Yield: 4 servings.

Easy Mushroom-Onion Burgers

Prep: 8 minutes • **Cook:** 13 minutes

*Crispy French fried onions cook inside these burgers and crown
a cheese and mushroom mixture slathered on top after grilling. Sandwich
the bounty in kaiser rolls for burgers your family won't soon forget.*

1 pound ground chuck
2 tablespoons Worcestershire sauce,
   divided
2 teaspoons Dijon mustard, divided
½ teaspoon pepper
1 (2.8-ounce) can French fried
   onion rings, divided

1 (3-ounce) package cream cheese,
   softened
1 (4-ounce) can sliced mushrooms,
   drained
3 kaiser rolls

• Combine ground chuck, 1 tablespoon Worcestershire sauce, 1 teaspoon mustard, pepper, and half of onion rings. Shape mixture into 3 patties. Grill, without grill lid, over medium heat (300° to 350°) 5 to 6 minutes on each side or until a meat thermometer inserted into thickest portion of 1 patty registers 160°.
• Meanwhile, combine remaining 1 tablespoon Worcestershire sauce, remaining 1 teaspoon mustard, cream cheese, and mushrooms. Spread mixture on cooked patties. Top with remaining onions. Broil 3 inches from heat 1 minute. Serve on rolls. Yield: 3 servings.

Jack Cheeseburgers

Prep: 27 minutes • **Cook:** 12 minutes

*Flavorful pockets of Monterey Jack cheese
and ripe olives are nestled in these hearty burgers.*

No Fuss
Entertaining

Make Ahead

**Kitchen
Timesavers**
Assemble these
patties ahead.
Cover and
refrigerate up
to 1 day. When
you're ready for
entertaining, just
pop them on the
grill, and cook
according to
directions.

1½ cups (6 ounces) shredded
    Monterey Jack cheese with
    peppers
⅓ cup chopped ripe olives
1¾ pounds lean ground chuck

¼ cup chopped onion
1 teaspoon salt
½ teaspoon black pepper
6 hamburger buns

• Combine cheese and olives; stir well. Shape cheese mixture into 6 balls; set aside.
• Combine ground chuck and next 3 ingredients in a large bowl; shape mixture
into 12 patties.
• Place a cheese ball in center of 6 patties; flatten cheese balls slightly. Top with
remaining patties, pressing edges to seal.
• Grill, covered with grill lid, over medium-high heat (350° to 400°) 5 to 6
minutes on each side or until done. Serve on buns. Yield: 6 servings.

30 Minutes or less Grilled Bacon, Cheese, and Tomato Sandwiches

(shown on page 266)
Prep: 16 minutes • **Cook:** 12 minutes

Editor's
Favorite

12 bacon slices
8 (½-inch-thick) French bread slices
¼ cup butter or margarine, softened
16 (½-ounce) thin slices provolone
    cheese (we used Sargento)

3 plum tomatoes, thinly sliced
24 large fresh basil leaves

• Microwave bacon in batches at HIGH 6 minutes or until crisp. Remove bacon,
and drain on paper towels. Set bacon aside.
• Spread 1 side of bread slices with butter; turn 4 slices, buttered side down, and
top each with 2 cheese slices. Top cheese evenly with tomato slices, bacon, half of
basil leaves, and remaining cheese slices; top with remaining basil leaves and bread
slices, buttered side up.
• Place a large skillet over medium heat until hot; add sandwiches, and cook, in
batches, 3 minutes on each side or until golden. Yield: 4 servings.

Double-Decker Egg Salad Sandwiches

Prep: 12 minutes • **Cook:** 20 minutes

A hearty helping of eggs, bacon, and spinach comes in each bite of these sandwiches.

4 large eggs
4 bacon slices
⅔ cup mayonnaise, divided
1 celery rib, diced
1 tablespoon minced sweet pickle relish
¼ teaspoon seasoned salt
½ teaspoon freshly ground pepper
12 very thin white or wheat sandwich bread slices, lightly toasted
1 cup packed fresh baby spinach

• Place eggs in a saucepan; add water to 1 inch over eggs, and bring almost to a boil. Cover, remove from heat, and let stand 15 minutes. Rinse eggs in cold water, and peel; chop eggs.
• While eggs cook, cook bacon in microwave at HIGH for 3 to 4 minutes or until done. Drain and crumble.
• Meanwhile, stir together ⅓ cup mayonnaise, celery, relish, seasoned salt, and pepper. Stir in chopped eggs and crumbled bacon.
• Spread remaining ⅓ cup mayonnaise evenly over 1 side of each bread slice.
• Spread 4 bread slices, mayonnaise side up, evenly with half of egg salad. Top evenly with half of spinach and 4 bread slices.
• Spread remaining egg salad on top of bread slice; top with spinach and remaining bread slices. Cut each sandwich into quarters. Yield: 4 servings.

Super Fast and Fresh

Make Ahead
Hard cook the eggs a day before, and chill overnight.

BLTs with a Twist

Prep: 13 minutes

*BLT gone gourmet! This sandwich is fit for a queen
with its unique blend of goat cheese, basil, garlic, and dried tomatoes.*

How-To Hints
Maximize the flavor
of bacon in this
sandwich by
heating your
precooked bacon
in the microwave
for 1 minute.

1 (4-ounce) package goat cheese, softened
1 tablespoon mayonnaise
¼ cup chopped fresh basil
2 garlic cloves, minced
¼ teaspoon salt
¼ teaspoon pepper
8 (1-ounce) sourdough bread slices, toasted

½ cup dried tomatoes in oil, drained and chopped
4 Green Leaf lettuce leaves
½ small red onion, thinly sliced
8 fully cooked bacon slices (we used Oscar Mayer Ready to Serve)

• Combine first 6 ingredients.
• Spread cheese mixture evenly on 1 side of bread slices. Sprinkle tomato evenly over coated side of 4 bread slices. Top evenly with lettuce, onion, bacon, and remaining bread slices, coated side down. Yield: 4 servings.

French Club Sandwiches

Prep: 13 minutes

*Tailgating takes a tasty turn when this winning cream cheese club
sandwich is served. This sandwich wraps and travels nicely chilled in a cooler.*

Double Delight
Double the
ingredients to
make 6 servings,
using 1 (16-ounce)
French bread loaf.

½ (8-ounce) container chive-and-onion cream cheese, softened
1 tablespoon mayonnaise
½ celery rib, chopped
¼ cup (1 ounce) shredded Cheddar cheese

1 (8-ounce) French baguette
½ pound thinly sliced cooked ham
3 dill pickle stackers (we used Vlasic)

• Combine first 4 ingredients, stirring until blended.
• Slice baguette in half horizontally, and spread cream cheese mixture evenly over cut sides of bread. Place ham on bottom half of baguette; top with pickles. Cover with top half of baguette. Cut baguette into 3 portions. Yield: 3 servings.

Ham-Swiss-and-Asparagus Sandwiches

Prep: 13 minutes • **Cook:** 5 minutes

12 fresh asparagus spears
3 tablespoons butter or margarine, softened
1 small garlic clove, minced
4 (6-inch) French rolls, split
3 tablespoons mayonnaise

¾ pound sliced cooked ham
2 (1½-ounce) Swiss cheese slices, cut in half diagonally
Green Leaf lettuce leaves
3 plum tomatoes, sliced

• Snap off tough ends of asparagus. Cook asparagus in boiling water to cover 3 minutes or until crisp-tender; drain. Rinse asparagus under cold water to stop the cooking process; drain and set aside.

• Stir together butter and garlic; spread on bottom halves of rolls. Spread mayonnaise over garlic mixture. Layer ham, asparagus, and cheese over mayonnaise; place sandwiches on a baking sheet.

• Broil 2 inches from heat 2 minutes or until cheese melts. Top with lettuce, tomato, and tops of rolls. Cut sandwiches in half diagonally. Yield: 4 servings.

Super Fast and Fresh

Menu Makings
Create a perfect summertime lunch by serving these ham delights with No-Squeeze Lemonade on page 166.

Grilled Chicken 'n' Cheese Sandwiches

Prep: 14 minutes • **Cook:** 6 minutes

2 cups chopped cooked chicken
⅓ cup golden raisins
¼ cup slivered almonds, toasted
¼ cup diced celery
½ cup mayonnaise

12 (¾-ounce) Monterey Jack cheese slices
12 whole wheat bread slices
¼ cup butter or margarine, softened

• Stir together first 5 ingredients. Place 1 cheese slice on each of 6 bread slices; spread evenly with chicken mixture, and top with remaining cheese and bread slices. Spread half of butter evenly on 1 side of each sandwich.

• Cook sandwiches, buttered side down, in a nonstick skillet or griddle over medium heat about 3 minutes or until lightly browned. Spread remaining butter evenly on ungrilled sides; turn and cook 3 minutes or until lightly browned. Yield: 6 sandwiches.

Kid Friendly

Fried Catfish Sandwiches

Prep: 15 minutes • **Cook:** 10 minutes

This crisp catfish is perfect sandwiched between savory onion buns.

Vegetable oil
¾ cup yellow cornmeal
¼ cup all-purpose flour
2 teaspoons garlic salt
1 teaspoon ground red pepper
4 catfish fillets (about 1½ pounds)

4 onion sandwich buns, split and
 toasted
Cocktail or tartar sauce
Lettuce leaves
4 tomato slices (optional)

• Pour oil to a depth of 3 inches in a Dutch oven; heat to 350°.
• Combine cornmeal and next 3 ingredients in a large shallow dish.
• Dredge fish in cornmeal mixture, coating well.
• Fry fish in hot oil 4 to 5 minutes on each side or until golden brown. Drain on paper towels.
• Serve on sandwich buns with cocktail sauce, lettuce, and, if desired, tomato. Yield: 4 servings.

Curried Tuna-Apple Sandwiches

Prep: 10 minutes

¼ cup mayonnaise
1 tablespoon lemon juice
½ teaspoon curry powder
⅛ teaspoon garlic powder
1 (6-ounce) can albacore tuna in
 water, drained and flaked

1 small Granny Smith apple,
 chopped
1 celery rib, chopped
¼ cup raisins
2 tablespoons diced onion
6 whole grain bread slices

• Stir together first 4 ingredients. Stir in tuna and next 4 ingredients. Spread mixture on 3 bread slices; top with remaining bread slices. Yield: 3 sandwiches.

Open-Faced Tuna Melts

Prep: 5 minutes • **Cook:** 5 minutes

1 (6-ounce) jar marinated artichoke
   hearts, drained and finely
   chopped
3 green onions, sliced
3 tablespoons mayonnaise
1 tablespoon lemon juice
½ teaspoon dried oregano

⅛ teaspoon black pepper
⅛ teaspoon ground red pepper
1 (6-ounce) can albacore tuna in
   water, lightly drained and flaked
2 English muffins, split and toasted
4 (1-ounce) provolone cheese slices

• Combine first 8 ingredients in a medium bowl. Divide mixture evenly among
muffin halves; top with cheese. Place on a baking sheet; broil 5 inches from heat 5
minutes or until golden brown. Yield: 2 servings.

**Super Fast
and Fresh**

Ideas for Two

Pimiento Cheese Finger Sandwiches

Prep: 10 minutes

Sharp Cheddar and red pepper pack a nice punch in these dainty sandwiches.

12 ounces sharp Cheddar cheese,
   shredded
½ cup mayonnaise
2 (4-ounce) jars diced pimiento,
   drained

⅛ teaspoon ground red pepper
¼ teaspoon salt
20 thin white crustless sandwich
   bread slices (we used IronKids)

• Process first 5 ingredients in a food processor until smooth, stopping to scrape
down sides. Spread mixture on half of bread slices; cover with remaining bread
slices. Cut each sandwich into 4 strips. Yield: 40 sandwiches.

**No Fuss
Entertaining**

**Simply
Southern**

**Secret
Ingredient
Savvy**
Be sure to shred
your own cheese
for this recipe.
Freshly shredded
cheese is more
moist and bonds
with other
ingredients better.

Pear-Walnut Salad

Prep: 8 minutes

*This autumn salad is proof positive that
opposites attract. The natural sweetness of the ripe, tender pears
plays perfectly off the tang of the blue cheese.*

1 (5-ounce) package mixed salad
   greens, torn
1 (6-ounce) package walnut halves,
   toasted (about 1½ cups)

1 cup jarred sliced Bartlett pears in
   light syrup, drained
½ cup crumbled blue cheese
½ cup sweet and sour dressing

• Combine first 4 ingredients in a large bowl; toss gently. Pour dressing over salad mixture just before serving; toss. Yield: 4 servings.

Apple-Spinach Salad

Menu Makings
This fruity
green salad
complements
French Onion
Sandwiches (page
289) nicely.

Prep: 5 minutes

1 (6-ounce) package fresh baby
   spinach
2 small Granny Smith apples,
   chopped

½ cup cashews
¼ cup golden raisins
½ cup sweet and sour dressing
   (we used Old Dutch)

• Combine first 4 ingredients in a bowl. Add dressing, tossing gently to coat. Yield: 4 servings.

Quick Baby Blue Salad

Prep: 13 minutes • **Cook:** 15 minutes

1½ cups pecan halves
2 tablespoons sugar
1 tablespoon Creole seasoning
2 (5-ounce) packages mixed salad greens (we used Dole Spring Mix)

1 (11-ounce) can mandarin oranges, drained
1 pint strawberries, quartered
¾ cup balsamic vinaigrette
1 (4-ounce) package crumbled blue cheese

• Place pecans on a baking sheet. Coat pecans with cooking spray. Combine sugar and Creole seasoning. Sprinkle over pecans; toss gently.
• Bake at 350° for 15 minutes or until pecans are golden brown, stirring once. Cool thoroughly.
• While pecans are baking, gently toss together greens, mandarin oranges, strawberries, balsamic vinaigrette, and crumbled blue cheese. Top with pecans. Yield: 7 servings.

Cantaloupe-Spinach Salad

Prep: 5 minutes

6 cups baby spinach leaves
1 large cantaloupe, cubed
½ cup pistachios, coarsely chopped

Pistachio-Lime Vinaigrette (page 312) or bottled vinaigrette

• Place spinach on individual serving plates; arrange cantaloupe on top, and sprinkle with pistachios. Serve with Pistachio-Lime Vinaigrette. Yield: 6 to 8 servings.

Apple-Broccoli Salad

Prep: 10 minutes

Crisp chunks of Red Delicious apple mingle amid the makings of a classic broccoli salad, adding a splash of color as well as a sweet crunch.

4 cups small fresh broccoli florets
½ cup raisins
½ cup chopped pecans, toasted
6 fully cooked bacon slices, crumbled

2 large Red Delicious apples, diced
1 small red onion, chopped
1 cup mayonnaise
½ cup sugar
2 tablespoons cider vinegar

• Combine first 6 ingredients in a large bowl.
• Combine mayonnaise, sugar, and vinegar; add to broccoli mixture, stirring to coat. Cover and chill. Yield: 6 servings.

Bing Cherry Salad

Prep: 2 minutes • **Cook:** 8 minutes • **Other:** 8 hours

1 (20-ounce) can crushed pineapple in juice, undrained
1 (16½-ounce) jar pitted Bing cherries, undrained

1 (12-ounce) can cola soft drink
2 (3-ounce) packages cherry gelatin
1 cup chopped pecans, toasted

• Drain pineapple and cherries, reserving juices. Bring reserved juices and cola to a boil in a saucepan over medium-high heat; stir in gelatin. Remove from heat; stir 2 minutes or until gelatin dissolves.
• Stir in pineapple, cherries, and pecans; pour into a lightly greased 6½-cup mold. Cover and chill 8 hours. Unmold onto a serving dish. Yield: 12 servings.

Fresh Raspberry-Spinach Salad

(shown on page 290)
Prep: 13 minutes

5 (6-ounce) packages fresh baby
    spinach
1 (14.4-ounce) can hearts of palm,
    drained and thinly sliced
1 medium-size yellow bell pepper,
    coarsely chopped

   Raspberry Vinaigrette (page 314) or
    bottled vinaigrette
2 cups fresh raspberries
2 (4-ounce) packages goat cheese,
    crumbled

• Combine first 3 ingredients in a large salad bowl. Pour vinaigrette over salad; toss gently. Top each serving evenly with raspberries; sprinkle with cheese. Serve immediately. Yield: 10 servings.

**No Fuss
Entertaining**

Big Batch

How-To Hints
This recipe makes a large batch, perfect for those big get-togethers. But if you aren't planning for a huge crowd, the salad's ingredients can easily be halved.

Tortellini Salad

Cook: 14 minutes • **Other:** 2 hours

2 (9-ounce) packages refrigerated
    cheese-filled tortellini
1 (12-ounce) jar marinated
    quartered artichoke hearts,
    drained and sliced
1 (8-ounce) jar dried tomatoes in
    oil, undrained and chopped

1 tablespoon fresh lemon juice
2 garlic cloves
1 teaspoon pepper
½ teaspoon salt

Make Ahead

• Cook pasta according to package directions; rinse with cold water, and drain well. Combine artichoke hearts and remaining 5 ingredients in a large bowl. Add pasta, and toss gently. Cover and chill salad at least 2 hours before serving. Yield: 8 servings.

Summer Vegetable-and-Orzo Salad

Prep: 9 minutes • **Cook:** 10 minutes • **Other:** 2 hours

Make Ahead ▶

Menu Makings
Simply add chopped cooked chicken to make this an easy-to-do main dish.

*It's amazing how many produce items you can buy prepackaged.
Try preshredded carrot for this recipe. To add a different taste to the dish,
use a different flavored vinaigrette or Italian dressing.*

1 cup uncooked orzo
1 sweet onion, chopped
3 tablespoons olive oil, divided
1 (10-ounce) package shredded carrot

1 large zucchini, chopped
1 large red bell pepper, chopped
¾ cup fat-free balsamic vinaigrette

• Cook orzo according to package directions. Drain and cool.
• Meanwhile, sauté onion in 1 tablespoon hot oil in a large nonstick skillet over medium-high heat 8 minutes or until browned.
• Combine orzo, onion, remaining 2 tablespoons oil, and remaining 4 ingredients in a large bowl. Cover and chill 2 hours. Yield: 4 servings.

Spinach Couscous Salad

Prep: 7 minutes • **Cook:** 6 minutes

5 Ingredients or Less ▶

Secret Ingredient Savvy
Add a fun twist to this recipe the next time you make it. Try Parmesan couscous and a three-cheese Italian vinaigrette.

2 (5.8-ounce) packages roasted garlic and olive oil couscous
3 cups fresh baby spinach
¾ cup golden raisins

4 green onions, sliced
¾ cup lite olive oil vinaigrette (we used Ken's Steak House)

• Prepare couscous in the microwave according to package directions. Fluff with a fork; cool uncovered.
• Combine couscous and next 3 ingredients in a large bowl. Pour vinaigrette over couscous mixture; toss gently to combine. Yield: 8 servings.

Guacamole Salad

Prep: 10 minutes

2 ripe avocados, peeled, seeded, and
   coarsely chopped
3 tablespoons picante sauce
¼ teaspoon salt
⅛ teaspoon pepper

1 small tomato, peeled, seeded, and
   finely chopped
2 tablespoons chopped onion
4 cups finely shredded iceberg
   lettuce

• Add first 4 ingredients to a food processor. Process until smooth, stopping once to scrape down sides. Stir in tomato and onion.
• Arrange shredded lettuce on a large serving platter or individual plates. Top lettuce evenly with avocado mixture, and serve immediately. Yield: 6 servings.

Italian Tossed Salad

Prep: 10 minutes

1 large head Red Leaf lettuce, torn
1 (14-ounce) can quartered
   artichoke hearts, drained
1 (4.5-ounce) can pitted ripe olives,
   drained

4 plum tomatoes, coarsely chopped
1 small red onion, thinly sliced
½ pound provolone cheese, shredded
   Parmesan Vinaigrette (page 313) or
   bottled vinaigrette

• Place lettuce and next 5 ingredients in a large bowl. Drizzle with Parmesan Vinaigrette, and toss gently to coat. Yield: 6 servings.

Simply Southern

Super Fast and Fresh

No-Cook Creation

Menu Makings
This salad works as an appetizer, atop a taco salad, or alongside Pronto Enchiladas (page 98).

No-Cook Creation

Two Meals in One
Instead of six side salads, make four main dish salads for a light supper. Just add cooked, cubed Italian meats from the deli.

Ranch House Salad

Prep: 5 minutes • **Cook:** 1 minute

**Super Fast
and Fresh**

Menu Makings
This classic
salad is a great
start to any
meaty entrée—
especially ones
from the grill.

Vegetable oil
2 corn tortillas, cut into thin strips
1 (8-ounce) package mixed salad
    greens
1 cup finely shredded red cabbage
½ cup (2 ounces) shredded
    Monterey Jack cheese

1 tomato, cut into wedges
1 avocado, sliced
Pecan Vinaigrette (page 313) or
    bottled vinaigrette

• Pour oil to a depth of ½ inch in a skillet; heat to 350°. Fry tortilla strips in hot
oil 1 minute or until crisp. Drain on paper towels.
• While oil heats, divide greens evenly onto each of 4 salad plates; top with
cabbage and cheese. Arrange tomato wedges and avocado over greens.
• Drizzle salads with Pecan Vinaigrette; top evenly with tortilla strips. Yield:
4 servings.

Spinach Salad with
Caramelized Pecans

Prep: 10 minutes • **Cook:** 3 minutes

**Super Fast
and Fresh**

*Sweet brown sugar, tart apple, and tangy blue cheese
complement each other nicely in this salad.*

1 tablespoon butter or margarine
½ cup pecan halves
1 tablespoon brown sugar
1 (6-ounce) package fresh
    baby spinach

1 large Granny Smith apple, thinly
    sliced
½ cup crumbled blue cheese
2 tablespoons olive oil
2 tablespoons white vinegar

• Melt butter in a small skillet over low heat; add pecan halves and brown sugar.
Cook, stirring constantly, 2 to 3 minutes or until caramelized. Cool pecans on
wax paper.
• Place spinach in a large serving bowl. Toss in pecans, apple, and blue cheese. Add
oil and vinegar, tossing gently to coat. Yield: 4 servings

Artichoke-Goat Cheese Salad

Prep: 10 minutes • **Other:** 20 minutes

1 (4-ounce) package goat cheese
1 (3-ounce) package cream cheese, softened
3 tablespoons chopped fresh dill
½ teaspoon salt
¼ teaspoon freshly ground pepper
1 (12-ounce) jar marinated quartered artichoke hearts
7 cups gourmet mixed salad greens

• Combine first 5 ingredients in a small bowl. Shape cheese mixture into a 5-inch log; cover and chill at least 20 minutes. Cut log diagonally into ½-inch-thick slices with a serrated knife, using a gentle sawing motion.
• While cheese mixture chills, drain artichoke hearts, reserving liquid. Chop artichoke hearts.
• Combine salad greens, artichoke, reserved artichoke liquid, and cheese slices in a large bowl, tossing gently to coat. Yield: 7 servings.

Squash Salad

Prep: 8 minutes • **Cook:** 2 minutes

This colorful vegetable array gives you the healthy benefits of steamed vegetables in record time, thanks to the microwave.

2 small yellow squash, thinly sliced
2 small zucchini, thinly sliced
1 red bell pepper, sliced into rings
1 small sweet onion, thinly sliced
¼ cup water
1 cup Italian dressing

• Place first 5 ingredients in a 1-quart glass bowl. Cover tightly with heavy-duty plastic wrap; fold back a small edge to allow steam to escape. Microwave at HIGH 2 minutes. Drain.
• Pour salad dressing over vegetables, tossing to coat. Cover and chill until ready to serve. Yield: 6 servings.

No Fuss Entertaining

Menu Makings
Serve this dressy salad with toasted baguette slices.

Super Fast and Fresh

Make Ahead

Microwave Miracle

Colorful Corn Salad

No-Cook
Creation

Make Ahead

Prep: 7 minutes • **Other:** 2 hours

A plethora of veggies sprinkle flavors throughout this vegetarian delicacy.

1 (16-ounce) package frozen whole
    kernel corn, thawed
1 small sweet onion, chopped
1 large tomato, seeded and chopped
1 large green bell pepper, chopped
¼ cup mayonnaise

½ teaspoon salt
½ teaspoon coarsely ground black
    pepper
¼ cup seeded and chopped
    cucumber (optional)

• Stir together corn and next 6 ingredients in a bowl, stirring until blended;
cover and chill 2 hours. Serve salad with a slotted spoon.
• Top each serving with chopped cucumber, if desired. Yield: 5 cups.

Broccoli Salad

Make Ahead

**Secret
Ingredient
Savvy**
If you don't have
capers on hand,
substitute 2 table-
spoons chopped
green olives
instead. And ¼ cup
pine nuts, toasted,
in place of the
pecans makes for a
nutty variation.

Prep: 15 minutes • **Other:** 30 minutes

Capers deliver a bit of tang to this crunchy salad.

4 cups chopped fresh broccoli
1 medium-size red onion, chopped
¼ cup chopped fresh dill
2 tablespoons capers, drained

Balsamic Vinaigrette (page 314) or
    bottled vinaigrette
¼ cup chopped pecans, toasted
    (optional)

• Toss together first 4 ingredients. Cover and chill 30 minutes. Drizzle with
Balsamic Vinaigrette, and sprinkle with pecans before serving, if desired. Yield:
about 5 cups.

Chickpea-and-Fennel Salad

Prep: 20 minutes • **Other:** 1 hour

½ cup Basil Vinaigrette (page 312) or bottled vinaigrette
½ teaspoon dried crushed red pepper
2 (15½-ounce) cans chickpeas, rinsed and drained*
2 medium fennel bulbs, thinly sliced

3 garlic cloves, minced
½ cup crumbled Gorgonzola cheese*
¼ cup minced fresh Italian parsley
Garnish: fresh fennel fronds

• Whisk together vinaigrette and red pepper in a bowl; add beans, fennel, and garlic, tossing gently to coat. Sprinkle with cheese and parsley. Cover and chill at least 1 hour. Garnish, if desired. Yield: 6 to 8 servings.

* Substitute 2 (15-ounce) cans navy beans and ½ cup crumbled blue cheese for chickpeas and Gorgonzola, if desired.

Green Bean, Walnut, and Feta Salad

Prep: 5 minutes • **Cook:** 10 minutes • **Other:** 1 hour

2 (16-ounce) packages frozen green beans
¾ cup olive oil
¼ cup white wine vinegar
1 tablespoon chopped fresh dill
½ teaspoon minced garlic
¼ teaspoon salt

¼ teaspoon pepper
1 small red onion, thinly sliced
1 (4-ounce) package crumbled feta cheese
1 cup coarsely chopped walnuts or pecans, toasted

• Microwave green beans 10 minutes on HIGH in a microwave-safe container, stirring after 5 minutes.
• Meanwhile, whisk together olive oil and next 5 ingredients.
• Toss together green beans, onion, cheese, walnuts, and vinaigrette in a large bowl.
• Chill 1 hour; toss just before serving. Yield: 8 servings.

Secret Ingredient Savvy

Select unblemished fennel bulbs with bright green fronds for the freshest flavor. Some grocery stores also label fennel as anise, but fennel is sweeter and more delicate than anise.

No Fuss Entertaining

Make Ahead

Basil Vinaigrette

Make Ahead ▷

Menu Makings
Serve this
vinaigrette with
Chickpea-and-
Fennel Salad
(page 303).

Prep: 3 minutes

For a crisp summer favorite, serve this dressing over a shrimp-pasta salad.

1½ cups loosely packed fresh basil
　　leaves
3 tablespoons olive oil
3 garlic cloves

¼ cup lemon juice
¼ teaspoon salt
¼ teaspoon freshly ground pepper
¾ cup olive oil

• Process first 6 ingredients in a blender until smooth, stopping once to scrape down sides. Turn blender on high; add ¾ cup olive oil in a slow, steady stream. Blend until smooth. Cover and store in the refrigerator. Yield: 1¼ cups.

Pistachio-Lime Vinaigrette

Make Ahead ▷

**Kitchen
Timesavers**
There's no need to
finely chop these
ingredients—the
blender does the
work for you.

Prep: 3 minutes

This vinaigrette is spicy sweet.

⅓ cup fresh lime juice
⅓ cup honey
¼ cup coarsely chopped red onion
1 teaspoon dried crushed red pepper

½ teaspoon salt
¼ cup fresh cilantro leaves
¾ cup vegetable oil
1 cup pistachios

• Process first 6 ingredients in blender until smooth. With blender running, add oil in a slow, steady stream. Turn blender off; add pistachios, and pulse until pistachios are finely chopped. Cover and store in refrigerator. Yield: about 2 cups.

Parmesan Vinaigrette

Prep: 4 minutes

⅓ cup shredded Parmesan cheese
⅔ cup vegetable oil
⅓ cup red wine vinegar
1 teaspoon Italian seasoning

1 teaspoon dried parsley
¼ teaspoon garlic powder
¼ teaspoon pepper
⅛ teaspoon salt

• Whisk together all ingredients in a small bowl. Cover and store in the refrigerator. Yield: 1¼ cups.

Make Ahead

Menu Makings
This vinaigrette adds the right touch to Italian Tossed Salad (page 299).

Pecan Vinaigrette

Prep: 5 minutes

Southerners enjoy pecans on virtually anything.
You'll be amazed by how this vinaigrette will enhance simple salads.

¼ cup white wine vinegar
2 tablespoons Dijon mustard
2 garlic cloves
½ teaspoon salt

½ teaspoon pepper
2 tablespoons dry sherry (optional)
1 cup olive oil
¼ cup chopped pecans, toasted

• Process first 5 ingredients and, if desired, sherry in a blender until smooth, stopping to scrape down sides. Turn blender on high; gradually add oil in a slow, steady stream until thickened. Stir in pecans. Cover and store in the refrigerator. Yield: 1¼ cups.

Make Ahead

Simply Southern

Menu Makings
Try this nutty dressing with Ranch House Salad (page 300).

Balsamic Vinaigrette

Prep: 3 minutes

Make Ahead ▶

Menu Makings
Broccoli Salad
(page 302)
becomes a zippy
creation with this
vinaigrette.

This traditional vinaigrette serves as a great staple for flavoring chicken and simple green salads.

⅓ cup balsamic vinegar	½ tablespoon sugar
¼ cup olive oil	½ teaspoon salt
1 garlic clove, minced	¼ teaspoon pepper

• Whisk together all ingredients in a small bowl. Cover and store in the refrigerator. Yield: about ⅔ cup.

Dijon Vinaigrette

Prep: 5 minutes

Make Ahead ▶

Menu Makings
Marinated Shrimp
Salad (page 310)
just isn't the same
without this
tangy dressing.

⅓ cup olive oil	2 teaspoons sugar
⅓ cup white wine vinegar	½ teaspoon dried basil
⅓ cup Dijon mustard	½ teaspoon salt
2 tablespoons paprika	¼ teaspoon freshly ground pepper

• Whisk together all ingredients in a large bowl until blended. Cover and store in the refrigerator. Yield: 1 cup.

Raspberry Vinaigrette

Prep: 2 minutes • **Cook:** 5 minutes

Menu Makings
Accent Fresh
Raspberry-Spinach
Salad (page 295)
with this fruity
vinaigrette.

1 cup firmly packed light brown sugar	¼ cup minced red onion
1 cup raspberry vinegar	1 teaspoon minced garlic
1 (10-ounce) jar seedless raspberry fruit spread	

• Combine all ingredients in a small saucepan. Cook over low heat until smooth, stirring constantly; cool. Yield: 2½ cups.

Honey-Pecan Dressing

Prep: 5 minutes

3 tablespoons sugar
1 tablespoon chopped sweet onion
½ teaspoon dry mustard
¼ teaspoon salt

½ cup honey
¼ cup red wine vinegar
1 cup vegetable oil
1 cup chopped pecans, toasted

• Pulse first 6 ingredients in a blender 2 to 3 times until blended. With blender running, add oil in a slow, steady stream; process until smooth. Stir in pecans. Cover and store in the refrigerator. Yield: 2½ cups

Fruit Salad with Honey-Pecan Dressing: Arrange fresh orange and grapefruit sections, sliced avocado, and sliced strawberries over Bibb lettuce leaves; drizzle with Honey-Pecan Dressing.

Blue Cheese-Buttermilk Dressing

Prep: 5 minutes

*Light mayonnaise and fat-free buttermilk help keep
this robust dressing light and healthy.*

1 (4-ounce) package crumbled blue
   cheese
1 cup fat-free buttermilk
½ to ⅔ cup light mayonnaise

3 to 4 tablespoons lemon juice
1 garlic clove, minced

• Stir together all ingredients in a small bowl. Cover and store in the refrigerator. Yield: 1¾ cups.

Cream of Mushroom-and-Leek Soup

Prep: 8 minutes • **Cook:** 13 minutes

How-To Hints
This soup will thicken upon standing. To thin soup, stir in a little extra milk to make it a desired consistency.

¼ cup butter or margarine
2¼ cups thinly sliced leek (about 3 leeks)
2 (8-ounce) packages sliced fresh mushrooms
½ teaspoon salt
2 tablespoons brandy*

1 (2.64-ounce) package original country gravy mix (we used McCormick)
1 cup half-and-half
1 (14-ounce) can chicken broth
½ teaspoon dried thyme

• Melt butter in a Dutch oven over medium-high heat. Add leek, mushrooms, and salt; sauté 4 to 5 minutes or until leek and mushrooms are tender. Add brandy, and cook, stirring often, 2 to 3 minutes.
• Stir in gravy mix and remaining ingredients, and cook 3 to 4 minutes or until thoroughly heated and slightly thickened. Serve immediately. Yield: about 4 cups.

* Substitute 2 tablespoons chicken broth for brandy, if desired.

Instant Gazpacho

Prep: 15 minutes

No-Cook Creation

Make Ahead

Menu Makings
Pair this light Mexican-style soup with Deep-Dish Taco Squares (page 95).

5 green onions, sliced
1 small red or green bell pepper, diced
1 small cucumber, diced
2 plum tomatoes, diced
1 cup Bloody Mary mix

¼ teaspoon salt
¼ teaspoon pepper
⅓ cup sour cream
½ teaspoon prepared horseradish
⅓ cup croutons

• Stir together first 7 ingredients. Chill 1 hour, if desired.
• Stir together sour cream and horseradish; chill, if desired.
• Ladle soup into bowls; sprinkle each serving with croutons, and dollop with sour cream mixture. Yield: 2⅓ cups.

Quick Bean Soup

Prep: 15 minutes • **Cook:** 15 minutes

Stovetop
Solution

Big Batch

Simply
Southern

A vast combination of beans makes this soup irresistible to bean lovers.
Onion and bell pepper add color and flavor to the mix.

1 large onion, chopped
1 small green bell pepper, chopped
2 teaspoons vegetable oil
1 (16-ounce) can kidney beans,
   rinsed and drained
1 (15-ounce) can pinto beans, rinsed
   and drained

1 (15-ounce) can black beans, rinsed
   and drained
2 (14½-ounce) cans stewed
   tomatoes, undrained
1 (14-ounce) can chicken broth
1 cup picante sauce
1 teaspoon ground cumin

• Sauté onion and bell pepper in hot oil in a large saucepan until tender. Add kidney beans and remaining ingredients; bring to a boil. Cover, reduce heat, and simmer 10 minutes. Yield: 10 cups.

Asparagus Soup

Prep: 15 minutes • **Cook:** 15 minutes

No Fuss
Entertaining

Menu Makings
This creamy
veggie soup is a
mellow start when
served before
Pan-Seared Steaks
with Roasted Red
Pepper Sauce
(page 204).

1 pound fresh asparagus
½ cup water
3 tablespoons butter or margarine
1 medium onion, chopped
3 tablespoons all-purpose flour

3 cups milk
1 teaspoon salt
½ teaspoon pepper
3 tablespoons sour cream

• Snap off tough ends of asparagus. Cut into 2-inch pieces.
• Cook asparagus in ½ cup boiling water 3 to 5 minutes or until tender; drain, reserving liquid. Set aside.
• Meanwhile, melt butter in a Dutch oven over medium-high heat; add onion, and saute 4 minutes or until tender. Add flour, and cook, stirring constantly, 5 minutes. Stir in reserved liquid until smooth. Add asparagus, milk, salt, and pepper; bring to a boil. Stir in sour cream. Cool slightly.
• Process mixture, in batches, in a blender until smooth, stopping to scrape down sides. Return to Dutch oven; cook until soup is thoroughly heated (do not boil). Yield: 5 cups.

20 Minutes or less Asian-Glazed Asparagus

(shown on page 326)

Prep: 3 minutes • **Cook:** 9 minutes

Editor's
Favorite

Stovetop
Solution

Super Fast
and Fresh

1 tablespoon cornstarch
¾ cup chicken broth
3 tablespoons soy sauce
1 garlic clove, minced

2 pounds fresh asparagus
2 tablespoons olive oil
⅛ teaspoon pepper
1 tablespoon sesame seeds, toasted

How-To Hints

Toast sesame seeds by spreading them out in a thin layer in a shallow pan. Bake at 350° for 4 to 6 minutes, stirring twice.

• Combine first 4 ingredients in a small saucepan. Bring to a boil; cook 1 minute, stirring constantly. Remove from heat; set aside.
• Snap off tough ends of asparagus. Cook asparagus in hot olive oil in a large skillet over medium-high heat, stirring often, 6 minutes or until crisp-tender. Add chicken broth mixture to asparagus; cook, stirring constantly, 1 minute or until thoroughly heated. Stir in pepper. Sprinkle with sesame seeds. Serve immediately. Yield: 4 to 6 servings.

30 Minutes or less Green Beans with Bacon and Mushrooms

Prep: 3 minutes • **Cook:** 25 minutes

Simply
Southern

Stovetop
Solution

1 (12-ounce) package sliced bacon
1 small onion, chopped
3 (9-ounce) packages frozen whole green beans, thawed

2 (4-ounce) cans sliced mushrooms, drained
1 tablespoon sugar

Kitchen Timesavers

To make preparation timely for this recipe, thaw the green beans in the refrigerator overnight so they'll be ready to cook when you are.

• Cook bacon in a large skillet until crisp; remove bacon, and drain on paper towels, reserving 1 tablespoon drippings in skillet. Crumble bacon, and set aside.
• Cook onion in reserved drippings, stirring constantly, until onion is tender. Stir in green beans, mushrooms, and sugar; cover and cook over medium heat 10 minutes. Spoon green beans into a serving dish; sprinkle with bacon. Yield: 8 to 10 servings.

Pesto Green Beans

Prep: 20 minutes • **Cook:** 10 minutes

No Fuss
Entertaining

2 pounds fresh green beans, trimmed
¼ cup butter or margarine
2 garlic cloves, pressed

1 teaspoon dried pesto seasoning (we used McCormick Gourmet Collection Pesto Seasoning)
½ teaspoon salt

Fix It Faster
Purchase trimmed fresh beans to save time, or buy baby green beans and leave them whole.

• Arrange green beans in a steamer basket over boiling water. Cover and steam 6 minutes or until crisp-tender.
• Melt butter in a large skillet over medium-low heat. Stir in garlic, pesto seasoning, and salt; sauté 2 minutes or until thoroughly heated. Toss butter mixture with beans in a bowl. Serve immediately. Yield: 8 servings.

Gratin of Broccoli in Béchamel

Prep: 10 minutes • **Cook:** 16 minutes

No Fuss
Entertaining

This fancy side combines broccoli with Gruyère cheese—sure to please any guest.

2¼ pounds fresh broccoli crowns, cut into spears
3 tablespoons butter or margarine
3 tablespoons all-purpose flour
2 cups milk
2 tablespoons stone-ground mustard

⅛ teaspoon salt
⅛ teaspoon freshly grated or ground nutmeg
⅛ teaspoon pepper
1 cup (4 ounces) shredded Gruyère cheese

• Arrange broccoli in a steamer basket over boiling water. Cover and steam 10 minutes or until crisp-tender. Remove from heat. Transfer broccoli to a lightly greased 13- x 9-inch baking dish.
• Meanwhile, melt butter in a heavy saucepan over medium heat; whisk in flour until smooth. Cook 1 minute, whisking constantly. Gradually whisk in milk; cook over medium heat, whisking constantly, until mixture is thickened and bubbly. Stir in mustard and next 3 ingredients. Pour sauce over broccoli; sprinkle with cheese.
• Broil 3 inches from heat 6 minutes or until lightly browned. Serve immediately. Yield: 8 servings.

Broccoli with Lemon Butter

Super Fast and Fresh

Prep: 5 minutes • **Cook:** 8 minutes

Lemon nicely accents this light, buttery side.

1 pound fresh broccoli crowns, cut into spears
3 tablespoons butter, melted
2 tablespoons lemon juice

½ teaspoon salt
⅛ teaspoon freshly ground pepper
Lemon wedges (optional)

• Arrange broccoli in a steamer basket over boiling water. Cover and steam 5 to 8 minutes or until crisp-tender. Drain; set aside.
• Combine butter and next 3 ingredients. Add broccoli; toss. Serve with lemon wedges, if desired. Yield: 4 servings.

Frosted Cauliflower

Secret Ingredient Savvy
Lose the fat but keep the taste of this creamy cauliflower side by substituting reduced-fat mayonnaise for regular.

Prep: 5 minutes • **Cook:** 25 minutes

1 cauliflower, broken into large florets
¾ cup grated Parmesan cheese
½ cup mayonnaise

1 tablespoon lemon juice
2 tablespoons Dijon mustard
1 tablespoon minced fresh parsley
3 green onions, thinly sliced

• Cook cauliflower, covered, in a saucepan over medium-high heat in a small amount of boiling water 8 to 10 minutes or until crisp-tender; drain. Place cauliflower in a lightly greased 2-quart baking dish.
• Stir together Parmesan cheese and remaining ingredients; spread evenly over cauliflower.
• Bake at 375° for 15 minutes or until lightly browned. Serve immediately. Yield: 6 servings.

Spinach with Herbs

Prep: 14 minutes • **Cook:** 14 minutes

Rosemary lends an aromatic touch to everyday spinach.

3 bacon slices
1 small onion, thinly sliced
2 (7-ounce) packages fresh baby
   spinach
¼ cup chopped fresh parsley

1 tablespoon white wine vinegar
1 teaspoon chopped fresh rosemary
½ teaspoon salt
⅛ teaspoon pepper

• Cook bacon in a large Dutch oven until crisp; remove bacon, and drain on paper towels, reserving 1 tablespoon drippings in pan. Crumble bacon; set aside.
• Sauté onion in hot drippings in pan 4 minutes or until tender. Add spinach, parsley, and next 4 ingredients; sauté 3 to 5 minutes or just until spinach wilts. Top with crumbled bacon. Serve immediately. Yield: 4 servings.

Super Fast
and Fresh

**Secret
Ingredient
Savvy**
Find packages of
fresh baby spinach
in the produce
section of your
supermarket along-
side packaged
salad greens.

Braised Greens with Chipotle-Chile Vinaigrette

Prep: 10 minutes • **Cook:** 23 minutes

One chipotle chile spices up this dish—the perfect complement to wilted greens.

2¼ cups low-sodium chicken broth,
    divided
2 tablespoons sherry vinegar
2 tablespoons fresh lime juice
1 tablespoon vegetable oil
½ teaspoon dried oregano
1 canned chipotle chile in adobo
    sauce

6 garlic cloves, minced
1 (1-pound) package prewashed
    chopped fresh mustard greens
1 (1-pound) package prewashed
    chopped fresh turnip greens

• Combine ¼ cup broth, vinegar, and next 4 ingredients in a blender; process until smooth.
• Bring 1 cup broth to a boil in a very large Dutch oven over medium-high heat. Add garlic; cook 2 minutes, stirring frequently. Add remaining 1 cup broth and greens; cover and cook 20 minutes or until wilted. Drain well. Serve with vinaigrette. Yield: 8 servings.

No Fuss
Entertaining

Big Batch

Simply
Southern

Chili Corn on the Cob

Prep: 10 minutes • **Cook:** 7 minutes

Microwave Miracle

Fix It Faster
If fresh corn is unavailable, use 8 half-ears of frozen corn instead. Just follow the package directions for cooking.

4 ears fresh corn, husks removed
¼ cup butter or margarine, softened
1 tablespoon chopped fresh chives

1 teaspoon chili powder
¼ teaspoon salt
¼ teaspoon pepper

• Wrap each ear of corn in plastic wrap; arrange, spoke fashion, on a glass plate.
• Microwave at HIGH 7 minutes, turning corn after 3½ minutes. Let stand 2 minutes. Meanwhile, stir together butter, chives, and chili powder. Remove plastic wrap; brush corn with butter mixture. Sprinkle with salt and pepper. Yield: 4 servings.

Glazed Stir-Fry Vegetables

Prep: 10 minutes • **Cook:** 7 minutes

Super Fast and Fresh

Menu Makings
These flavorful vegetables are great alongside Asian Grilled Flank Steak (page 50).

1 teaspoon chile oil
1 medium potato, peeled and cut into thin strips
3 cups broccoli florets
1 medium-size red bell pepper, cut into 1-inch pieces

2 tablespoons sugar
2 teaspoons cornstarch
3 tablespoons fresh lemon juice
½ cup water

• Heat oil in a large skillet or wok over medium-high heat 2 minutes. Add potato, and stir-fry 2 minutes. Add broccoli and bell pepper, and stir-fry 2 minutes or until crisp-tender.
• Stir together sugar and next 3 ingredients until smooth. Add mixture to vegetables, and stir-fry 1 minute or until thickened and bubbly. Yield: 4 servings.

Onion-Gruyère Gratin

Prep: 5 minutes • **Cook:** 16 minutes

*We used Vidalia onions for this creamy gratin—their sweetness
accentuates the flavor of the Gruyère cheese.*

6 medium onions, cut into ½-inch-
   thick slices (about 3 pounds)
3 tablespoons whipping cream
1 teaspoon all-purpose flour
½ teaspoon salt
⅛ teaspoon ground nutmeg
1 cup (4 ounces) shredded Gruyère
   cheese

• Place onion slices in a lightly greased 11- x 7-inch baking dish. Cover tightly
with heavy-duty plastic wrap; fold back a small corner to allow steam to escape.
Microwave at HIGH 10 minutes or just until onion is tender. Drain onion;
return to dish.
• Whisk together whipping cream and next 3 ingredients in a small bowl. Pour
cream mixture over onion, stirring to coat. Cover and microwave at HIGH
1 minute; stir. Sprinkle onion with cheese.
• Broil 3 inches from heat 5 minutes or until cheese is golden. Serve immediately.
Yield: 6 servings.

**Simply
Southern**

**No Fuss
Entertaining**

**Microwave
Miracle**

Menu Makings
Serve this upscale
gratin with Spicy
Beef Fillets
(page 205).

Squash Casserole

Prep: 5 minutes • **Cook:** 33 minutes

This creamy Southern side gets a flavor boost from Ranch-style dressing mix.

2 (16-ounce) packages frozen sliced
   yellow squash
1 cup chopped onion
1 cup mayonnaise or salad dressing
3 large eggs, lightly beaten
½ cup crushed unsalted saltine
   crackers
1 (0.4-ounce) envelope buttermilk
   Ranch-style salad dressing mix
1 cup (4 ounces) shredded sharp
   Cheddar cheese
1 cup soft breadcrumbs
1 tablespoon butter or margarine,
   melted

• Cook squash with onion according to directions on squash package, omitting
salt; drain well, pressing between paper towels. Combine squash mixture, mayonnaise, and next 4 ingredients in a lightly greased shallow 2-quart casserole.
• Combine breadcrumbs and butter; sprinkle over top. Bake at 350° for 20 to
25 minutes. Yield: 8 servings.

**Simply
Southern**

**No Fuss
Entertaining**

Big Batch

Zucchini Patties

Big Batch

Kid Friendly

Prep: 9 minutes • **Cook:** 6 minutes per batch

*Picky eaters will be so busy gobbling up these tasty patties
that they'll never guess veggies are hidden inside.*

1½ cups shredded zucchini (about 2 medium)	2 tablespoons finely chopped onion
¼ cup all-purpose flour	2 tablespoons mayonnaise
¼ cup grated Parmesan cheese	1 teaspoon seasoned salt
2 large eggs, lightly beaten	1 tablespoon butter

• Squeeze zucchini between layers of paper towels to remove excess moisture. Combine zucchini, flour, and next 5 ingredients in a bowl. Stir well.
• Melt butter in a large skillet over medium heat; spoon 2 tablespoons batter for each patty into skillet. Cook 3 minutes on each side or until browned. Yield: 10 patties.

Italian-Topped Tomatoes

Big Batch

Kid Friendly

Secret Ingredient Savvy

New Dijon varieties such as chipotle and dried tomato offer new taste sensations. Use your choice of flavors in this simple tomato bake.

Prep: 7 minutes • **Cook:** 15 minutes

2 tablespoons Dijon mustard	¼ cup Italian-seasoned breadcrumbs
3 medium tomatoes, cut in half crosswise	¼ cup shredded Parmesan cheese
⅛ teaspoon salt	2 tablespoons butter, melted
	1 teaspoon chopped fresh parsley

• Spread mustard evenly over cut side of each tomato half; sprinkle evenly with salt. Place tomato halves, cut sides up, in an 11- x 7-inch baking dish.
• Combine breadcrumbs and remaining ingredients in a small bowl. Gently spoon breadcrumb mixture evenly over each tomato. Bake at 450° for 12 to 15 minutes or until browned. Serve immediately. Yield: 6 servings.

Honey-Baked Tomatoes

Prep: 10 minutes • **Cook:** 35 minutes

8   medium tomatoes, cut into
    1-inch slices
4   teaspoons honey
2   white bread slices

1   tablespoon dried tarragon
1½   teaspoons salt
2   teaspoons freshly ground pepper
4   teaspoons butter

• Place tomato slices in a single layer in a lightly greased aluminum foil–lined 15- x 10-inch jellyroll pan. Drizzle with honey, spreading honey into hollows.
• Process bread in a blender or food processor until finely chopped.
• Stir together breadcrumbs and next 3 ingredients; sprinkle evenly over tomato slices. Dot with butter.
• Bake at 350° for 30 minutes or until tomato skins begin to wrinkle.
• Broil 5 inches from heat 5 minutes or until tops are golden. Serve warm. Yield: 8 servings.

No Fuss Entertaining

Make Ahead

Kitchen Timesavers
Prepare the crumb topping the day before the party.

Greek Tomatoes

Prep: 5 minutes

These superquick tomatoes get a Greek accent from capers and feta cheese.

4   medium tomatoes, cut into
    ¼-inch-thick slices
¼   cup capers, rinsed and drained
4   ounces crumbled feta cheese

¼   cup minced fresh parsley
    Coarsely ground pepper
2   tablespoons olive oil

• Place tomato slices on a platter. Sprinkle with capers and next 3 ingredients; drizzle with oil. Yield: 6 servings.

Super Fast and Fresh

No-Cook Creation

Garlic Mashed Potatoes

20 Minutes or less

Microwave Miracle

Kid Friendly

Simply Southern

Menu Makings

This classic side dish calls for Chicken-Fried Steak 'n' Country Gravy (page 10).

Prep: 6 minutes • **Cook:** 9 minutes

3 tablespoons butter or margarine	1⅓ cups milk
4 garlic cloves, pressed	½ teaspoon salt
2⅔ cups frozen mashed potatoes (we used Ore Ida)	¼ teaspoon freshly ground pepper

• Place butter in a 1½-quart microwave-safe bowl. Cover and microwave at HIGH 30 seconds or until butter melts. Add garlic; cover and microwave at HIGH 1½ minutes or until garlic is tender. Stir in potatoes, milk, salt, and pepper. Cover and microwave at HIGH 7 minutes or until thickened, stirring after 3 minutes. Serve immediately. Yield: 4 servings.

Souper Macaroni and Cheese

30 Minutes or less

Kid Friendly

Secret Ingredient Savvy

For a spicier flavor, substitute nacho cheese soup for Cheddar cheese soup.

Prep: 5 minutes • **Cook:** 25 minutes

Kids will love this cheesy blend topped with fried onion rings.

8 ounces uncooked elbow macaroni	½ cup milk
1 (10¾-ounce) can Cheddar cheese soup, undiluted	½ teaspoon prepared mustard
1 (8-ounce) package shredded American and Cheddar cheese blend	¼ teaspoon pepper
	1 (2.8-ounce) can French fried onion rings

• Cook macaroni according to package directions, including salt; drain.
• Stir together cheese soup and next 4 ingredients. Stir in macaroni. Spoon macaroni mixture into a lightly greased 11- x 7-inch baking dish.
• Bake at 400° for 10 minutes or until thoroughly heated. Top with French fried onion rings, and bake 3 more minutes. Yield: 6 servings.

20 Minutes or less

Pasta with Greens

Prep: 5 minutes • **Cook:** 15 minutes

Editor's Favorite

Toasted pine nuts add satisfying crunch to this sensational side.

8 ounces uncooked fettuccine
1 (16-ounce) package frozen chopped collard greens or other greens
2 to 3 garlic cloves, minced
3 tablespoons olive oil
½ teaspoon salt

¼ teaspoon freshly ground pepper
½ cup freshly grated Parmesan cheese
⅓ cup pine nuts, toasted
Garnishes: freshly grated Parmesan cheese, toasted pine nuts

• Cook pasta according to package directions, including salt; drain and set aside.
• Meanwhile, cook greens according to package directions; drain and set aside.
• Cook garlic in olive oil in a large skillet over medium-high heat until tender, but not brown. Add greens, salt, and pepper; cook until heated.
• Combine pasta, greens mixture, ½ cup Parmesan cheese, and ⅓ cup pine nuts in a large serving bowl. Garnish, if desired. Yield: 4 servings.

Rice Pilaf

Prep: 5 minutes • **Cook:** 30 minutes

1 tablespoon olive oil
1 cup uncooked long-grain rice
2½ cups chicken broth

½ cup coarsely chopped walnuts or pecans, toasted

• Heat olive oil in a large skillet over medium-high heat until hot. Add rice; sauté 3 to 5 minutes or just until rice is lightly browned.
• Meanwhile, bring broth to a boil in a large saucepan. Gradually add rice to broth; cover, reduce heat, and simmer 25 minutes or until liquid is absorbed and rice is tender. Stir in walnuts. Yield: 4 servings.

Menu Makings
This simple side dish pairs nicely with a high-flavored entrée. Try it with Pan-Seared Steaks with Roasted Red Pepper Sauce (page 204).

Royal Raspberry Tea Cakes

Prep: 25 minutes • **Cook:** 20 minutes per batch

No Fuss
Entertaining

Make Ahead

1 cup butter, softened
½ cup powdered sugar
2 teaspoons vanilla extract

2 cups all-purpose flour
¼ teaspoon salt
¾ cup seedless raspberry preserves

Secret Ingredient Savvy
Give these cookies another flavor just by using your favorite preserves in place of the raspberry.

• Beat butter and sugar at low speed with an electric mixer until creamy. Add vanilla extract, beating until blended.
• Combine flour and salt in a small bowl; gradually add to butter mixture, beating just until blended after each addition.
• Shape dough into 1-inch balls; place 2 inches apart on lightly greased baking sheets. Press thumb or end of a wooden spoon into each ball, forming an indentation; fill evenly with raspberry preserves.
• Bake at 325° for 15 to 20 minutes or just until edges begin to brown. Remove to wire racks to cool. Yield: 2½ dozen.

Almond Tea Cookies

Make Ahead

Prep: 5 minutes • **Cook:** 12 minutes per batch

*Full of almonds, these chunky cookies are
great to serve with afternoon tea.*

2½ cups sliced almonds
¾ cup sugar
¼ cup all-purpose flour

⅓ cup butter, melted
1 egg white, lightly beaten
½ teaspoon vanilla extract

• Combine all ingredients in a large bowl, stirring gently to blend. Drop by tablespoonfuls onto parchment paper-lined baking sheet (do not use wax paper).
• Bake at 350° for 10 to 12 minutes or until golden. Cool completely on baking sheets. Remove from paper, and store in an airtight container. Yield: 2½ dozen.

Marvelous Macaroons

30 Minutes or less

Prep: 8 minutes • **Cook:** 22 minutes

2⅔ cups sweetened shredded
    coconut
⅔ cup sugar
¼ cup all-purpose flour

¼ teaspoon salt
4 egg whites
1 teaspoon almond extract
1 cup slivered almonds

• Combine first 4 ingredients in a medium bowl; stir well. Add egg whites and almond extract; stir well. Stir in almonds.
• Drop dough by teaspoonfuls onto lightly greased cookie sheets.
• Bake at 325° for 22 minutes or until golden. Remove immediately to wire racks to cool completely. Yield: 2 dozen.

Make Ahead

Secret Ingredient Savvy
Almonds are the key ingredient for a classic macaroon. This version is the ultimate loaded with both almond extract and slivered almonds.

Chocolate Macaroons

Prep: 20 minutes • **Cook:** 10 minutes per batch

Two favorites—chocolate and coconut—come together in these cookies that'll have you raving.

1 cup semisweet chocolate morsels
1 cup sweetened flaked coconut
½ cup finely chopped walnuts

2 egg whites
¼ teaspoon salt
½ cup sugar

• Heat chocolate in a medium-size heavy saucepan over low heat until melted, stirring occasionally. Cool to room temperature. Stir in coconut and walnuts.
• Beat egg whites and salt at high speed of an electric mixer until foamy. Gradually add sugar, 1 tablespoon at a time, beating until stiff peaks form and sugar dissolves (2 to 4 minutes). Fold egg white mixture into chocolate mixture.
• Drop by heaping teaspoonfuls onto baking sheets lined with aluminum foil.
• Bake at 350° for 10 minutes. Remove cookies to wire racks, and cool completely. Yield: 3 dozen.

Make Ahead

Angel Fluff Brownies

Prep: 10 minutes • **Bake:** 25 minutes

Kid Friendly

**Secret
Ingredient
Savvy**

Mix in your
favorite pudding
flavor for fun
variations.

1 (3.4-ounce) package chocolate
   instant pudding mix
⅔ cup granulated sugar
½ cup all-purpose flour
2 large eggs

⅓ cup butter or margarine, melted
¼ cup whipping cream
1 teaspoon vanilla extract
½ cup chopped walnuts, toasted
Powdered sugar (optional)

• Stir together first 8 ingredients until blended. Spoon into a lightly greased
8- or 9-inch square pan.
• Bake at 350° for 25 minutes or until edges pull away from pan. Cool in pan on
a wire rack. Sprinkle with powdered sugar, if desired. Yield: 16 brownies.

Creamy No-Bake Bars

Prep: 12 minutes • **Other:** 8 hours and 30 minutes

Kid Friendly

**No Fuss
Entertaining**

Make Ahead

How-To Hints
Once these freeze,
cut them into
bars, and wrap
individually with
plastic wrap for a
ready-made treat.

1 cup chopped pecans
1 cup sweetened flaked coconut
2½ cups crisp rice cereal, crushed
1 cup firmly packed light brown
   sugar

½ cup butter or margarine
1 quart vanilla ice cream, softened

• Bake pecans and coconut separately in shallow pans at 350°, stirring occasionally,
5 to 10 minutes or until toasted. Combine pecans, coconut, and cereal in a
medium bowl.
• Bring brown sugar and butter to a boil in a small saucepan over medium heat,
stirring constantly; boil, stirring constantly, 1 minute. Pour sugar mixture over
cereal mixture, stirring until coated.
• Press half of cereal mixture into a 9-inch square pan lined with plastic wrap;
freeze until firm. Spread with ice cream; press remaining cereal mixture over ice
cream. Cover and freeze 8 hours or until firm; freeze until ready to serve. Yield:
16 servings.

Turtle Bar Cookies

Prep: 15 minutes • **Cook:** 21 minutes

2 cups all-purpose flour
1 cup firmly packed brown sugar
½ cup butter or margarine, softened
1 cup pecan halves

⅔ cup butter
½ cup firmly packed brown sugar
1 cup milk chocolate morsels

• Combine first 3 ingredients in a mixing bowl; beat well. Pat mixture firmly into an ungreased 13- x 9-inch pan. Arrange pecans over crust.

• Combine ⅔ cup butter and ½ cup brown sugar in a saucepan. Bring mixture to a boil over medium heat, stirring constantly; cook 3 minutes, stirring constantly. Spoon mixture over pecans. Bake at 350° for 15 to 17 minutes or until golden and bubbly.

• Remove from oven; sprinkle top with chocolate morsels. Let stand 2 to 3 minutes or until slightly melted. Gently swirl chocolate with a knife, leaving some morsels whole (do not spread); cool. Cut into bars. Yield: 20 cookies.

Make Ahead

How-To Hints
These cookies are fun to make with this easy "frosting!" Simply sprinkle chocolate morsels on top of the hot brownies, and swirl the melted chocolate gently with a knife after a couple of minutes. The result is a quick, rich frosting.

Pumpkin Gingerbread

Prep: 15 minutes • **Cook:** 30 minutes

We love the holiday inspiration pumpkin adds to this all-time favorite that's quick and easy to prepare.

¼ cup butter or margarine, softened
⅔ cup firmly packed brown sugar
3 egg whites
1 teaspoon vanilla extract
1¼ cups self-rising flour

½ teaspoon ground ginger
1 teaspoon ground cinnamon
1 cup canned pumpkin
6 tablespoons dark corn syrup
Powdered sugar

• Beat butter at medium speed with an electric mixer until creamy. Gradually add brown sugar, beating well. Add egg whites, 1 at a time, beating until blended. Stir in vanilla.

• Combine flour, ginger, and cinnamon.

• Combine pumpkin and corn syrup; add to brown sugar mixture alternately with flour mixture, beginning and ending with flour mixture, and blending well after each addition. Pour into a lightly greased 8-inch square pan.

• Bake at 350° for 25 to 30 minutes or until a wooden pick inserted in center comes out clean. Cut into squares. Sprinkle servings with powdered sugar. Yield: 9 servings.

Editor's Favorite

Streusel Blueberry Shortcake

Make Ahead ▶

Prep: 15 minutes • **Cook:** 18 minutes • **Other:** 40 minutes

3 cups biscuit mix
⅔ cup milk
¼ cup butter or margarine, melted
½ cup firmly packed brown sugar
½ cup chopped pecans

¼ cup butter or margarine
1 (8-ounce) container frozen
  whipped topping, thawed
2 pints fresh blueberries

• Combine first 3 ingredients in a large bowl; stir until a soft dough forms. Spread dough evenly into two lightly greased 8-inch square pans.
• Combine brown sugar and pecans; cut in ¼ cup butter with a pastry blender until mixture is crumbly. Sprinkle nut mixture over dough.
• Bake, uncovered, at 400° for 18 minutes or until a wooden pick inserted in center comes out clean. Cool in pans on wire racks 10 minutes; remove from pans, and cool completely on wire racks.
• Place 1 cake layer on a serving plate. Spread half of whipped topping over layer, and arrange half of blueberries on top. Repeat procedure with remaining cake layer, whipped topping, and blueberries. Chill cake until ready to serve. Yield: 1 (8-inch) cake.

Caramel-Apple Shortcakes

No Fuss Entertaining ▶

Prep: 15 minutes • **Cook:** 18 minutes

Fix It Faster
Substitute store-bought sponge cake cups for the Cinnamon-Crunch Shortcake, if desired.

1 tablespoon butter
5 Gala apples, peeled and sliced
½ cup apple juice
3 tablespoons brown sugar
¼ teaspoon ground cinnamon

Bottled caramel sauce
1 recipe Cinnamon-Crunch
  Shortcakes (page 361)
Whipped cream

• Melt butter in a large skillet over medium-high heat; add apple, tossing to coat. Stir in apple juice, brown sugar, and cinnamon. Bring to a boil; reduce heat to low, and simmer 10 to 15 minutes or until apple slices are tender.
• Pour ½ cup caramel sauce over apples, tossing to coat. Split Cinnamon-Crunch Shortcakes in half. Layer half of shortcake halves with apple mixture and whipped cream. Top with remaining shortcake halves. Drizzle with additional caramel sauce. Yield: 12 servings.

Cinnamon-Crunch Shortcakes

Prep: 20 minutes • **Cook:** 15 minutes

*These sweet shortcakes form a lovely base for any kind of fruit—or try
the Fruit Compote below.*

2½ cups all-purpose baking mix
 3 tablespoons granulated sugar
 ½ cup milk
 4 tablespoons butter, melted and
      divided

 ¼ cup chopped pecans
 2 tablespoons brown sugar
 ¼ teaspoon ground cinnamon

• Stir together baking mix, granulated sugar, milk, and 3 tablespoons butter until a
soft dough forms. Turn out onto a lightly floured surface; knead 3 to 4 times.
• Pat dough to a ¼-inch thickness; cut with a 2¾-inch round biscuit cutter. Place
on lightly greased baking sheets.
• Combine pecans, brown sugar, cinnamon, and remaining tablespoon butter; pat
onto biscuit tops.
• Bake at 375° for 12 to 15 minutes or until lightly browned. Yield: 12 servings.

Cinnamon-Crunch Shortcakes with Fruit Compote: Prepare 1 recipe Cinnamon-
Crunch Shortcakes. Melt 1 tablespoon butter in a large nonstick skillet over
medium-high heat. Stir in ½ cup apple juice; ¼ cup firmly packed brown sugar;
2 ripe Bosc pears, peeled and sliced; 2 Rome apples, peeled and sliced; ¼ cup
dried cranberries; and ¼ teaspoon ground cinnamon. Bring to a boil; reduce heat
to low, and simmer, stirring occasionally, 10 to 15 minutes or until fruit is tender.
Split each baked shortcake in half. Layer half of shortcake halves with fruit compote and whipped cream; top with remaining shortcake halves.

Chocolate Éclair Cake

Prep: 15 minutes • **Other:** 8 hours

One box of graham crackers contains three individually wrapped packages of crackers; use one package for each layer of this indulgent dessert.

1 (14.4-ounce) box honey graham crackers
2 (3.4-ounce) packages French vanilla instant pudding mix
3 cups milk

1 (12-ounce) container frozen whipped topping, thawed
1 (16-ounce) container ready-to-spread chocolate frosting

• Line bottom of an ungreased 13- x 9-inch baking dish with one-third of honey graham crackers.
• Whisk together pudding mix and milk; add whipped topping, stirring until mixture thickens. Spread half of pudding mixture over graham crackers. Repeat layers with one-third of graham crackers and remaining pudding mixture. Top with remaining graham crackers. Spread with chocolate frosting. Cover and chill 8 hours. Yield: 12 servings.

No-Cook Creation

5 Ingredients or Less

Kid Friendly

How-To Hints

To lighten, use reduced-fat graham crackers, sugar-free pudding mix, fat-free milk, and fat-free frozen whipped topping.

Toffee Temptation

Prep: 15 minutes • **Other:** 2 hours

1 (3.4-ounce) package vanilla instant pudding mix
2 cups milk
1 (15-ounce) package cream-filled sponge cakes (we used Twinkies)

1 (8.4-ounce) package chocolate-covered toffee candy bars, crushed
½ (8-ounce) container frozen whipped topping, thawed

• Prepare pudding according to package directions using 2 cups milk.
• Meanwhile, slice cakes in half horizontally. Line an 11- x 7-inch dish with bottom halves of cakes, cut sides up. Sprinkle with ½ cup candy.
• Spoon pudding over candy. Arrange top of cakes over pudding, cut sides down. Spread with whipped topping; sprinkle with remaining candy. Cover and chill 2 hours. Yield: 10 servings.

No-Cook Creation

5 Ingredients or Less

Birthday Party Brownie Cakes

Prep: 10 minutes • **Cook:** 20 minutes

1 (21-ounce) package family-style brownie mix (we used Duncan Hines)
½ cup vegetable oil
¼ cup cranberry juice
2 large eggs

Toppings: semisweet chocolate morsels, candy-coated chocolate pieces, chopped pecans, candy sprinkles
Powdered sugar (optional)
Ice cream (optional)

• Stir together first 4 ingredients until smooth. Spoon batter into 12 lightly greased muffin cups. Sprinkle with desired toppings.
• Bake at 350° for 20 minutes or until a wooden pick inserted in center comes out clean. Remove from pan, and cool on a wire rack. If desired, sprinkle with powdered sugar, and serve with ice cream. Yield: 12 servings.

Cherry Dumpling Dessert

Prep: 10 minutes • **Cook:** 25 minutes

Sweet dumplings bake atop a simple cherry filling for one of the easiest desserts you can make. Spoon it like a cobbler.

3 (14½-ounce) cans tart red pitted cherries, undrained
1 cup plus 2 tablespoons sugar, divided
2 cups all-purpose flour
1 tablespoon plus 1 teaspoon baking powder

1 teaspoon salt
¼ cup butter or margarine
¾ cup milk
Half-and-half (optional)

• Combine cherries and ½ cup sugar in a large Dutch oven; stir well. Bring mixture to a boil.
• Meanwhile, combine flour, baking powder, and salt; cut in butter with pastry blender until mixture is crumbly. Add remaining sugar, stirring just until blended. Add milk, stirring just until dry ingredients are moistened.
• Carefully drop dough by heaping tablespoonfuls into boiling cherry mixture. Cover and cook over medium heat 25 minutes or until dumplings are done. Serve with half-and-half, if desired. Yield: 8 servings.

Caramel-Apple Pie

Prep: 10 minutes • **Cook:** 30 minutes

Editor's Favorite

Big Batch

No Fuss Entertaining

Put the finishing touch on an autumn supper with this caramel-apple dessert.

8 medium-size red cooking apples, peeled, cored, and thinly sliced
½ cup granulated sugar
1 teaspoon apple pie spice
1 cup firmly packed brown sugar
¾ cup all-purpose flour
½ cup butter or margarine
¾ cup quick-cooking oats, uncooked
Ice cream

• Place apple in a lightly greased 13- x 9-inch pan. Combine granulated sugar and apple pie spice; sprinkle over apple, and toss gently.
• Combine brown sugar and flour; cut in butter with pastry blender until mixture is crumbly. Stir in oats. Sprinkle brown sugar mixture evenly over apple mixture. Bake at 400° for 30 minutes. Serve warm with ice cream. Yield: 12 servings.

Coconut Cheesecake Pie

Prep: 17 minutes • **Other:** 2 hours

Make Ahead

How-To Hints
It's easy to make a homemade graham cracker crust using a 9-inch pieplate. Simply combine 1 (5⅓-ounce) packet graham crackers, crushed, ¼ cup sugar, and ¼ cup plus 2 tablespoons butter or margarine, melted. Firmly press crumb mixture evenly in bottom and up sides of your 9-inch pieplate, and you're ready for the filling.

Look for cream of coconut near the piña colada and margarita mixes.

1 (8-ounce) package cream cheese, softened
1 cup cream of coconut
1 (3.4-ounce) package cheesecake instant pudding mix
1 (7-ounce) package sweetened flaked coconut
1 (8-ounce) container frozen whipped topping, thawed
1 (9-ounce) ready-made graham cracker crust (we used Keebler's deep dish)
1 cup whipping cream
Garnish: sweetened flaked coconut

• Beat cream cheese and cream of coconut at medium speed with an electric mixer until smooth. Add pudding mix, beating until blended.
• Stir in coconut; fold in whipped topping. Spread filling mixture evenly into crust; cover and chill 2 hours or until set.
• Beat whipping cream with an electric mixer until soft peaks form, and spread evenly over top of pie. Garnish, if desired. Yield: 1 (9-inch) pie.

Blueberry Yum Yum

Prep: 15 minutes • **Cook:** 23 minutes • **Other:** 8 hours and 45 minutes

*You'll have everyone sayin' yum yum when you serve this blueberry treat.
This dessert makes for a happy tummy!*

1½ cups self-rising flour	¾ cup sifted powdered sugar
1 cup firmly packed light brown sugar	½ teaspoon vanilla extract
¾ cup butter or margarine, softened	1 (12-ounce) container frozen whipped topping, thawed
1½ cups chopped pecans, toasted	2 (21-ounce) cans blueberry fruit filling
1 (8-ounce) package cream cheese, softened	

• Combine flour and brown sugar; cut in butter with a pastry blender until mixture is crumbly. Stir in pecans. Press mixture into a lightly greased 13- x 9-inch baking dish.
• Bake at 375° for 23 minutes. Cool in pan on a wire rack.
• Beat cream cheese, powdered sugar, and vanilla until smooth; stir in whipped topping. Spread cheese mixture evenly over prepared crust. Spoon fruit filling evenly over cream cheese layer. Cover and chill at least 8 hours. Yield: 15 servings.

Speedy Blackberry Cobbler

Prep: 6 minutes • **Cook:** 28 minutes

*Sugar cookie dough is put to clever use in this recipe to form
a crispy dough atop this cobbler.*

4 cups fresh blackberries	9 (¼-inch-thick) slices refrigerated sugar cookie dough (we used Pillsbury Sugar Cookie dough)
¾ cup sugar	
¼ cup all-purpose flour	1 tablespoon sugar
1 teaspoon lemon zest	
1 teaspoon fresh lemon juice	

• Combine first 5 ingredients in a medium bowl; pour into a lightly greased 8-inch baking dish. Microwave at HIGH 8 minutes or until bubbly, stirring once.
• Place cookie slices over berries; sprinkle evenly with 1 tablespoon sugar. Bake at 375° for 20 minutes or until golden. Yield: 6 servings.

No Fuss Entertaining

Kid Friendly

Fix It Faster
If you can't wait to enjoy this dessert, quickly cool the crust in the fridge or freezer before adding filling ingredients.

Simply Southern

Menu Makings
Serve warm with ice cream.

Apple Shortbread
Crisp

Apple Shortbread Crisp

Prep: 7 minutes • **Cook:** 36 minutes

The buttery, crispy shortbread cookie topping on this dessert will leave you wanting more.

2 (12-ounce) packages frozen apple chunks (we used Stouffer's Harvest Apples)
6 tablespoons butter or margarine
20 shortbread cookies, crushed (we used Keebler Sandies Simply Shortbread)
½ cup chopped walnuts
¼ cup firmly packed light brown sugar
1 teaspoon ground cinnamon, divided
¼ teaspoon ground nutmeg
2 tablespoons light brown sugar
Vanilla ice cream

• Prick plastic wrap covering apple chunks several times with a fork; microwave at MEDIUM (50% power) 7 minutes or until apple is thawed. Let stand 2 minutes.
• Meanwhile, melt butter in a large skillet over medium heat; add cookie crumbs and walnuts. Cook, stirring constantly, 2 minutes. Remove from heat, and stir in ¼ cup brown sugar, ½ teaspoon cinnamon, and nutmeg.
• Combine 2 tablespoons brown sugar and remaining ½ teaspoon cinnamon; sprinkle in a lightly greased 1-quart baking dish. Sprinkle half of apple over brown sugar mixture; top with half of cookie crumb mixture. Repeat layers with remaining apple and crumb mixture.
• Bake at 375° for 25 minutes or until golden. Serve warm with vanilla ice cream. Yield: 6 servings.

Simply Southern

Editor's Favorite

Menu Makings
This makes the ideal harvest dessert after a meal of Spinach with Herbs (page 331), Pecan Chicken (page 14), and simple mashed potatoes.

Caramel-Apple Pizza

Prep: 8 minutes • **Cook:** 15 minutes

Big Batch

Kid Friendly

*Treat your family to pizza for dessert. They'll love the
sugar cookie crust layered with cream cheese and apples. And don't forget
to top it off with your favorite caramel topping.*

½ cup water
1 tablespoon lemon juice
5 medium Braeburn or Fuji apples,
    peeled and thinly sliced
1 (18-ounce) package refrigerated
    sugar cookie dough

2 (8-ounce) packages cream cheese,
    softened
1 cup firmly packed brown sugar
1 teaspoon vanilla extract
¼ cup caramel topping

• Combine ½ cup water and lemon juice in a medium bowl; add apple slices.
• Press cookie dough evenly onto an ungreased 12-inch pizza pan. Bake at 350°
for 15 minutes or until golden. Cool crust in pan on a wire rack.
• Beat cream cheese, brown sugar, and vanilla at medium speed with an electric
mixer until smooth. Spread over cookie crust.
• Drain apple slices; arrange over cream cheese layer. Drizzle with caramel
topping. Yield: 16 servings.

Fresh Fruit
Pizza

Fresh Fruit Pizza

Prep: 23 minutes • **Cook:** 13 minutes

The lemon curd not only holds the fruit in place, it serves as an exquisite anchor for all the flavors. You may have never imagined such a pizza. Now you'll never forget it. It's best served the day it's made.

1 (18-ounce) package refrigerated
    sugar cookie dough
2 tablespoons seedless raspberry jam,
    melted

¾ cup Lemon Curd
2 cups fresh raspberries
2 cups fresh blackberries
2 cups fresh sliced strawberries

• Press cookie dough into a 12-inch pizza pan coated with cooking spray. Bake at 350° for 13 minutes or until golden brown. Cool completely on a wire rack.
• Spread jam over crust. Spread Lemon Curd over jam; arrange raspberries, blackberries, and strawberry slices on top. Serve immediately. Yield: 12 servings.

Lemon Curd

Prep: 6 minutes • **Cook:** 7 minutes • **Other:** 1 hour

For a lime-curd variation, substitute lime rind and juice for the lemon rind and juice.

¾ cup sugar
1 tablespoon grated lemon rind
2 large eggs

⅔ cup fresh lemon juice (about 3
    large lemons)
2 tablespoons butter or margarine

• Combine first 3 ingredients in a saucepan over medium heat, stirring with a wire whisk. Cook until sugar dissolves and mixture is light in color (about 3 minutes).
• Stir in lemon juice and butter; cook 4 minutes or until mixture thinly coats the back of a spoon, stirring constantly with whisk. Cool. Cover and chill (mixture will thicken as it cools). Yield: 1⅓ cups.

Note: Lemon Curd can be stored in the refrigerator for up to 1 week. You can easily double the recipe and freeze half of it in a zip-top freezer bag. Thaw in the refrigerator, and use within 1 week of thawing.

Soft-Serve Chocolate Ice Cream

Prep: 4 minutes • **Other:** 20 minutes

Cool off on triple-digit summer days with this frozen chocolate delight. Serve it with either a spoon or a straw.

1 (14-ounce) can sweetened condensed milk	6 cups chocolate milk
½ cup instant malted milk powder	1 (16-ounce) container frozen whipped topping, thawed
1 cup chocolate syrup	

• Combine first 4 ingredients; fold in whipped topping. Pour mixture into freezer container of a 1-gallon hand-turned or electric freezer. Freeze according to manufacturer's instructions. Yield: about 4 quarts.

Blackberry Custard

Prep: 15 minutes • **Cook:** 7 minutes • **Other:** 2 hours

This chilled, berry-topped custard was a winner of top honors in our test kitchen.

¾ cup sugar	½ teaspoon vanilla extract
⅓ cup all-purpose flour	1 cup whipping cream
Dash of salt	2 tablespoons sugar
4 egg yolks	2 cups fresh blackberries
2 cups milk	

• Combine first 3 ingredients in a heavy saucepan; whisk in egg yolks and milk. Cook over medium heat, whisking constantly, 5 to 7 minutes or until thickened. Remove from heat; stir in vanilla. Pour into a serving dish; cool. Cover and chill 2 hours.
• Beat whipping cream at medium speed with an electric mixer until foamy; gradually add 2 tablespoons sugar, beating until soft peaks form. Spread over custard. Top with fresh blackberries. Yield: 4 servings.

Easy Tiramisu

Prep: 20 minutes • **Other:** 8 hours

1 (16-ounce) package mascarpone cheese	1 cup brewed espresso
1¼ cups whipping cream	2 tablespoons dark rum
¼ cup powdered sugar	2 (3-ounce) packages ladyfingers
1½ teaspoons vanilla extract	4 (1-ounce) bittersweet chocolate baking squares, grated

• Beat first 4 ingredients at high speed with an electric mixer 30 seconds or just until blended.
• Stir together espresso and rum.
• Arrange 1 package of ladyfingers in bottom of a 3-quart bowl or trifle dish; brush with half of espresso mixture. Layer half of mascarpone cheese mixture over ladyfingers; sprinkle with half of grated chocolate. Repeat layers. Cover and chill 8 hours. Yield: 8 servings.

Make Ahead

No-Cook Creation

Secret Ingredient Savvy
Substitute 2 (8-ounce) packages cream cheese, softened; ⅓ cup sour cream; and ¼ cup whipping cream, beaten until blended, for 16 ounces mascarpone cheese, if desired.

Peanut Butter Pudding

Prep: 5 minutes • **Cook:** 6 minutes • **Other:** 2 hours

½ cup sugar	½ cup half-and-half
2 tablespoons cornstarch	¾ cup creamy peanut butter
¼ teaspoon salt	1 teaspoon vanilla extract
1½ cups milk	Garnish: whipped cream

• Combine first 3 ingredients in a medium-size heavy saucepan; gradually whisk in milk and half-and-half.
• Bring to a boil over medium heat, whisking constantly. Boil, whisking constantly, 1 minute. Remove from heat. (Pudding will be thin.)
• Add peanut butter and vanilla, whisking until smooth. Pour into a bowl; place plastic wrap directly over warm pudding. Chill at least 2 hours. Garnish, if desired. Yield: 2½ cups.

Make Ahead

Ideas for Two

Kid Friendly

The Quick & Easy Kitchen

5 Habits of Highly Efficient Cooks

1 Organize Your Kitchen

• **Pick a day to clean and organize** your kitchen. Store the utensils you use regularly in a convenient place on your counter so you don't have to dig through drawers to find what you need. Get rid of the equipment and utensils that you never use.

• **Use racks, shelves, and bins** to neatly store equipment and ingredients.

• **Group similar items** together in your pantry.

• **Group all measuring items** (cups, spoons) together near where you prepare foods for cooking.

• **Alphabetize your spices and seasonings** so they're easy to find. If you have room, dried seasonings keep best in the freezer. If you store them in a cabinet, just place them in a cool area away from heat or light.

• **Keep a notepad** in the kitchen to jot down ingredients that need to be replaced.

• **Clean out your refrigerator** and store the items you use the most in the front and in the door racks.

2 Plan Ahead

• **Try to plan and shop for a week's worth of meals.** It might take a few extra minutes initially, but once you're in the habit of planning weekly menus, you'll save time and reduce the stress of coming up with meal ideas at the last minute.

• **Stock your kitchen** with quick cooking staples. Many are listed by food category on page 389.

• **Read through the recipes** you want to prepare and gather everything you need before you start cooking.

• **When you're preparing** breadcrumbs or toasting nuts for a recipe, prepare extra and freeze in zip-top freezer bags.

• **When the price is right,** stock up on standard items you know you'll use and you have room to store.

• **Avoid last-minute stops** to pick up an item or two; you'll spend more time and money than you planned.

• **Make out a grocery list before you go** to the supermarket and stick to the list. You'll buy less and spend less time in the store.

• **Make your grocery list according to the order of aisles** in the store (see page 389). Follow that order, and you'll backtrack less.

• **Microwave** to get a jump start on cooking. Use the microwave to thaw foods or to pre-cook casseroles or meat you'll finish cooking in the oven or on the grill.

• **Chop and freeze ½-cup portions** of red or green bell pepper, onion, and parsley in zip-top freezer bags.

3 Strategize Cleanup

• **Get in the habit of cleaning as you cook.** You'll be delighted that the dishes are halfway done when you're finished with dinner.

• **Soak dirty dishes** in hot, soapy water as you prepare meals so you won't have to scrub so much later.

• **Use spray-on oven cleaner** on extra dirty pots and pans to ease cleanup.

• **Use a graduated measuring spoon.** It's one spoon that adjusts for the measurement you need so you don't have to mess up a whole set.

• **Measure dry ingredients** before wet ones so you can use the same measuring cups and spoons without washing between measuring.

• **Measure or sift ingredients** onto wax paper or paper towels for easy cleanup.

• **Prevent messy splatters** by setting a metal colander upside down over a skillet of simmering food. The colander holes allow steam to escape.

• **Use plastic freezer bags** to marinate meat or poultry. Turn the bag occasionally to completely coat the food.

• **Line baking pans** or broiler pans with aluminum foil for quick and easy cleanup when roasting meat, chicken, fish, or vegetables. You'll have very little mess to clean off the pans after removing the foil.

• **Chop a small amount** of an ingredient with a chef's knife instead of dirtying a food processor.

• **Use a zip-top plastic bag** to make crumbs for toppings. Place cereal or cookies in the bag; crush the contents of the bag into crumbs with your hands or a rolling pin.

• **Beat eggs in a mixing bowl** first, and then add the other ingredients to save cleaning an extra bowl.

4 Know Your Grocery Options

• **Buy small amounts** of shredded carrots, celery sticks, cauliflower or broccoli florets, and sliced mushrooms from the salad bar to save cleaning and slicing time. If you need larger amounts, look for bagged shredded or baby carrots, cauliflower or broccoli florets, and sliced mushrooms in the produce section.

• **Buy prepackaged** frozen chopped onion and green bell pepper.

• **Purchase products that combine more than one ingredient,** such as Creole, Italian, Mexican, and Greek spice blends (Mrs. Dash has several good blends). Canned Mexican-, Italian-, or Cajun-style stewed tomatoes (you get tomatoes, onions, peppers, and the seasonings in a single can) are also a good choice. Besides saving on cooking time, these products save you storage space and the time it takes to put away groceries.

• **Buy bags of precut, prewashed salad greens,** such as spinach leaves, romaine hearts, mixed salad greens, and cabbage, to save cleaning and preparation time.

Continued on following page

• Peeled raw shrimp and peeled cooked shrimp are the quickest cooking forms. Follow the chart below for weight and measure comparisons, which are especially helpful if you want to start with unpeeled fresh shrimp instead.

Shrimp Choices

Unpeeled, raw		Peeled, raw		Peeled, cooked
⅔ pound	=	½ pound	=	⅓ pound
1 pound	=	¾ pound	=	½ pound
1⅓ pounds	=	1 pound	=	⅔ pound
2 pounds	=	1½ pounds	=	1 pound
2⅔ pounds	=	2 pounds	=	1⅓ pounds
4 pounds	=	3 pounds	=	2 pounds

• Chopped cooked chicken is available in many forms, and we call for it often in our recipes. Below are some helpful conversions when purchasing different chicken products.

Chicken Choices

Amount and type		Amount chopped, cooked
1 pound uncooked boneless, skinless chicken	=	3 cups
5.5-ounce cooked boneless chicken breast half	=	1 cup
1 (6-ounce) package grilled chicken strips	=	1⅓ cups
1 (9-ounce) package frozen chopped cooked chicken	=	1⅔ cups
1 (2-pound) deli-roasted chicken	=	2 to 3 cups
1 (3-pound) raw chicken, cooked	=	3 cups

5 Be a Speed Shopper

If you want to be a true speed shopper, determine your shopping style by this clever analysis and plan your supermarket strategy accordingly.*
• **Dasher:** Runs into the store on the way home every night to pick up something for that night's dinner. Frequents the deli and frozen food sections and grabs whatever

looks good. Opts for a basket rather than a cart. Generally has less than 8 items; uses the express aisle.
• **Gatherer:** Travels up and down every aisle grabbing items that might be thrown together for a meal. Subject to impulse buys and advertised specials. Sometimes ends up with a cart full of groceries but still can't figure out what to cook for supper.
• **Hunter:** Enters a detailed weekly grocery list into the palm pilot and meticulously searches for each and every item on the list. Not uncommon for this shopper to visit several stores on the quest for one item. Often seen with coupons.

Whatever your shopping style, you can make your selections quickly and move on if you know where to find the foods you need in each section of the store. Our plan on the next page will help you simplify your shopping whether you're shopping for the month, week, or just for the night.

This is more than a grocery list—it's a strategic plan for shopping. We've identified the key areas of the store where you'll find quick cooking staple products for many of the recipes in this book. Although the specific layouts will be different, most stores will have these same areas. Familiarize yourself with your local grocery and plan your grocery list around the store's layout.

This sample layout of a grocery store highlights key sections of the store. In each section, there is a list of the products in that section that we recommend you keep on hand to be a superfast chef extraordinaire. Start in the bottom left and work your way through the store. The order in which you move through the sections isn't crucial, except that we do recommend that you add frozen foods and dairy products to your cart last.

The **Hunters** and **Gatherers** will probably go to each section. The **Dashers** may only hit a few. Either way, you've saved yourself the time of going up and down every aisle.

One key point to keep in mind for this strategy to work: stock up on staples. If you shop once for the staples and condiments that you use frequently, you won't have to spend time doing that each time you visit the store. Use this chart as a general staples guide for items you need to keep on hand for ultimate quick and easy meals, menus, and entertaining.

When you're finished shopping, have your grocer bag like items together (frozen, refrigerated, or pantry products), and put-away time in your kitchen will be quicker.

Based on research done for the national Cattleman's Beef Association.

Speed Shopper's Supermarket Staples

Freezer
- ❑ Fruit, whole and sliced
- ❑ Vegetables
- ❑ Onions, chopped frozen
- ❑ Peppers, chopped frozen
- ❑ Seasoning blend (chopped frozen onion, peppers, celery, and parsley)
- ❑ Potatoes, hash browns and cooked mashed
- ❑ Chicken, chopped cooked
- ❑ Shrimp, peeled raw or cooked
- ❑ Ice cream
- ❑ Whipped topping

Refrigerated Section
- ❑ Butter
- ❑ Cheese, sliced
- ❑ Cheese, preshredded and blends
- ❑ Fresh pasta
- ❑ Milk
- ❑ Bread products
- ❑ Eggs
- ❑ Sour cream and yogurt
- ❑ Fruit juice
- ❑ Potato products
- ❑ Dips and spreads

Meat/Poultry/Seafood
- ❑ Chicken, chopped cooked boneless chicken tenders and breasts
- ❑ Beef, ground chuck
- ❑ Beef, precooked crumbles
- ❑ Pork chops and tenderloins
- ❑ Bacon
- ❑ Shrimp, peeled and/or cooked
- ❑ Premarinated meats and poultry
- ❑ Sausage

Deli/Bakery
- ❑ Roasted chicken
- ❑ Breads/rolls
- ❑ Sliced meats
- ❑ Salad bar items

Condiments & Miscellaneous
- ❑ Dressing, Italian, Greek, Ranch, and Honey Mustard
- ❑ Honey
- ❑ Ketchup
- ❑ Mustard, Dijon and regular
- ❑ Oils, vegetable and olive
- ❑ Salsa
- ❑ Soy sauce
- ❑ Vegetable cooking spray
- ❑ Worcestershire sauce
- ❑ Chili sauce

Spices
- ❑ Chili powder
- ❑ Crab/shrimp boil
- ❑ Creole seasoning
- ❑ Dried minced onion
- ❑ Garlic salt and powder
- ❑ Greek seasoning
- ❑ Italian seasoning
- ❑ Lemon-pepper seasoning
- ❑ Mexican seasoning
- ❑ Pepper, black, ground red, dried crushed red
- ❑ Seasoned salt and pepper

Pasta, Rice, Grains, Nuts
- ❑ Pasta: Couscous, macaroni, thin spaghetti, rotini
- ❑ Rice: Boil-in-bag rice and rice mixes
- ❑ Pecans, chopped
- ❑ Quick-cooking oatmeal and grits

Canned Goods
- ❑ Broth and soups
- ❑ Veggies
- ❑ Pasta sauce
- ❑ Fruits
- ❑ Tomatoes, diced regular and Mexican-style, Cajun-style, Italian-style
- ❑ Tomato sauce
- ❑ Bell peppers, roasted
- ❑ Instant potato flakes

Produce
- ❑ Fruits, whole and jarred
- ❑ Garlic, cloves and jarred minced
- ❑ Potatoes, baking and round red
- ❑ Broccoli florets
- ❑ Cauliflower florets
- ❑ Onions, Spanish, green, and red
- ❑ Peppers, green, red, and yellow
- ❑ Salad greens, packages of premixed washed
- ❑ Spinach, package of washed leaves
- ❑ Vegetables, packages of single and mixed cut

Ready, Set, *Go!*

Microwave Vegetable Chart

Cooking vegetables in the microwave is the best way to preserve nutrients and flavor, and is often the quickest way to cook them. Cook all vegetables at HIGH power in a baking dish covered with dish lid. If you use heavy-duty plastic wrap to cover the dish, be sure to turn back one corner to allow steam to escape.

Food	Microwave Time*	Special Instructions
Asparagus, 1 pound	2 to 4 minutes	Snap off tough ends of spears. Add 2 tablespoons water.
Beans, green, 1 pound	10 minutes; stand 5 minutes	Trim ends; cut beans into 1-inch pieces. Add ½ cup water.
Broccoli spears, 1 pound	6 to 7 minutes	Arrange in a circle, spoke-fashion, with florets in center; add ¼ cup water.
Carrots, baby, 1 pound	6 minutes; stand 2 minutes	Add ¼ cup water.
Cauliflower florets, 1 pound	6 to 7 minutes; stand 2 minutes	Add ¼ cup water.
Corn on the cob, 2 (large) ears 3 ears 4 ears	 6 to 7 minutes 7 to 8 minutes 8 to 9 minutes	Cut ears in half. Arrange end-to-end in a circle; add ¼ cup water.
Onions, 1 pound, peeled and quartered (2 medium)	4 minutes; stand 2 minutes	Add 2 tablespoons water.
Potatoes, sweet/baking (9-ounce) 1 potato 2 potatoes 4 potatoes	 3 to 5 minutes 5 to 7 minutes 10 to 12 minutes	Pierce skins and arrange end-to-end in a circle; let stand 5 minutes after cooking.
New potatoes, 1 pound	6 to 8 minutes	Pierce if unpeeled; add ¼ cup water.
Spinach, 10-ounce package fresh leaves	2 to 3 minutes	Rinse leaves before cooking; leave leaves damp.
Squash, yellow/zucchini, 1 pound, sliced (4 medium)	6 minutes	Add ¼ cup water.
Squash, acorn, 1 pound, (1 medium)	4 minutes	Pierce skin.
Turnips, 1 pound, peeled and cubed (3 medium)	6 to 7 minutes	Add ¼ cup water.

✱ These times are based on times in a 1,000 watt microwave oven. Your times may vary if your oven has a different wattage.

Metric Equivalents

The recipes that appear in this cookbook use the standard United States method for measuring liquid and dry or solid ingredients (teaspoons, tablespoons, and cups). The information on this chart is provided to help cooks outside the U.S. successfully use these recipes. All equivalents are approximate.

Metric Equivalents for Different Types of Ingredients

A standard cup measure of a dry or solid ingredient will vary in weight depending on the type of ingredient. A standard cup of liquid is the same volume for any type of liquid. Use the following chart when converting standard cup measures to grams (weight) or milliliters (volume).

Standard Cup	Fine Powder (ex. flour)	Grain (ex. rice)	Granular (ex. sugar)	Liquid Solids (ex. butter)	Liquid (ex. milk)
1	140 g	150 g	190 g	200 g	240 ml
¾	105 g	113 g	143 g	150 g	180 ml
⅔	93 g	100 g	125 g	133 g	160 ml
½	70 g	75 g	95 g	100 g	120 ml
⅓	47 g	50 g	63 g	67 g	80 ml
¼	35 g	38 g	48 g	50 g	60 ml
⅛	18 g	19 g	24 g	25 g	30 ml

Useful Equivalents for Dry Ingredients by Weight

(To convert ounces to grams, multiply the number of ounces by 30.)

1 oz	=	¹⁄₁₆ lb	=	30 g
4 oz	=	¼ lb	=	120 g
8 oz	=	½ lb	=	240 g
12 oz	=	¾ lb	=	360 g
16 oz	=	1 lb	=	480 g

Useful Equivalents for Length

(To convert inches to centimeters, multiply the number of inches by 2.5.)

1 in				=	2.5 cm			
6 in	=	½ ft		=	15 cm			
12 in	=	1 ft		=	30 cm			
36 in	=	3 ft	=	1 yd	=	90 cm		
40 in				=	100 cm	=	1 m	

Useful Equivalents for Liquid Ingredients by Volume

¼ tsp	=							1 ml	
½ tsp	=							2 ml	
1 tsp	=							5 ml	
3 tsp	=	1 tbls			=	½ fl oz	=	15 ml	
	=	2 tbls	=	⅛ cup	=	1 fl oz	=	30 ml	
	=	4 tbls	=	¼ cup	=	2 fl oz	=	60 ml	
	=	5⅓ tbls	=	⅓ cup	=	3 fl oz	=	80 ml	
	=	8 tbls	=	½ cup	=	4 fl oz	=	120 ml	
	=	10⅔ tbls	=	⅔ cup	=	5 fl oz	=	160 ml	
	=	12 tbls	=	¾ cup	=	6 fl oz	=	180 ml	
	=	16 tbls	=	1 cup	=	8 fl oz	=	240 ml	
	=	1 pt	=	2 cups	=	16 fl oz	=	480 ml	
	=	1 qt	=	4 cups	=	32 fl oz	=	960 ml	
						33 fl oz	=	1000 ml	= 1 l

Useful Equivalents for Cooking/Oven Temperatures

	Fahrenheit	Celsius	Gas Mark
Freeze Water	32° F	0° C	
Room Temperature	68° F	20° C	
Boil Water	212° F	100° C	
Bake	325° F	160° C	3
	350° F	180° C	4
	375° F	190° C	5
	400° F	200° C	6
	425° F	220° C	7
	450° F	230° C	8
Broil			Grill

Index